Landscape with Figures

Landscape with Figures

Figures

The Final Part of his Autobiography

L.T.C. ROLT

ALAN SUTTON PUBLISHING LTD

First published in the United Kingdom in 1992
Alan Sutton Publishing Limited
Phoenix Mill · Far Thrupp · Stroud · Gloucestershire

First Published in the United States of America in 1993
Alan Sutton Publishing Inc.
83 Washington Street · Dover · NH 03820

Paperback edition first published 1994

Reprinted 1995

British Library Cataloguing-in-Publication Data

Rolt, L.T.C.
    Landscape with figures.
    I. Title
    620.0092

    ISBN 0-7509-0593-X

Library of Congress Cataloging in Publication Data applied for

Cover picture: detail from Dolgoch Viaduct *by Felix Kelly. Private
Collection.*

Typeset in 11/13 Imprint.
Typesetting and origination by
Alan Sutton Publishing Limited.
Printed in Great Britain by
WBC, Bridgend, Mid Glam.

Contents

For
Sonia, Richard and Timothy

Introduction

This is the third part of the autobiography *Landscape with Machines* by L.T.C. Rolt (originally entitled *Gifts of Gradual Time*) of which the first titles, *Landscape with Machines* and *Landscape with Canals* have remained in print in one form or another since they were first published.

Why has this volume been so long in joining the others, particularly as there has been pressure over the years from readers who want to know the end of the story?

There is very little to say by way of explanation other than that, to the writer's family, after an initial flutter of indecision, it seemed best to let time go by. Better we felt to let time pass while we settled down to this, to us, most personal of testaments: one in which the retrospective summing up of a life was attempted by its protagonist.

It is now nearly two decades since the death of the author and the events described, the old passions and feelings and their outcome in action have slipped imperceptibly into history.

We have not changed the viewpoint of the book except to add a necessary note where needed. Therefore a subject which was felt so deeply by a professional author, such as Public Lending Right, is left to appear as it did to him. It was introduced a matter of weeks after his death although, as it was not based on copyright, of no direct benefit to him or his heirs. Many of the enterprises inspired by the campaigns described here have consolidated and given inspiration to yet others in a way that clearly could not have been foreseen by him.

I am glad the gentle but persistent pressure from the present publisher, and the encouragement from the author's old friend and reader, has resulted in letting the story of one man's account of the things he cared for, and the struggles and campaigns of the time to ensure that some of them survived, be completed.

Sonia Rolt, 1992

Preservation cannot be a one-sided affair of people vaguely wishing that 'developers' or 'they' wouldn't pull things down. Only the example of each individual patiently living out a faith in his cultural roots by inhabiting – say – the most beautiful old building he can find in the locality, can we hope to turn the tide of such destruction.

Alison Smithson, *The Euston Arch*, 1968

Foreword

This book, like its two predecessors, is mainly concerned with the English landscape and with the machines – say rather those manifestations of the Industrial Revolution – which have captivated me throughout my life. Yet I think the reader will find that, as I have grown older and acquired a philosophy of life and a greater understanding of the Industrial Revolution, the conflict between these two loves – between the two halves of my own nature, if you like – has become less divisive and bewildering. Very briefly, I have learned that, where the machines are concerned, it is the quality that counts.

As in the earlier volumes, with the exception of the final chapter of this book, I have attempted so far as possible to deal with events as they occurred and with my reactions to them at that time no matter how jejune they may now appear to be. In other words, I have attempted to evoke the past without benefit either of hindsight or foresight; to avoid the temptation to nudge the reader into looking 'now on this picture, now on that'. This can blur the truth besides being tiresome for the reader. Not that I possess the gift of total recall; I have had the benefit of my writings at different periods which provide a guide to what I was thinking and of my reactions to events at any particular time.

The last chapter of this book has been written wholly from the standpoint of the present. As it took three chapters of the first book to describe the events of a mere two years of my adolescence, it may surprise the reader to find that this chapter deals with some events that happened as long as fifteen years ago. I accounted for those three early chapters by advancing the theory that the stream of time does not flow past us at a constant rate, but appears to flow faster as we grow older because, metaphorically speaking, our hearts beat slower. That certain events of the last fifteen years should appear to me as 'now' as I write these words, therefore seems as logical as that two years should become a whole epoch when I was young.

Writing an autobiography is an act of self-indulgence which I did not think I would ever perpetrate. As a biographer I take for granted the reader's interest in such great men as I choose to write about, but why should I assume a like interest in my own small doings? My only excuse is that some of my activities have not been without influence on present and future events. This being so it may prove to have been worth while historically to put them on the record.

L.T.C.R., April 1974

1
Narrow Canals to Narrow Rails

Cradled in the mountains of Merioneth the Talyllyn was the 'Sleeping Beauty' of Britain's railways. The concern fell into a trance very soon after its birth in 1866 and it continued so until 1950. Nothing changed except that the course of the line came to resemble some disused country lane rather than a railway. Down this overgrown way, on the original rails, hidden, yet at the same time held to gauge by the thick grass, there reeled at very infrequent intervals an original tall-chimneyed locomotive hauling an equally original train of Victorian four-wheelers. Owing to the state of the permanent way – if such it could be called – this Talyllyn train made a curious and totally unrhythmical clattering noise, while it proceeded with a strange undulating and swaying motion as though the coaches were a string of towed boats surmounting a succession of small waves. Seen in its setting of mountains, this lost railway had a certain magical quality about it which makes me wonder sometimes whether we did right to disturb it. Yet, had we not done so when we did, it is certain that its sleep would very soon have become the sleep of death. One could not perpetuate so deep and precarious a state of trance.

Although there is no documentary evidence to prove it, I am now convinced that the Talyllyn Railway owes its existence to the belief that there was gold to be found in the vicinity of the remote Bryn Eglwys slate quarry, perched high in a cleft of the mountains surrounding Cader Idris. Since 1847 slate had been worked here on a small scale by John Pughe and his descendants, the slate being carried by pack-horse over the mountains to Aberdovey for shipment by sea. In 1863, however, the Pughe family sold the quarry to a group of Manchester business men headed by the brothers William and Thomas McConnel, owners of the largest cotton-spinning business in Manchester. At this time the cotton trade was badly hit by the effects of the American Civil War and the McConnel brothers were looking eagerly for some promising alternative investment, or, in modern parlance, they were seeking to diversify their business. In order to acquire and develop Bryn Eglwys, the brothers formed the Aberdovey Slate Company in January 1864 with a capital of £75,000. In the following year capital was increased to £112,500 of which £15,000 was allocated to the construction of the Talyllyn Railway to provide a rail link between the quarry and the Welsh coast. It was the first narrow gauge railway in the world to be constructed at the outset for steam traction.

Although there was good slate to be found at Bryn Eglwys, extraction by underground methods was difficult and costly and, like other quarries in the area, production would always remain small scale compared with the mammoth quarries further to the north at Penrhyn and Dinorwic. It is hard to see why these astute Lancashire business men were prepared to stake this very considerable capital sum on the future of this small quarrying concern. The answer is that gold-lust is a disease that can infect even the keenest of brains. The Pughe family are said to have held the firm belief that there was gold to be found at Bryn Eglwys, but one feels that this may have been expressed tongue-in-cheek for the benefit of would-be English purchasers. Certainly, in the vicinity, occasional veins or outcrops of white quartz occur containing little golden flecks of pyrites or 'fool's gold'. Such quartz veins often indicate the presence of gold, though there is no evidence that gold has been found anywhere in the area. Yet the McConnel brothers would have been encouraged to believe the Pughes' story by an extraordinarily rich strike at the Clogau Mine between Dolgelley and Barmouth. This Clogau Mine had originally been sunk in an abortive search for copper, but in 1860 it became a gold mine when the vein of gold was discovered. Within three years gold to the value of £43,783 had been produced from this one small working and by 1865 the mine was paying out £22,575 per annum in dividends. Nor was this a mere flash in the pan. As late as 1904 Clogau produced 18,417 ounces of gold from 14,384 tons of ore. So the McConnel brothers' expectation of finding gold at Bryn Eglwys was not so fanciful as one might suppose. Yet, not only was there no gold, but even the slate-quarrying venture failed to come up to expectations and, in 1883, the Abergynolwyn Slate Company, as it was then called, went into voluntary liquidation. Thereafter the quarry was worked upon a much more modest scale by William's son, W.H. McConnel, until 1911 when he sold out to Henry (later Sir) Haydn Jones.

With this background of commercial failure, it is easy to see why the Talyllyn Railway became a sleeping beauty. What is much more difficult to understand is why it was endowed at the outset with the dignity of a statutory railway company intended for public passenger traffic. It could so easily have been built as a mineral line by way-leave agreement like the railways which served the Penrhyn and Dinorwic quarries, but for some reason this did not suit the McConnels. They went through the whole costly and time-consuming ritual of promoting an Act of Parliament, a proceeding that subsequently entailed an inspection of the line by the Board of Trade, prior to opening, to ensure the safety of the travelling public. One can only think that in the first flush of enthusiasm for their new venture only the best was good enough. They had to have a real railway which had been blessed by parliament or none at all.

I first became acquainted with the Talyllyn Railway in the summer of 1943 when Angela and I decided not to spend my annual leave at Llanthony as usual but to seek pastures new. After much brooding over maps we agreed that the vicinity of Cader Idris and Talyllyn Lake in Merioneth looked intriguingly wild and mountainous and we succeeded in booking rooms at a small farm called Minfford near the head of the lake. We reached this retreat from Tardebigge by taking the train to Dolgelley and thence by taxi.

I did not – and do not – consider that the mountain landscapes of Wales, beautiful though they are, can rank with those of the Welsh border. By comparison with the latter, the mountains, though they may be much higher and wilder, seem to lack that majesty that comes from outline and symmetry. Similarly, the valleys seem never so rich as in the border country; the trees have a stunted look; the pastures, though green enough, look poorer and there is never an arable field to be seen. Consequently, there is lacking that striking contrast between wild highland and rich lowland which makes the landscape of the border so uniquely beautiful. Again, by comparison with such border towns as Hay, Presteigne, Clun or Bishops Castle, the small towns of real Welsh Wales seem bleak and dreary. To walk, as we did, down the single long main street of Towyn when a storm of wind and rain was funnelling through it off the sea, made me feel homesick for England. There were few people about, and those that there were stood huddled in shop doorways watching despondently as the curtains of rain drove past. This all-pervading moisture darkened still further the funereal hues of the dour nineteenth-century houses, all purple slate and dark, rough-dressed stone. This was our first impression of Towyn. We had come in from Minfford by bus with the idea of travelling back to Abergynolwyn on the train, but when we finally reached the Wharf station it was to find a rain-smudged hand-written notice pinned to the board by the entrance proclaiming NO TRAIN TODAY. It subsequently transpired that the only serviceable locomotive had broken down and, as the return bus had left by this time, there was nothing for it but a long walk home.

We walked back along the line and very soon it stopped raining although the mountain ridges were still lost in swirling mists. In this way we learnt more about the Talyllyn Railway than we would have done had we been able to travel over it. So alarming was the state of the track that I marvelled that any train could possibly run without becoming derailed, not once but several times, on the journey between Towyn and Abergynolwyn. It was made the more alarming by the fact that as the line climbed up the valley, clinging to a narrow mountain ledge, there was an almost sheer drop on the valley side of the rails. When we finally reached Abergynolwyn station, nearly seven miles from Towyn, it was growing late and we were faced with a further five miles of hard slogging along the road home to Minfford. In those petrol-less days, Welsh roads were deserted and there seemed little prospect of a lift. We were lucky, however, for no sooner had we reached the road than a car stopped and picked us up. It turned out to be a friendly district nurse bound for one of the farms near Minfford.

I must not paint too black a picture of this Welsh holiday. Although it is true that it left us with no desire to repeat it, nevertheless the weather on the whole treated us kindly and we had some memorable mountain walks. One day I recall particularly. We had taken the morning bus over the pass into the Corris valley. This set us down opposite the little railway station at Corris and no sooner had we alighted than I glimpsed a plume of steam coming up the valley towards us. This turned out to be Corris Railway locomotive No.3* hauling a few empty wagons with a diminutive brake-van coupled in rear. So apposite was this arrival that it might have been specially staged for our benefit. Ever since I had first travelled on the Glyn Valley Tramway as a boy, narrow gauge railways held a peculiar fascination for me, partly, I think, because they were small and individualistic, not to say idiosyncratic, and partly because, almost invariably, they were to be found in mountainous or remote settings, difficult country which only the narrow gauge could penetrate economically. As I admired this brave and unexpected sight, I little thought

* An 0–4–2 tank locomotive built for the railway in 1878 by the Hughes Engine Co. of Loughborough, later the Falcon Engine & Car Works and now later of the Brash Company.

that in a few years the Corris Railway would cease to exist and that, through my agency, this entire train, locomotive, wagons, brake-van and all, would enjoy a fresh lease of life on the Talyllyn Railway.

We walked back from the Corris valley over the mountains by Bryn Eglwys to Abergynolwyn. I recall that at the summit of the pass we came upon a remote mountain farm that had obviously only lately been abandoned. The door hung open and within we found the pathetic remnants left behind after long occupancy. There were Victorian dresses and a whole series of black-bordered memorial cards commemorating members of the family who had 'passed on', each bearing a photograph and an appropriate text. The house stood open to the four winds and even on this fine day a mountain breeze sighed about its walls and rattled a loose casement upstairs as we looked through these dour reminders of mortality. The effect upon us was indescribably melancholy and we were glad to be out in the sunlight and on our way once more. Curiously enough, although I recall most vividly this eerie, empty house, the Bryn Eglwys quarries failed to leave any impression at all on my mind although they must have been working at this time, albeit in a very desultory fashion owing to the war. I clearly remember skirting the margin of the small reservoir which supplied the quarry with waterpower*, but after this my mind is like an unexposed negative.

Though the quarry failed to register, the Talyllyn Railway certainly did. Five years later a mental picture of that grass-grown, wavering track sprang most vividly to mind as I sat in the Inland Waterways Association office in Gower Street and leafed through the pages of the Bill which was to nationalize Britain's transport. The IWA had procured a copy of the Bill to see how it was going to affect the canal system, but I soon found myself turning to the section dealing with

---

* The reservoir supplied Pelton wheels which drove the slate saws and, via a wooden launder, an overshot waterwheel which drove an air compressor to supply power to the underground workings.

railways where I came upon a list of the companies, additional to the 'big four', which would be taken over if the Bill became law. The list was extremely comprehensive, indeed I could think of only one statutory railway company – the Talyllyn – which had been omitted. It was by no means the first time in railway history that this obscure railway had been overlooked.*

A few days before this, I had been listening to a party political broadcast during which a labour party spokesman had assured me how wonderful it would be when I, as one of the citizens of Great Britain, owned the railway system instead of a bunch of acquisitive capitalists. How different it would be, when railways were run for the benefit of all! Because I was old enough to remember the pride and efficiency of the old pre-grouping companies, the spit-and-polish of their locomotives and rolling-stock which spoke so eloquently of that tremendous *esprit de corps* that existed throughout the railway service, I doubted the truth of this socialist dogma. Instead of 'our railways' it seemed to me that they were far more likely to become nobody's railways under nationalization. They would fall into neglect and decay just because they had become political pawns about which nobody felt responsible and nobody cared. It was with such gloomy thoughts in mind that I reflected what a fine thing it would be if at least one independent railway could survive to perpetuate, if only upon a small scale, the pride and the glory of the old companies. Why not the Talyllyn? Why not indeed? But then I thought of that seven miles of worn out track . . . As a romantic it seemed a brave notion, but as a practical engineer it seemed madness to attempt to re-animate a railway so run down that it had become so much scrap metal. Then a compromise occurred to me for which there was a good precedent in the north of England.

---

* For example, it was the only public railway which ignored the Board of Trade's instruction to install continuous brakes on its trains following the Armagh disaster. I imagine the management did not deliberately disobey the order but either failed to read it or forgot about it.

The first event ever organized for IWA members was an excursion in 1947 on a 'trip boat' on the Lancaster Canal ending at the bottom of the Tewitfield Locks near Carnforth. I seized this opportunity to pay my first visit to the neighbouring Ravenglass & Eskdale Railway in Cumberland. This had been built and opened in 1875 with the backing of the Whitehaven Iron Mines Ltd as a 3 ft gauge line for the purpose of carrying iron ore and granite from mines and quarries in Eskdale. This staple iron ore traffic soon failed but, by dint of carrying an increasing amount of holiday passenger traffic during summer seasons, 'Ratty', as the railway was known affectionately by the locals, struggled along until 1913 when it finally closed down. The closure of the granite quarry the previous year had proved to be the last straw. In 1915, however, the derelict railway was leased for a trial period of three years to a concern called Narrow Gauge Railways Ltd. This company operated miniature railways at seaside resorts and one of its directors was W.J. Bassett Lowke, a name revered by every railway-minded school-boy*. Using most of the original permanent way materials, the gauge of the railway was then reduced to fifteen inches and the line worked by miniature locomotives designed by Henry Greenly. These *Greenly* locomotives were of 'main line' type correctly scaled down to 15 inch gauge, and while they charmed the children at Rhyl or elsewhere, they were scarcely man enough for the seven steeply-graded miles of line in Eskdale. Consequently, since 1924, when the shipowners Sir Aubrey Brocklebank and Henry Lithgow took over the company, there was a tendency to increase the size of locomotives and stock to 'over-scale' proportions as advocated by that Victorian engineer, Sir Arthur Heywood who held that 15 inches was the smallest practicable gauge and who had designed and built the Eaton Hall Railway for the Duke of Wesminster. (It was at Eaton

* I had been privileged to welcome the idol of my schooldays, W.J. Bassett Lowke, with his wife, aboard *Cressy* on one occasion. They took tea with us while *Cressy* was lying at Gayton Arm End, Blisworth.

Hall that I had glimpsed, as a very small boy, Heywood's *Katie* and was captivated immediately.) Under this new regime the Beckfoot granite quarry had been re-opened and special high capacity bogie vehicles were introduced to convey the stone down to a new crushing plant which was built at Murthwaite, $2\frac{1}{2}$ miles from the lower terminus at Ravenglass. To obviate the transhipment of crushed stone at Ravenglass, this $2\frac{1}{2}$ miles of line was 'gauntleted' by standard gauge track. It was to handle traffic over this section that Kerr Stuart of Stoke-on-Trent built an 0–6–0 standard gauge diesel-mechanical locomotive of 90 hp in 1930.*

The early history of the Ravenglass & Eskdale was so like that of the Talyllyn that I saw no reason why the parallel should not be carried still further. Conversion to a miniature gauge might prove to be a cheaper, quicker and more economical solution than any attempt to restore the worn out railway to its original state. The old track could be sold for scrap and replaced by new rail of a lesser weight per yard, laid to a gauge of only $10\frac{1}{4}$ inches. I reckoned that scaled-down versions of narrow gauge locomotives running on this slim gauge should be capable of hauling as many passengers as the original Talyllyn locomotives had done in their prime. For example, I had in mind a 2–8–2 locomotive which Kerr Stuart had once built for the 2 ft gauge Gwalior Light Railway of India. This had a tractive effort of 15,206 lbs; suppose a scaled down version of such a prototype on the $10\frac{1}{4}$ in gauge . . .

I did not envisage scrapping the original Talyllyn locomotives and coaches. They could form the nucleus of a narrow gauge railway museum at Towyn and become 'operable relics', running over a length of original track laid between the two

---

* This locomotive, one of the first of its type, was designed by my uncle, Kyrle Willans and, as a young apprentice, I drove it on test before despatch to Ravenglass. I stood on the footplate of this locomotive once more in 1973 after an interval of forty-three years; it is now working for a firm near Lichfield and is still giving good service.

stations at Towyn. The whole project would be manned by volunteers recruited from the ranks of railway enthusiasts. I argued that, unlike the members of the Vintage Sports Car Club, railway enthusiasts had, hitherto, been denied any practical creative outlet other than model-making and would, therefore, be only too glad of the opportunity to assist in the construction, maintenance and day-to-day running of a public railway; the more so as most of them were condemned by the age to wholly uncreative jobs in normal life.

The more I thought about this scheme the more promising it seemed and, during the winter of 1947/8, I discussed it at some length with two railway-minded friends of mine at Banbury, Bill Trinder and Jim Russell. Bill Trinder ran a radio shop in the town and I had first met him just before the war when I had bought a portable radio from him for *Cressy*. It was Bill who introduced me to Jim Russell, an ex-GWR employee who had since become a professional photographer. They were quite excited by the idea and at their suggestion we consulted Messrs Fuller and Franklin of Basset Lowke Ltd of Northampton as to who was the best person to advise us about the feasibility and cost of converting the line. They told us that an engineer named David Curwen was the best person in England to help us, so we drove down to Baydon, the next village to Aldbourne in the Wiltshire Downs and reputedly the highest village in the county, where we found David building miniature steam locomotives in a small workshop down a rough track near the village. He estimated that conversion would cost around £10,000 which seemed a very large sum at that time but was probably only a fraction of the expense of restoring the existing line to perfect order. I was at once very impressed with David both as an engineer and as a person. I think we took an immediate mutual liking to each other and he proved to be one of the very few intimate friends I made as a result of this railway venture. Our friendship was later cemented when, although I played no part in bringing them together, David married my cousin Barbara Willans.

An outcome of this visit to Wiltshire was that in 1949 David

came north and spent a couple of nights with me aboard
Cressy at Pont Cysyllte while Angela was on holiday in
Venice. We got up at first light on the morning after his arrival
and, in perfect late summer weather, had a splendid run into
Wales in my Alvis. Our object was to catch the morning train
back to Towyn from Abergynolwyn, but though we arrived in
time and waited patiently in the little station shelter, the train
never appeared. As we eventually discovered, *Dolgoch*, the
only workable locomotive, had broken her frame, putting an
end to the train service for a week or more. So we spent an
afternoon exploring the abandoned 'ghost town' of Bryn
Eglwys before returning to *Cressy*.

Over the next two years Bill, Jim and I paid several visits to
Towyn in the course of which we talked to old Sir Henry
Haydn Jones, who had owned both the quarry and the railway
since 1911 and was now aged eighty-five, trying in vain to
interest him in our project. He intended to keep the railway
running so long as he lived, he said, but he was not prepared
to spend any money on it. It was abundantly clear that there
was nothing further we could do but watch the situation until
Sir Haydn died, for it was certain that when he did so his
executors would be forced to sell the railway for scrap.

In September 1949, to my surprise, a nostalgic article on
the Talyllyn Railway appeared in the *Birmingham Post*. The
anonymous writer extolled the beauties of a railway which, he
said, was obviously on its last legs and ended with a plea to the
government or British Railways to do something about it.
This seemed much too good an opportunity to miss, so I
replied with a letter in which I said: 'Surely it is a sorry
symptom of the decline of individual initiative at the present
time that we so often grumble and say: "Why don't they do
something about it?" and so seldom pause to consider whether
we might not be doing something about it ourselves.' Then,
without going into details, I went on to say that a scheme was
afoot to ensure the future of the railway and would anyone
interested please write to me. I promised to keep them
informed of developments, including the date of a possible

future meeting in Birmingham. As a result, I received a surprising number of letters which I filed as a possible 'bank' of future members. They would serve precisely the same purpose as my *Narrow Boat* 'fan' letters had done when the IWA was launched.

As it happened, these letters did not lie in the file for very long. But in the meantime, Jim Russell, who was more closely in touch with Birmingham railway enthusiasts than either Bill Trinder or myself, told us that it was their considered opinion that the idea of the conversion of the railway was most unlikely to attract support and that only a plan to preserve the existing railway would prove sufficiently popular. Against my own judgement I allowed myself to be persuaded by this argument, though no one knew better than I did what an immense gamble we were taking. In the event, it would take seven years to re-lay the whole of the old line and not until then could it be said with confidence that the future of the railway was assured.

I was working *Cressy* through one of the locks on the Oxford Canal on my way north to Market Harborough in 1950, when I received verbally the news that Sir Henry Haydn Jones was dead. It was now or never. As soon as we moored that evening at Twyford Wharf, just south of Banbury, I typed a letter to Mr Arthur of Machynlleth, the solicitor to the Haydn Jones estate, outlining our new proposals for the Talyllyn Railway which were: that a society should be formed to preserve the railway; that the executors should allow the railway to be run by this society for a trial period of three years and that the railway company should be administered by a joint board consisting of directors nominated by the society and by the executors. I urged that the executors should come to no irrevocable decision before I had had time to organize a meeting in Birmingham to discuss the formation of such a society. While I was at Market Harborough I received a very satisfactory reply to my letter confirming that no decision would be made pending the outcome of the Birmingham meeting.

Such ready acquiescence was entirely due to the advice given by our friend, Edward Thomas. Having first joined the

Talyllyn Railway in 1897 as a seventeen-year-old assistant clerk to his father, Hugh, who was then manager, Edward Thomas, in effect if not in name, succeeded his father after the railway had been acquired by Sir Henry Haydn Jones. To anticipate, he subsequently became one of the two representatives of the executors on the Board (the other being Sir Haydn's widow), a post which he relinquished owing to advancing years in 1967 having notched up a record seventy years in the service of the railway company. When he died in 1972 at the age of ninety-two I mourned his passing for, where this railway project was concerned, I could have had no more loyal ally. From my first visit with Bill Trinder and Jim Russell in 1948, it became clear to us that, in our efforts to save the railway, Edward Thomas was wholeheartedly on our side. So, when it came to winning over Lady Haydn and her solicitor to what must have seemed to them – as it did to many others – a completely crack-brained idea, his advocacy proved far more effective than any Englishman's could conceivably have been.

The fateful Birmingham meeting was fixed for 11 October 1950 at the Imperial Hotel. I sent a circular letter to all those who had responded to my earlier letter in the *Birmingham Post*; what is more, that paper announced the meeting on its front page, for in 1951 the concept of volunteers preserving and running a railway made news because it was then wholly novel. As a result we had a full house. Bill Trinder chaired the meeting very ably and was supported on the platform by Jim Russell, myself and Edward Thomas. We were surprised and delighted by his response to our suggestion that he should attend, for already Edward Thomas had reached his seventieth year and never left his native Towyn if he could possibly avoid it. Yet he needed no second bidding to make the long journey to Birmingham where his eloquent speech on behalf of the railway undoubtedly influenced the decision to form a Talyllyn Railway Preservation Society, there and then, by inviting volunteers from the floor to join with the 'three musketeers' from Banbury in setting up a committee.

20th September, 1950

Dear ....

TAL-Y-LLYN RAILWAY

As you are no doubt aware, the Tal-y-Llyn Railway is the last surviving independent Statutory Railway Company in Britain. It is also the last of the once numerous independent Welsh narrow gauge lines still carrying passenger traffic. Built in 1865 and retaining its original locomotives and rolling stock, the railway is of great historical interest, is within measurable distance of achieving its centenary and traverses some of the finest scenery in Wales

Owing to the recent death of the owner and Manager of the railway, Sir Haydn Jones, it is extremely unlikely that the railway will re-open for traffic in 1951 unless some practical and financial help is forthcoming. This despite the fact that its popularity with holiday makers is such that demand frequently exceeds present carrying capacity.

It is felt that all who are in any way interested in railways will endorse the view that it would be deplorable if the year 1951 should be marked by the permanent closure of this unique and historic railway. For this reason a meeting has been arranged at which it is hoped to found an organised body which will ensure that the railway shall continue as a going concern. This meeting will be held at the Imperial Hotel, Temple Street, Birmingham at 7-0p.m. on Wednesday, 11th October, 1950. The organisers cordially invite you to this meeting and hope you will make every effort to attend.

Lady Haydn Jones has graciously expressed her willingness to consider any practicable proposals which may be put forward at this meeting, and it is hoped that her legal representative will be present.

Yours Truly,

Original circular letter advising correspondents to attend the meeting at which the first Railway Preservation Society was founded

To cut a long story short, following this Birmingham meeting, Bill Trinder, Pat Garland and myself met Lady Haydn Jones and Edward Thomas in Arthur's office at Machynlleth where an arrangement, very similar to that suggested in my letter to Arthur, was agreed upon. However, one vital addition was suggested by Pat Garland, a Birmingham accountant who acted as Hon. Treasurer to the venture for many years. This was the setting up of a private limited company known as Talyllyn Holdings Ltd, to hold the shares in the Talyllyn Railway Company. But for this device, in order to legalize the new joint administration which I had proposed, it would have been necessary to amend the Talyllyn Railway Act of 1865, a very costly and tedious legal proceeding. Not having a legal mind and knowing nothing of the intricacies of company law, this was a difficulty I had never envisaged. Its ingenious solution meant that the railway could still boast that it operated under its original 1865 Act of Incorporation.

While the Talyllyn Railway had been struggling towards rebirth, its neighbour the Corris Railway had practically disappeared from the face of the earth. In the early spring of 1947, exceptional floods on the Dovey had undermined the piers of the bridge by which the railway crossed that river in order to gain access to Machynlleth station, its point of traffic interchange with the ex-Cambrian. The line had been sold to a local scrap-dealer who soon tore it up, but not before the rolling-stock and the two surviving locomotives had been moved down the valley and over the weakened bridge into Machynlleth station yard. One of these locomotives was No. 3, which I had seen on my first visit to Corris during the war; the other, No. 4, was a standard type built by Kerr Stuart in 1921. This type, known to the works as a 'Tattoo' had become very familiar to me during my apprenticeship with that firm. Because the Corris was of the same uncommon gauge as the Talyllyn, it seemed to me absolutely vital that we should acquire these two locomotives and so solve our motive power problem. Not only were they close at hand but we should thereby avoid the costly task of re-gauging. This was the last job which we, the trio from Banbury, undertook to negotiate before handing over to the committee, two of whom had sportingly agreed to put up the purchase price of the engines provided we could get them for a reasonable figure. There was no time to be lost, for it was remarkable that they had survived the demise of the railway for so long before being sold for scrap. Accompanied by David Curwen we paid a hurried visit of inspection to Machynlleth yard. Partially covered by old wagon sheets and with all the cab spectacles and gauge glasses shattered by vandals, the two locomotives looked very neglected and forlorn. It was clear that they needed considerable repair, particularly No. 4 which looked as though she had been out of use for a long time. Nevertheless, we decided they were well worth having.

The Corris Railway having become the concern of the Western Region, there followed, hard on this inspection, an excursion from Banbury to Swindon Works where we found the engineers responsible so sympathetic that I believe, had they still been representatives of the GWR, they would have given us the locomotives. But now that the company had been nationalized their freedom of action was as cabined and confined as that of civil servants, a state of affairs they obviously deeply resented. However, after some discussion among themselves, they informed us that they had decided they could safely write them off their books at £25 a piece. No matter how bad their condition was, we felt we could not go far wrong at that, so we accepted on the spot and drove back to Banbury in high good humour. Both locomotives are still giving good service and run on the Talyllyn under the names of *Sir Haydn* and *Edward Thomas* respectively.

From all this it will have become clear how I was able to walk out of the last disastrous meeting of the IWA in Birmingham, straight into a meeting of the new committee of the TRPS in Pat Garland's office in Waterloo Street. The idea of this railway venture had first occurred to me in the early days of the IWA when I had no notion of the storm that lay ahead. Even when I had resigned as Hon. Secretary in 1949, Sir Henry Haydn Jones was still alive and, as there was still no indication when the project might mature, it had not entered into my calculations. Not until I was heading for Market Harborough and it had become clear that my association with the IWA was drawing to an end did the Talyllyn Railway scheme, suddenly and providentially, come alive to provide an alternative outlet for my energies just at the very moment when it was most needed. In retrospect, this sequence of events seems almost miraculously providential.

At that meeting of the TRPS committee, someone asked the question: who was going to be in charge of the railway during the critical summer season of 1951? Strangely enough, this was a problem which had never occurred to me. Clearly, at this early stage in the proceedings we could not possibly afford to advertise for a salaried manager. The members of the committee first eyed each other round the table and then every eye finally came to rest on me and I realized that I was the only one present who was what is called a self-employed person with no ties. I nodded, 'Alright', I said, 'I'll do it, provided the Society can make some contribution towards my expenses', whereupon the amount of £30 per month was agreed upon — scarcely a princely sum, but I hoped it would serve to keep the wolf from the door until the autumn when I could resume my writing.

It was little more than eighteen months since I had resigned as Hon. Secretary of the IWA, largely because it was taking up more of my time than I could afford; so on the face of it, it seemed crazy to commit myself to five months of full-time work for a pittance. Crazy from a monetary, materialistic point of view, perhaps, and yet in the circumstances in which I found myself at that time, I could not have made a better move. The IWA débâcle, coinciding as it did with the breakdown of my marriage and the loss of *Cressy*, had left me feeling completely alone and disorientated, and, filled with self-pity. For this disease, some totally absorbing occupation that filled every day from dawn till dusk in an entirely new environment was without doubt the best cure. For me it was the equivalent of the traditional palliative of going out on safari in darkest Africa.

I have written in detail of my experiences during that first crucial 1951 season in my book *Railway Adventure* and it would therefore be superfluous to repeat it here. So those who have not read that book must take my word for it, that from May to the end of September the task of keeping the trains running against every kind of odds, both human and mechanical, totally absorbed all my thought and energy. That the railway staggered through the season successfully was entirely due to the unfailing support and good advice I received from my predecessor, Edward Thomas, plus the labours of a small and dedicated team of friends and members who stood by me loyally throughout the season. These were David Curwen, my cousin Barbara his wife, and a young man named John Snell who had volunteered to work for nothing on the railway after leaving school at Bryanston and before going up to Oxford. David acted as Chief Mechanical Engineer in charge of the running shed and repair shop at Towyn Pendre with John as his assistant while Barbara frequently helped me out at the Wharf terminus. All four of us stayed together in lodgings at Dolgoch, half way up the line, throughout that ever-memorable summer. In addition two volunteer members of the Society, Bill Oliver and 'Maggie' Maguire assisted by other volunteers performed wonders as permanent way men by holding the worn out track together against all the laws of probability.

In addition to this band of stalwarts, we inherited from the old regime the Welsh permanent staff, but in the event they only provided the human problem, the last straw that almost broke the camel's back. When I first arrived they had seemed to me pleasant and willing enough so that I was surprised when Edward Thomas warned me that I would find them: 'Very difficult people, you know, yes indeed!' I reflected gloomily that if he, a fellow Welshman who had known them all their lives, had found them difficult, what hope had I.

What hope, indeed! Within weeks both walked out on me without any warning whatever. David, John and I arrived at Towyn from Dolgoch one morning to find the locomotive that was to haul the morning train cold and without a driver. David Curwen, instead of working in the shop, was compelled to act as driver while he trained his fireman, John Snell, to succeed him.

It later became obvious that these 'difficult people' bitterly resented our new regime and thought that by letting us down without warning they would make the Society's failure certain. But when the reaction of the stubborn Englishmen was merely to close ranks and, by a prodigious feat of improvisation, to carry on as though they had never been, their resentment seemed to know no bounds. One of them, who lived in a cottage beside the railway, made a jolly practice of pouncing, like some old man of the sea, upon new and unsuspecting volunteers who had come down to work on the railway and informing them that I was mad, that my crazy attempt to run a railway which was obviously unsafe was bound to end in disaster, and the sooner they dissociated themselves from the railway and returned whence they had come the better. Looking rather white about the gills, one volunteer turned up at the Wharf station office one evening and reported to me an encounter of this kind. It had been a frightening tirade, he said, so venomous that he feared the man might do the railway some serious mischief. I succeeded in calming him down, told him of Edward Thomas's warning to me, and assured him that no wild talk of that kind was going to prevent the trains from running so long as I was in charge.

In 1951 I was much too fully occupied with practical problems to concern myself with the more unpleasant quirks of human nature, though I was also not unaware of a certain jealousy in the ranks of railway enthusiasts. They were saying in effect: 'Rolt, Rolt, he's a canal man, isn't he? What's he doing muscling in on our pitch and what does he know about railways, anyway?' For the same reason I was also impervious to the final purge of the heretics following the hard-won victory of the IWA establishment. I had intended continuing to pay my IWA subscription even though I had no intention of playing any further active part in the organization, but it was not to be. One day, while I was busy issuing tickets to passengers for the morning train, a letter arrived from the Bloomsbury office of the IWA. This solemnly informed me that by decision of the Council I had been expelled from the Association. I read this hastily, then tossed it aside and went on date-stamping tickets, reflecting that a year ago such a letter would have infuriated me in view of the efforts I had made to get the IWA off the ground. Yet now, so remote and so ludicrous did the whole canal quarrel seem that it had become 'a tale told by an idiot, full of sound and fury, signifying nothing'. I subsequently learned that, with one exception, all the signatories to that heretical manifesto had been similarly excommunicated. The exception was the Earl of Lucan.* Apparently Bloomsbury, inveterately snobbish, could not summon sufficient courage to expel a belted earl, thus creating an anomalous situation which Pat Lucan promptly and honourably remedied by resigning.

My unfortunate experience in the IWA had one definite effect upon the TRPS which was somewhat ironical because,

---

*   Pat Lucan was the kindest and most courteous of men who became my friend and one of my most loyal supporters. As Lord Bingham he had joined the IWA in its earliest days and soon joined the committee. Soon afterwards he succeeded to the Earldom. He acquired an old and rather tired looking ex-Grand Union motor boat and with this he became quite the most intrepid of the early IWA 'trail-blazers'. My exploits on the Stratford and Welsh Canals fall into insignificance beside Pat Lucan's epic east-west voyage through the Kennet & Avon culminating in a journey up the Severn estuary from Avonmouth to Sharpness, or his voyage across the Wash from the Nene to the Great Ouse. It must be said, however, that whereas *Cressy* was a floating home with all our precious possessions on board, *Hesperus*, as she was ominously called, was a holiday boat and was not even converted. While Pat and his wife occupied the motor cabin, their family camped under canvas in the hold. When under way they looked the scruffiest crew imaginable.

as a direct result of it, as the years went by and I eventually became Chairman of the Railway Company and the Preservation Society, I found myself fettered by my own rules. It came about in this way. After that historic meeting in Birmingham when it had been decided to form the TRPS, I had hurried home and, there and then, had drafted out a publicity leaflet and a set of Rules and Constitution for the Society for approval at the first meeting of the newly formed committee – or council as it was later called. As I did so, I recalled wryly that it was only five years since I had undertaken precisely the same job for the nascent IWA. With this very much in mind, I devoted much thought to the Rules and Constitution of this latest venture in order to ensure that no single individual cock could ever succeed in imposing his will on the organization and so make the Talyllyn Railway his private dunghill. I produced a democratic document which I believed to be proof against such 'take-overs' and so it has proved. Of the many similar preservation societies which have since sprung up, the TRPS remains to this day by far the most democratic. The Society really does own and run the railway unlike many others which are little more than supporters' clubs with, at best, token minority representation on the managing body of the railway.

But as the railway and society flourished and grew over the years and the amount of business increased, so the defects of this democratic system I had devised became the more apparent. In order to satisfy Society members that their wishes were truly represented, we had to have a huge and unwieldy council and a plethora of sub-committees. As a result, decision-making became exasperatingly slow and difficult. Even so, when a decision was eventually reached, it was often bitterly contested by the membership who would claim that the council were out of touch and unrepresentative. Sometimes, things would reach such a farcical pitch that the impossible course of holding a plebiscite of the whole membership seemed the only way of reaching an acceptable decision. When I became Chairman I frequently used to chafe against this slow and infinitely laborious method of policy-making. Too often it meant that the decision, when at last it was reached, was but an emasculated version of the original proposition. Representing the lowest, rather than the highest common denominator of the intelligence of all those present, it simply proved the truth of the old saying that a camel is a horse designed by a committee. So, ironically, I was ultimately hoist with my own petard as colleagues like Pat Garland and Pat Whitehouse, the Hon. Secretary, who had joined the venture at its beginning, jokingly pointed out. When I grew impatient of delay they would remind me that I had brought such a state of affairs upon myself since I had been the chief architect of the Constitution, including the manner in which the Society controlled the Railway Company.

Yet, when I look back on my eighteen years of active association with the Talyllyn Railway, despite the fact that they yielded more frustration and pain than reward where I was concerned, I would not have changed the set-up even if I could. For it seems to me that my experience of these two organizations, the IWA and the TRPS, typifies in microcosm the perennial, unsolved dilemma that besets all human government. Impatient of the inefficiencies, the compromises and delays inseparable from the cumbersome democratic machine, there is an understandable tendency to streamline and simplify that machine in an attempt to make its action speedier. The logical end of this road is to leave decision-making to some super-man regardless of the fact that, according to the inexorable law that absolute power corrupts absolutely, even the wisest of men in such circumstances soon begins to display symptoms of paranoia or megalomania.

In order to draw a moral, I have been anticipating the future and must now return to the events of 1951. It was a most significant year in my life. It had begun with the final dissolution of the way of life I had so long dreamed about and finally achieved just before the war; it ended in what was to prove to be the start of a new life immediately after the summer season on the Talyllyn Railway was over.

Whereas under the old regime trains had only run on three days of the week, we had succeeded, against all the laws of probability, in maintaining a five-days-a-week service from the beginning of June to the end of September. But it had all been pretty exhausting, and I heaved a mighty sigh of relief when the last train of the year appeared under the bridge and ground safely to a standstill at the Towyn terminus. I must say, too, that I felt very glad to be leaving Towyn behind me when, a few days later, I headed eastwards up the familiar valley through the mountains in my old 12/50 Alvis; my destination was Shrewsbury station where I had arranged to meet Sonia South off a train due in from Birmingham in the late afternoon.

2
Beginning a
New Life

Sonia South had been among the first to join the IWA and her unique position soon earned her a place on the committee. She had been a member of that early deputation, led by A.P. Herbert, which had visited the Minister of Transport during the bitter January of 1947. In my – largely unsuccessful – campaign to improve conditions for the working boaters she became my right hand, for the simple reason that she had first hand knowledge of those conditions such as no one else possessed outside the ranks of those who had been born in a boat cabin and who could seldom speak for themselves. I had thus grown to know Sonia well during my last IWA years and soon came to realize that, though she was highly intelligent and much better read than I was, she was by no means the rather frightening, left-wing blue-stocking I had supposed her to be at first sight in the foyer of that cinema in Birmingham towards the end of the war.

Sonia was an orphan. She had never known her father, while her mother had died just before the war in tragic circumstances which had affected her outlook on life profoundly. Trained for the stage by Michel St Denis at his London Theatre Studio, she had only a brief theatrical career – the London Village Players, the Players' Theatre, OUDS Shakespearean productions under the direction of Neville Coghill – before the war intervened. Lodging with an aunt in London, she had then got a job as an Aeronautical Inspection

Directorate inspector at the Hoover factory which was manufacturing components for the aircraft industry. This was her
first experience of what life inside a modern factory was like
and she hated it so much that she soon fled, as I had done from
Rolls Royce, joining the ranks of the 'idle women' under the
command of Kit Gayford, crewing pairs of Grand Union
boats between London and Birmingham. Unlike me, therefore, her experience of canals and canal boaters was gained the
hard way. Indeed, as I subsequently learned from her and
from other members of that select sisterhood, *Cressy* and her
bath (which they glimpsed through a window as they chugged
past) became a fabled dream of luxury, to be regarded with
that mixture of envy and scorn such as the muscled driver of
the huge 'artic' reserves for the owner of the Rolls Royce as it
sweeps silently past him on the motorway. It certainly did not
escape us that by these amateur Amazons of the cut we were
regarded as mere drones. And yet, despite the fact that her
initiation was so much more rugged than mine, the canals and
their nomadic population had the same fascination for her as
for me. She certainly proved this, for whereas I was content to
dabble my feet in the shallow margins of the canal, she had
plunged straight into the deepest part of the channel by
marrying a boater who could neither read nor write. By so
doing she moved on from the ranks of the 'idle women' into
the class of the real professionals. The cabin of the butty boat
Warwick*, drawn by the motor *Cairo*, became her home from
then on. She and her husband worked this pair of boats
two-handed between London and Birmingham or the Coven-
try coalfield, and, as anyone who has ever been on a canal even

---

* When *Warwick* had to be docked at Braunston her place was temporarily
taken by *Sunny Valley*, the boat which was renamed and repainted for
the Ealing film. At the time Barbara Jones painted the splendid picture
which appears as a frontispiece to my book, *Inland Waterways of
England*, Sonia was occupying *Sunny Valley* and the pot plant which
appears beside the cabin chimney was hers. Boaters do not normally go
in for pot plants!

for a brief holiday will appreciate, working a pair of boats two-handed on such a trip as this was the toughest possible form of professional boating. Not only was it extremely hard work, but it was also dangerous because keeping pace with more adequately-manned pairs (which were in the majority) involved taking unwarrantable risks at the locks. In these circumstances it is no wonder that the cabin on *Cairo* was always available to guests, particularly those with canal experience, and both Angela and I successively made a trip with them to experience at first hand what real boating involved. With such a third hand to lock-wheel (set the locks in advance) and generally help with the locks, most of the hazards and stress of working two-handed were obviated.

From this it will be understood why, during the first years of the IWA, Sonia's knowledge and experience was so uniquely valuable to anyone as concerned as I was to improve conditions for the working boaters. However, she, like me, was expelled as a heretic from the Association. The last canal assignment we undertook together before I left narrow canals for narrow rails was to arrange a meeting with some prominent official in the Transport & General Workers Union in Birmingham, whose name I now forget. Most of the boaters were members of the TGWU and we both felt that the union ought to be on our side in our efforts to improve working conditions on the canals so as to enable the boaters to earn a better livelihood. Sonia maintained that the union failed to help because its officials were completely out of touch with, and therefore did not understand, the peculiar working conditions obtaining on the waterways. She thought that this state of affairs might be remedied if the union could be persuaded to form a special 'Inland Waterways Branch' to deal with the boaters' problems. This was the reason for our meeting in Birmingham. Sonia, less disillusioned about trade unions than I, was optimistic but, alas, our mission was as completely abortive as I had feared it might be. I was left wondering why the TGWU had the nerve to go on collecting dues from impoverished boaters when this official made it abundantly clear to us that his organization just did not want to know about their problems. So far as he was concerned the canal community was an anachronism and, like the gipsy community, the sooner it could be tidied away the better. The fact was, of course, that the union was geared to cope with the never-ending demands of dissatisfied wage-earners for more money for less work; the needs of such a strongly individualistic community as the canal boaters were something entirely alien to its experience.

After this frustrating interview was over we had tea together in some squalid Birmingham café before we parted. It was during this simple meal that I looked up from my plate to find Sonia regarding me with the deepest compassion and tenderness. Although in all my thirty-nine years, no woman had looked at me in quite that way before, there could be no mistaking the meaning of that glance. I felt unworthy and deeply abashed. As I learned subsequently, she had only recently admitted this disturbing truth to herself; disturbing because she had determined, as a result of a bitter example, never to give all the heart for love. In other words, in any relationship with the opposite sex she had determined that her will should remain in control of events and that she would never permit herself to be swept away on a tide of emotion.

At the time this meeting took place I was still living on *Cressy* although it had already become clear that my marriage was breaking up and that *Cressy*'s days were numbered. In such a state of disorientation, this sudden and totally unexpected discovery had an effect on me which I can only liken to the sensation of one who comes out of a bitter-cold night into the comfort and warmth of a fire. Yet, at the same time, I found myself confronting a deeply bewildering and disturbing situation. So much so that I fear Sonia could read no answering comfort in my eyes but only trouble and dismay. It was in this unsatisfactory and turbulent state of mind, and with no more said, that we went our separate ways, she to New Street station, I to Snow Hill to return to *Cressy*.

I was alone on my boat at the time, so I had ample opportunity for self-questioning in an attempt to reach the right answer to what for me was an agonizing problem, so many were the pros and cons. Where Sonia and myself were concerned I now realized with hindsight that during our purely platonic association within the IWA, we had been totally unaware of the fact that, to coin a metaphor, the voltage between our two psychical poles had been steadily rising until, that evening in Birmingham, the current had suddenly sparked across with the alarming suddenness of a lightning flash out of a clear blue sky, disconcerting us both. Such an experience had never happened to either of us before, and for my part I questioned whether it was the real thing or whether it was merely an infatuation which was liable to end as suddenly as it had begun. Since I was experiencing the agonies of a broken marriage at the time, the prospect that the whole thing might happen all over again was something I could not bring myself to contemplate. There was also the thought that there were not two but four people involved in this dilemma and that to jeopardize the happiness of our respective partners for the sake of a mere infatuation would be unthinkable. Moreover, I was only too well aware that infatuation – call it the illusion of love if you like – is a chimera which is particularly prone to lead astray people in our situation. Precisely because they recognize each other as fellow victims of failed marriages, both are at once desperately seeking, and eager to give, solace.

I was not so worried about my marriage from this point of view because Angela had already made it clear by word and action that our relationship was drawing to a close. What caused Sonia and myself so much distress was the future of her husband, that simple, blameless man who could neither read nor write. She had willed their marriage in fulfilment of a consciously conceived romantic theory of which he had been the victim. This decision she had taken against the advice of all her friends, new and old, who could see nothing but disaster ahead for a marriage between two people having such a vast disparity of intellect and temperament. The boaters, too, had shaken their heads over the marriage but for a different reason. Naturally they could not evaluate Sonia's stature as a person although she was very popular with them, but they knew her as someone 'off the bank', as they termed it, and in their long experience mixed marriages between boaters and girls off the bank only very rarely proved lasting. Either the woman left the man, or the man concerned left the canals and, to please his wife, took a job ashore. The reason for this was very simple; no girl off the land could stand the conditions of life afloat; the close confines of a narrow boat cabin, the long hours of physical toil in every kind of weather which had to go on even when she was in an advanced state of pregnancy. To do this the boaters said, you had to be born in a boat cabin; only then did the work seem second nature which meant that you were able to appreciate its undoubted compensations including the sense of belonging to a close-knit community whose bonds were strengthened by shared rigour and stubborn independence. As one from 'off the bank', Sonia had performed manfully (literally), but now at last she had come to realize that her friends on the land and on the canal had both been right after all. She dared not contemplate the psychological and physical stresses and strains to which she would be subjected if she attempted to prolong her boating life much longer. This despite the fact that she had had no children. These made the burden of most boaters' wives very much heavier until they were old enough to become active members of the crew. But this knowledge caused her to grieve over the future of her husband who was immensely proud of her and who, if she left him, would become the innocent victim of an experiment in living that she had deliberately willed.

Yet the knowledge that she would have had to leave her husband, whether or not I had ever swum into her ken, could not lighten my load of guilt. For those contemplating such a step, the 'innocent party' is always a problem, particularly if he or she is a likeable person who has done no wrong to the other partner. In my case, however, it was more than

ordinarily difficult, in fact the situation must have been almost
unique. Few people can appreciate what a handicap illiteracy
is in the modern world. When it came to knowledge of the
natural world based on acute powers of observation exercised
on many slow journeys, the canal boaters far surpassed
modern urban man; yet on the other hand, Sonia's husband
had great difficulty in finding his way across London by
himself, owing to his inability to read destination boards and
the multiplicity of direction signs. Where I was concerned, it
was like a strong man taking unfair advantage of one seriously
handicapped; I felt as one who had eaten of the Tree of
Knowledge and was contemplating mortal injury to another
who still walked the Garden in a state of innocence. This may
sound a gross exaggeration, but it is the nearest I can get to
expressing my feeling at that time. On top of this, I felt it must
appear that I was dealing an underhand blow at that unique
community I had so long admired. Further – though this I
minded less – there was the thought that it must seem to my
late associates in the IWA that my close collaboration with
Sonia was simply a cover for a prolonged seduction aimed to
entice a boater's wife away from him under pretence of helping
his fellows.

Throughout the long summer of 1951 Sonia and I never
met – we were far too fully occupied – though we exchanged
long letters almost daily in which we debated the doubts and
the problems which I have mentioned. Her letters were hastily
scribbled in snatched moments of leisure in the small cabin of
Warwick and subsequently posted at strategic points on the
canal that I knew only too well; at Sutton Stop, Sampson
Road, Warwick Two, Buckby, 'Maffers', Bulls Bridge or
Limehouse Dock. To these I replied at length, writing by
candlelight at night in the privacy of my bedroom at Dolgoch;
candlelit because the house was lit by a small hydro-electric
plant powered by a mountain stream. In summer the water
supply to this plant ran out about 10.30 p.m., the light slowly
fading away like some stage twilight effect. In September a
letter arrived from Sonia telling me that, come what might,

she had finally determined to leave the boats and to lodge with friends who lived in Braunston until she could decide what next to do. Physically, this would be a simple move because her personal possessions were very few – necessarily so. To this I replied with the question as to whether it would be possible for us to stay together for a week on neutral territory after the Talyllyn Railway season ended as this might surely help us to decide upon the future. Such vital questions could not be settled by correspondence and to this she agreed.

I cogitated long and earnestly, poring over maps, to decide where this trysting place should be. Llanthony I at once ruled out – it was too filled with old associations; there I would be continually reminded of times past. No, it must be somewhere entirely new to us both, an empty pitcher waiting to be filled with our own memories. After a great deal of thought I had decided upon the Anchor Inn which stands high on the Kerry Hills between Clun and Newtown on the westernmost extremity of the Shropshire March. In later years I often drove past this lonely inn as it lay on one of my alternative routes between Gloucestershire and Towyn, but in 1951 I had never set eyes on it so it was a shot in the dark. In reply to my letter of inquiry, Mrs Phoebe Moody, the mistress of the Anchor, wrote that she would be delighted to put us up for a week in early October, so this was how I came to be heading west towards Shrewsbury from Towyn on this fine autumn day.

Although Sonia's train arrived punctually at Shrewsbury in the late afternoon, the shadows were beginning to lengthen as we drove south down the Welsh border through that eerie lead-mining district of the Stiperstones and so on by Bishops Castle to Clun. There we turned westwards to follow the valley of the little Clun river across Offa's Dike until, climbing steadily, we came to the Anchor. By the time we reached the inn it was almost dark. We found that we were the only guests and that Mrs Moody had prepared for us a delicious dinner of jugged hare which we ate before the cheerful fire in the small dining room.

The Anchor Inn lies athwart the junction of the roads from
Clun and Beguildy to Newtown. It presents only its northern
gable end at first floor level to the Clun road, thus appearing to
crouch beside that road in so insignificant a fashion that a
traveller from England could hurry past without being aware
that there was an inn there. It came into existence in the days
when cattle in great number were exported from Wales to
England 'on the hoof', for it stands upon what was once one of
the great trunk drove roads between the two countries.
Although the inn is in Shropshire, it is almost within a stone's
throw of the Welsh border with the effect that it attracts many
a thirsty Welshman on a Sunday. Why it was ever called the
Anchor is unknown. Anything further removed from any
maritime associations than the top of the Kerry Hills it would
be difficult to find. Perhaps the name was adopted to suggest a
safe harbour, for the inn certainly becomes a place of refuge
amid these desolate hills in winter, especially when, as
frequently happens, snowdrifts block the border roads. Seen
from the lower, Beguildy, road it is apparent that the Anchor
is much larger than it appears from other vantages. Extending
round three sides of a courtyard, at the time of our visit it was
equipped to withstand a long siege with ample covered stores
of fuel, and a general store and grocery whose well-stocked
shelves seemed primarily intended to meet the emergency
needs of the inn itself rather than those of the few scattered
farms in the vicinity.

That evening drive from Shrewsbury to the Anchor marked
the beginning of the most memorable week of my life. I cannot
explain precisely why this was so because there are times when
even the most honest autobiographer must be reticent. I will
only say that any lingering suspicion I might have harboured,
that ours might be merely a brief infatuation, very soon blew
away and by the end of the week I had become convinced that
the foundations of a true and lasting relationship had been
laid. I also discovered for the first time how such a relationship
can miraculously sharpen one's five senses and so cause the
magical doors of perception to open. Those who insist upon

regarding the lover with sympathy or indulgence as one temporarily besotted, or as suffering from an acute mental illness whose symptoms are delusions and hallucinations are, in my view, mistaken. Why should people whose senses are trammelled by space and time into a grey prison belittle those who, temporarily at least, are privileged to perceive in all its rich colour, brilliance, and beauty, the transfigured world that exists in an eternal now beyond such arbitary confines? It is this world that children and mystics can see and it has been claimed that modern synthesized drugs have made it accessible to all. Although I have never tried them, I do not believe in such 'instant mysticism' drugs any more than I believe that a medium has the power to make the dead speak. For I am told that a uniquely significant thing about the strange and glittering world conjured up by drugs is its utter lack of humanity. It is essentially a world of things, colours and essences in which people do not exist, the creation of some supreme egotist designed to charm the self alone. This is not the world which the child, the mystic and the lover share; the visionary landscapes that Blake or Palmer depict are filled with life, be it human or superhuman In Thomas Traherne's superb evocation of the child's timeless vision of the world where 'all things abided eternally as they were in their proper places', it was not only the green trees, when first seen, that transported and ravished him but the people also. 'I knew not', he says, 'that they were born or should die.'

So it was, certainly for me and I believe for us both, during that week. The weather was fine and our routine simple. Each day, with one exception, we set out with our packets of sandwiches to walk over the high, bare hills. Although the Kerry Hills afford some splendid prospects looking westward over Wales, they do not stand comparison with the landscape splendours of the Black Mountains further to the south. The Kerrys lack the superb symmetry and shape of the Black Mountains; they are a mere inchoate upheaval of the earth, most of which has become enclosed sheep walk while the highest, unenclosed portion is not true moorland but a bare expanse of bent grass. The Kerrys have also suffered severely from that inhuman monster the Forestry Commission.* Yet we asked no more; it was for us an enchanted landscape from which we were loth to retreat as dusk fell despite the lure of a warm fire and Mrs Phoebe Moody's superlative cooking. Only two incidents on these walks come to mind. One was the discovery of a grassy bank starred with the purple and gold blossoms of late flowering wild pansy, a flower which, although it is not described as rare, for some reason I had not seen before although I had walked much on the high pastures and waste places which are its natural habitat. The other memorable occasion was when we saw, nestling in a high fold of the hills far from any road, a small and apparently ruinous shepherd's or crofter's stone-built cottage. To anyone familiar with such remote districts the sad evidence of rural de-population and the decline of subsistence farming is a commonplace, but in this case our assumption was false. Whenever I pass such an empty or ruinous house curiosity gets the better of me, but as we were approaching this one we were startled to hear sounds of movement within accompanied by an unmistakable male cough. We stole silently away over the soft turf without inquiring further, leaving the identity of the occupier forever a mystery. I was reminded of Mr Tod's house at the top of Bull Banks or the cottage of the solitary of Llanbedr which Francis Kilvert describes so graphically in his diary.

The one exception to this daily walk was when we decided to drive down to Clun one morning, having taken a liking to the little town when we had passed through it on arrival. It seemed typical of that enchanted week that, all unknowing, we should have picked on the day of Clun's annual carnival. It might have been staged for our especial benefit; for we arrived

* Along the road to Newtown a plantation had just been clear felled. This had been so close planted that there was no ground cover beneath the trees with the inevitable result that the rain had already begun to leach the precious top soil away down the steep slope. The road in places was covered with silt that looked like brown drifts of snow, eloquent evidence of man's folly.

just as the procession was forming. We watched it pass over
the ancient river bridge and up the short, steep pitch into the town.
To the jaundiced eye, for all I know, it may have looked pretty
tatty, but for us all the participants resembled the people described
by Traherne: '. . . young men glittering and sparkling angels, and
maids strange seraphic pieces of life and beauty.'

Our week together ended when I drove Sonia to the Low
Level station at Wolverhampton, travelling through Much
Wenlock and Ironbridge, and having done so, headed the
Alvis southwards towards my home in Gloucestershire. The
big question was, what now? Sonia was bound for her friends
at Braunston where she was welcome to a bed whenever she
needed it. As for myself, it looked as though I should be
staying with my mother at Stanley Pontlarge for an indefinite
period. There could be no question of our setting up house
together even in the most modest fashion because we simply
could not afford it. In April, before I went down to Towyn,
my bank balance had looked fairly healthy but it had been
plummeting downward ever since and, what was worse, there
was no best-seller in the pipe-line to reverse this situation.
Sonia, now that she had left the boats, had no income
whatever.

It was my friend Melville Russell-Cooke who, bless her,
rescued us from this dilemma. She and my cousin David, the
painter, were going to spend the winter at Kilsalla, her house
on the coast of County Mayo, near Westport. Would we, she
asked, like to keep her house at Leafield warm while they were
away? More than this, she made it clear that she had no
objection to our using her house for that dreary charade that
was then necessary to provide the required evidence for
divorce. On the strength of this, one of my old VSCC friends
nobly volunteered to play the part of witness and was invited
down to Oxfordshire for the weekend, while I drove over to
Braunston and collected Sonia.

Although it may sound a gross abuse of hospitality, that
winter we spent together at Leafield turned out to be a
strange, dream-like, and not by any means wholly pleasurable

period in our lives. Not only did we have to learn to live with each other and to make the many small adjustments which this implies; not only did we both suffer acute pangs of remorse on account of our previous partners, but we had to act out these exacting parts on a stage that was completely foreign to us. From the cramped confines of a boat cabin and the austerity of my Welsh farm bedroom with its horse-hair mattress and uncertain light, we had suddenly been dropped, like a couple of poor church mice, into the lap of luxury. This world of central heating and constant hot water where even the bathroom had a fitted carpet was something outside our experience. Moreover, everything in that house reflected Mel's unerring good taste, and in this respect she reminded me of Anna whom I had known before the war. Furniture, china and glass all delighted the eye and the touch, while on the walls hung valuable pictures; here and there a sombre, stormy landscape by Vlaminck, a strikingly sinister portrait by the Australian artist, Sidney Nolan, who had then still to make his reputation; over the fireplace a small but exquisite Jack Yeats showing a train on the West Clare line running along the shore of the Shannon estuary between Kilrush and Kilkee at dusk. So alien were these trappings of what the media are pleased to call 'gracious living' that we felt as though we had suddenly been transported to another planet. Past struggles, Sonia with the recalcitrant locks and the mud banks of a badly maintained canal, and I with the manifold ills of a worn out railway, seemed to have been relegated to a region of remote fantasy. Only my ancient Alvis, slumbering in the unaccustomed luxury of the garage next door and incontinently dropping gobbets of black oil upon its pristine floor, served to remind us of the world we had so lately left. We went on shopping expeditions to Witney and, more rarely, to Oxford; we walked in the forest of Wychwood on a bitter, misty day in the dead of winter when all the world was rimed with frost, and in the evenings or in bad weather I tried to make up for time lost during the summer by writing a book which, in the event, was not conspicuously successful.

It was during this weird interregnum at Leafield that I was asked by the committee of the TRPS whether I would be prepared to take charge of the Talyllyn Railway again during the coming 1952 summer season. I considered this invitation long and carefully, not only on financial grounds but also because I knew I should no longer have the skilled and unfailingly willing and cheerful support of David Curwen in the loco shed and repair shop at Pendre. In association with a financial partner, David had bought himself a small general engineering business in Devizes and had told me he could not come to Towyn again. It was not that I doubted my ability to keep the locomotives steaming. No self-respecting Stuart apprentice could possibly admit to such a doubt. It was a simple matter of geography. I could not be in two places at once. From my experience last summer I knew that it would be quite impossible for me to be 'shedmaster' at Pendre and at the same time look after the passenger side of things by issuing tickets at Towyn Wharf station and acting as guard on the trains when, as often happened, no suitable volunteer offered himself for this duty. So far as I could see the railway would only become workable if Sonia was prepared to take charge at Wharf, leaving me free to keep mechanical matters under control at Pendre. This, Sonia was perfectly prepared to do, so it seemed an ideal and – from the point of view of the railway – most economical solution to the staff problem, always provided the puritanical Welsh made no objection to the CME and the Traffic Manager 'living in sin', for there was no prospect of our respective divorces being made absolute by the summer. Strangely enough, although this did prove a stumbling block, the objection came from certain English members of the TRPS committee and not from the Welsh. For many weeks this question made it very doubtful whether or not we should go to Towyn at all, though if we had not I do not know what would have become of the railway because the TRPS was then in no financial position to advertise the posts of two senior staff and pay them the rate for the job.

In 1951, the prospects for a successful season were very nearly ruined when, at the eleventh hour, the TRPS committee got cold feet and forbade me to re-open the line throughout to traffic despite the fact that I had already advertised the service. Then it had been Edward Thomas who had saved the day by remarking: 'If I had been told by Lady Haydn to run the railway this season, I should have done so without any of your assistance.' This forthright rejoinder instilled some Dutch courage into the doubters and I was given the signal to go ahead. Now, for the second time this indefatigable little Welshman proved himself my stout ally, although I like to think that it was the future of the Talyllyn Railway that was uppermost in his mind. It was the occasion of a Board meeting at Towyn at which both he and Lady Haydn were present. It was getting perilously near the start of summer services on the railway, but the Society representatives were still earnestly debating our scandalous situation until Edward Thomas, as he afterwards told me, spoke up saying that he thought the proposed staffing arrangement was an excellent one and that our private lives were nothing whatever to do with the Railway Company. Faced with such a forthright pronouncement from an elderly chapel-going Welshman, his fellow directors capitulated there and then and, without more ado, Sonia and I found ourselves in charge at Wharf and Pendre stations respectively. For reasons of economy we did not stay in digs as I had done the previous season but hired a caravan and obtained permission to park it in a field at Dolgoch. Here we lived pretty well except that Sonia found shopping for food difficult owing to sheer lack of time. We rarely found time even to speak to each other during the five working days except when I called for her at the Wharf station to take her out for a hurried lunch at a small café in the town.

Those who want to read a full account of this 1952 summer season on the railway will find it in the last chapter of *Railway Adventure*. After so long a spell of boating on the canals, it must have been a strange experience for Sonia suddenly to find herself issuing tickets and acting the part of a passenger guard on a train. The latter was rather a unique role for, unlike all other passenger brake-vans, that on the Talyllyn was equipped with a minute ticket office from which tickets were issued at all intermediate stations. To withdraw the right ticket, date stamp it and deal with change in a dark little cubby-hole, perhaps while the train was in motion, causing the van to rock and plunge like a ship in a seaway, called for considerable presence of mind combined with sheer physical agility. Yet I was able to spend most of my time in the little loco shed and workshop at Pendre, secure in the knowledge that the traffic department was in capable hands.

A great deal had been done on the railway since the previous winter to make my life easier. The track layout at the Wharf terminus had been re-designed in a way that made working much safer.* A private telephone line had been installed between the Wharf and Pendre which meant that, in the event of difficulty or emergency, Sonia and I could now communicate with each other. No longer was it necessary to drive pell-mell through the streets of Towyn with howling tyres or, failing a car, send a volunteer hot-foot along the track as David and I had had to do in the past John Alcock, Chairman of Hunslets of Leeds, the locomotive builders who had taken over Kerr Stuart's goodwill and manufacturing rights in 1931, had most generously undertaken to overhaul the ex-Corris Kerr Stuart locomotive No. 4 at his works and deliver it back in time for the start of the season. This meant that I no longer had to rely upon one 86-year-old-locomotive (*Dolgoch*) to maintain the service. Yet in spite of these improvements, there

---

* There was no means of running the engine round its train in 1951. Instead, the only means of getting the engine to the head of the train was as follows: the engine propelled the stock up the incline out of the station where the latter was then held on the brakes while the locomotive retired into a siding. Then the train was allowed to run back by gravity into the platform road. If no one was on hand to apply the guard's brake at the right moment the entire train would have leapt over the end of the Wharf to block British Rail's Cambrian Coast Line.

were still many unexpected vicissitudes to cope with and in one respect – the state of the permanent way – my anxieties were greater than in the previous season. For the need to run more trains in order to earn more revenue for rehabilitation was taking more out of the track in terms of wear and tear than we could possibly put into it. By a superhuman effort we had managed to re-lay so far approximately half-a-mile of track, leaving over five and a half miles in a worse state than ever before despite crude 'first-aid' cobbling measures. This appalling track was racking the locomotives and stock to pieces and there was a constant and growing risk of derailment. Derailments, in fact, did occur during both seasons though fortunately they caused no serious injury, human or mechanical. Yet it was only too clear that we were fighting a losing battle against wear and tear and for the life of me I could not see how this vicious circle was ever to be broken. It called for a massive re-laying programme which was quite beyond the Society's resources.

Despite the hazards of an appalling track, we won through once again, more by luck than judgement, to the end of the summer season on 30 September, by which time the number of passenger journeys stood at 22,866, an increase of 7,238 over the previous year.* But despite this successful result and the fact that at one stage we had seriously thought of finding a house near the railway, we finally decided for various reasons, notably the financial one, that I should announce forthwith that I was giving up the job of Railway Manager so as to allow the Society the maximum of time to find a successor. I remained a member of the committee and acquired the honorary title of 'Superintendent of the Line'.

As in the previous year, the end of the season was marked by the Annual General Meeting of the Society at Towyn. In

* When these figures are compared with that of 5,235 passenger journeys for 1950, the last year of the old regime, the reason for the increased wear and tear can be better appreciated. It is also enlightening to compare these figures with that of the 170,690 passenger journeys for 1972.

1951 it had struck me that this occasion had fallen pretty flat.
The platform party seemed to be so busy congratulating each
other on the conclusion of a successful season that they had
not spared a thought for, or even a cursory mention of, those
who had born the burden and heat of the day. In this I was not
thinking of myself but of my friend David Curwen. Knowing
as I did then that it was only due to the almost miraculous
feats of mechanical improvisation he had performed at Pendre
which had kept the trains moving, I thought it disgraceful
when his name did not receive a mention from those who, at
the beginning of the season, had doubted whether the railway
should be re-opened at all. So I was determined that this
AGM weekend should not fall flat where we were concerned;
at least we would make it the occasion for a little private
celebration, so I invited down Hugh and Gunde Griffith and
my friend John Morley, of pre-war Vintage Sports Car Club
days, who had presented the railway with two of his firm's
electric ballast tampers. They stayed at the Tyn y Cornel hotel
beside Talyllyn Lake, where we joined them. By these
participants, this occasion has gone down in history as the 'lost
weekend'. At one stage in the proceedings I am told that Hugh
and I were to be seen in a stationary boat in the middle of the
lake, each rowing hard in opposite directions and both singing
lustily some traditional Welsh air, though not using the
orthodox words.

We stayed on for a week or so in our caravan at Dolgoch,
partly to recover from the party and partly to explore the area
which we had not the time to do during the season. We
travelled on the Snowdon Mountain Railway, visited the
Dinorwic slate quarries and the Gwynffynydd gold mine.
Visiting the latter was a very strange experience. The gold
mine is in a remote situation in a deep and narrow valley near
the headwaters of the river Mawddach some hundreds of feet
below the road from Dolgelly to Trwsfynydd. When I stopped
and switched off my engine at the head of the rough track that
follows the floor of the valley towards the mine, silence seemed
to fall like a heavy blanket. This was broken by the barking of

a dog and presently a man emerged from a solitary cottage that we had assumed to be empty and approached the car. 'Have you been sent by Mr Roberts?' he inquired eagerly, and when I shook my head he was visibly downcast. He then explained that the mine was on the point of re-opening; it only awaited the arrival of a particular part which the mysterious Mr Roberts had ordered from America before work would be in full swing again. As I had done my homework and knew that the mine had lain derelict since 1929, I must have looked a little sceptical for he waved his arm in a dramatic gesture towards the mountain ahead, declaiming passionately: 'I can take you in there and show you visible gold'. He lowered his voice and repeated the words 'visible gold' with extraordinary emphasis and awe as though he were describing some holy presence made manifest. It was obvious to us both that the man's wits were crazed and I pondered why it was that a near-useless metal should have been capable of wielding such power over the minds of men since the beginning of time. After all, but for gold-lust there might have been no Talyllyn Railway. We shook off our crazy friend somehow and walked past the burnt out ruins of the ore-crushing mill up to the mouth of the adit. Beside it stood the old Dolgelly lock-up which had been rebuilt up here to serve as a strong room for the gold. We noticed the recent footprints left on the muddy floor of the adit, presumably by those hypnotized by the prospect of 'visible gold'. The massive iron door of the gaol was bolted and barred, but someone under the influence of the same lure had actually quarried a hole through its immensely thick wall, presumably in the fond belief that some gold might have been left behind when the mine closed.

By mid-October our hired caravan at Dolgoch was becoming distinctly chilly, especially as the sun only cleared the rim of the mountain for a couple of hours either side of noon. Soon Dolgoch would lose the sun altogether. So we returned the caravan to its owner and became nomads again, poorer than when we had come down to Wales in the spring. This time it was an aunt of Sonia's who came to our rescue. A sterling character she had acted *in loco parentis* towards Sonia since the death of her mother and now she invited us to stay over the winter in her house at Roehampton. It was here, in January 1953, that our elder son Richard first saw the light.

It was during this winter in London that the President of the TRPS, David Northesk, and I were between us able to solve the problem of the rapidly deteriorating permanent way. I discussed this with David, explaining that only massive aid could save the day, and he had the brilliant idea that a contingent of TA Royal Engineers from Longmoor might come down to Towyn and re-lay track for us as a training exercise. An ex-Guardsman himself, David knew all the right doors to knock on, but he wanted me beside him to explain the position in some detail and to emphasize just how vital to the railway's future the job was. I remember talking long and earnestly to some high-up in the War Office, but this was the first time I had ever tiptoed timidly along the so-called 'corridors of power' and I was somewhat bewildered by the ramifications of this strange old-boy network. However, our ploy was successful and it was agreed that a Longmoor detachment would visit the railway next summer although, owing to a most absurd hitch, this very nearly failed to come about. The man responsible for this hitch was none other than Vic Feather, that doughty champion of the trade-union movement. How he got to hear of our scheme I do not know; but like some Don Quixote clad in rusty nineteenth-century armour, he came thundering down upon our pathetic little Talyllyn windmill shouting: 'Unfair to railway workers'. But soon the forces of reaction, led by David Northesk, became locked in combat and eventually Vic Feather and his TUC cohorts beat a retreat. Perhaps it dawned upon them that they were making themselves more than usually ridiculous.

TA contingents from Longmoor paid three visits to the Talyllyn Railway: in the summer of 1953, during the winter of 1953/54 and again during the 1954 summer season. Unfortunately they could not completely re-lay the line because we could not afford enough replacement rail at that time, but

most of the trouble and danger was due, not to the fact that the
rails were badly worn, but that all the sleepers were rotten so
that there was virtually nothing to hold the rails to gauge but
the thick grass that had spread itself all over the formation. We
were able to provide plenty of sleepers which we bought
second-hand from British Railways and then sawed in half so
that one sleeper made two for the narrow gauge. At the loss of
some revenue in fares, the army were given total occupation
on both their summer visits. They tore out the old track, ran a
bulldozer along the formation to remove the grass and level it
off and then laid out the replacement sleepers, spiked the old
rails firmly to them and re-ballasted. Altogether, the army
re-laid two miles of track during these three visits of which a
quarter of a mile was re-railed as well as re-sleepered. At the
end of 1954 there were still substantial lengths of track sorely
needing attention, while the railway as a whole still left a lot to
be desired. Yet this massive help from the army undoubtedly
broke the vicious circle and, to mix metaphors, turned the tide
in our favour.

As spring came in, some good friends of Sonia's offered us
the use, as a flat, of the upper floor of their house at Aller Park
on the north Devon coast, on the Cornish border near
Morwenstow. Feeling we had already leant too heavily on her
aunt's kindness, we accepted gladly and set off one March
morning from Roehampton bound for Devon feeling like some
tinker family on the move with all our worldly possessions on
board plus a two months old baby. My car was even then
twenty-nine years old, but never in its history can it, or any
other 12/50 Alvis duck's back for that matter, have borne such
a burden. The boot in the pointed tail (which has a greater
capacity than one might suppose) was stuffed with belongings
including a basket for the baby; bulging suitcases were
strapped onto each running board. Sonia sat beside me with
Richard in her lap. So far as I can remember he never
complained throughout the long journey. Perhaps he was
already displaying a taste for vintage cars; certainly he soon
showed his distaste for modern ones by turning a bright shade

of green within five miles and then being violently sick. My old car would have to perform two more similar moving operations before our nomadic existence finally came to an end.

Aller Park was set four-square to the winds on the top of a treeless headland, one of a series of promontories with deep valleys between that north Devon and Cornwall thrust out, like so many aggressive knuckles, to meet the challenge of the Atlantic. The saw 'From Padstow Point to Lundy Light is a watery grave by day or night' is not a time-honoured local adage but an invention of the celebrated Parson Hawker of Morwenstow, but it is none the less true for that. The west window of our upstairs sitting room looked down upon one of the most savage stretches of coast in all Britain. On all but the calmest days we lived within sound of the ceaseless warfare waged between stubborn rock and great Atlantic roller, an unending thunder of battle.

In addition to our sitting room, I had the use of a little writing room with a desk set beneath a window that faced south. Whenever, momentarily stuck for the right word, I looked up, I found the prospect from this window very satisfying. Down below was the deep valley of the Marsland stream, the boundary between Devon and Cornwall. Its lower slopes were covered by dense wood of scrub oaks whose tops were so evenly brushed and combed by strong winds off the sea funnelling up the valley that it had the appearance of a green fleece, recently clipped. On the bare slopes above this wood and therefore directly on a level with my eye a man was at plough with a tractor, slowly transforming the smooth green slope of this first Cornish headland into a corduroy of red earth, a white scatter of gulls wheeling at his back. I used to reflect that if I had had the sea instead of mountains in my genetic back-ground, I would doubtless find this majestic landscape as spell-binding as the Black Mountains. Yet although I admired its quality, it failed to move me and sometimes its air of desolation and savagery oppressed me.

After we had stayed for a while at Aller Park, we came to the conclusion that the time had come when we could batten upon the kindness of Sonia's friends and relations no longer. We decided that, money or no money, we should try to find a home of our own somewhere along the Welsh border. To this end, I made a lightning foray from Aller Park up the border as far as Ludlow, where I learnt from a house agent that Laurel Cottage at Clun was to be let furnished for a very modest rental. At least this would be a very convenient base from which to look for something more permanent that we could make our own; also Clun was a place of very pleasant memories for us so I took Laurel Cottage on the spot without consulting Sonia.

So earliest summer saw our Alvis caravan once more upon the move, this time bound north from the west country for Clun. Laurel Cottage was a simple, square stone house of indeterminate date but probably Regency. It was on the eastern edge of the town facing a narrow lane which had not been built up on the opposite side with the effect that it had an uninterrupted view to the east over green fields. Later, we had the chance to purchase Laurel Cottage, but after much thought we decided against it. Because the house was built into rising ground at the back, its rooms got no sun except in the early morning which would make it very gloomy in winter. Owing to this rising ground it was almost impossible to build a garage or even form a parking bay and the lane itself was far too narrow to admit parking. Finally there were persistent rumours of a new council estate to be built in the green field opposite. Nevertheless, despite these disadvantages, present or to come, it was a pleasant, comfortable, friendly little house in which we were very happy during our brief occupation.

Besides Laurel Cottage, we viewed and contemplated purchasing a number of houses in the border country, but either they were quite beyond our financial reach even with the aid of a mortgage or, if they were within our means, they invariably suffered from one or more serious snags. At this point the reader may well ask, if he has not asked long before, what about my family house at Stanley Pontlarge? What indeed!

Unlike Sonia's aunt, my mother had not proffered a helping
hand. Nor would I have been particularly anxious to grasp it if
she had, for I knew that the house was bitterly cold in winter.
There was no electric light and no telephone. My mother had
never used the latter instrument in her life and when one rang
in her vicinity she would regard it as though it were a
poisonous snake. In the long winter evenings the house was
not only chill but in almost perpetual darkness as my mother
groped her way around or sat and read, crouched over a small
fire, by the light of a small wick paraffin lamp. She cooked on
the same two wick paraffin stove which I remembered from
boyhood. It was now blackened with age and fumed and
smoked atrociously. Through the whole house the walls and
ceilings were blackened by the paraffin fumes which could be
smelt in every room.

My mother had been a source of great anxiety to me ever
since my father died in 1941. It had never occurred to her to
take a job and she had continued to live, on her miniscule and
dwindling income from investments, in a house that was not
only much too big for her, but which she could not afford to
repair. Her sole interest and her great labour of love was the
garden which she kept immaculately but in such a way that it
demanded the maximum amount of hard work. So concentrated was her mind upon horticulture that she seemed
blissfully unaware that the house was in an advanced state of
dissolution. Through loss of the oak hanging-pegs or failure of
the cleft laths, stone slates were slipping from the roofs; in
winter, snow blew under the roof creating miniature snowdrifts in the attics which, melting, had brought down the
plaster ceilings in the bedrooms beneath; owing to the failure
of the flashing between the roof of one wing and the gable end
of the other, whenever there was a storm from the north rain
streamed down one wall of a bedroom and into the kitchen
below. My mother seemed oblivious to these defects, which
was perhaps just as well since she lacked the means to have
them put right. Since 1941 this state of affairs had been a
mounting anxiety to me, yet my mother would not entertain

any suggestion of change in her way of life. So a large question mark hung, not only over our future but over that of my mother and the house in Gloucestershire. I realized that if we did succeed in finding a house of our own, this would do nothing to solve the problem of what was to be done about my mother. Could I ignore it until the roof of the house fell about her ears as it undoubtedly would do given a few more years?

At the eleventh hour I received an overture from my mother saying that she would like to see us and also her grandson whom she had not yet set eyes on. Accordingly we motored over from Clun and spent the day with her at Stanley Pontlarge. This visit marked the beginning of discussions between my mother and myself whereby she finally consented to make over the house to me by deed of gift while I, in return, agreed to build a small 'dower house' for her in our orchard about 100 yards distant from the old house. I drew a succession of ground plans of such a house until I arrived at something which suited her and then handed over the approved sketch to an architect. In the late autumn of 1953, my mother went to lodge with a friend in the neighbouring village while we moved into the old house and commenced to dig the foundations of the new with our own hands. The house was built (or rather the operation was directed) by an old Winchcombe builder who had always worked for my family. He was able, conscientious and cheap, but he was old and slow and undependable so that the house, though it was of the most modest description, seemed as though it would never be finished. After interminable, frustrating delays it was finally completed at the end of 1954 and my mother was able to move in. As can be imagined, this was a very difficult transition period for all concerned.

Years before, I think it must have been in 1943, I remembered discussing the problem of what I should do about my solitary mother and the decaying family home with H.J. Massingham. He had replied without hesitation; it was my heritage, and therefore a responsibility which I could not and should not evade. At the time I stowed this advice away in the

back of my mind as one hiding away an unwelcome letter in
the hope that it will disappear. For at the time my thoughts
were all of *Cressy* and I could not see any future beyond her
eventual end. And as for Angela, I already knew her to be such
a restless mortal that I realized she would never be content to
settle down to a conventional life 'on the bank', as the canal
boaters say. Yet here was I, at the age of forty-four, and after
years of peripatetic existence either in digs or on a canal boat,
settling down to a conventional and static way of life 'on the
bank'. At least I had salved my conscience by accepting at last
Massingham's advice which had been niggling away at the
back of my mind. I had accepted my responsibilities and
returned like a homing pigeon to Stanley Pontlarge. But I
would have my work cut out to restore and maintain my
ancient heritage.

Wick paraffin lamps and paraffin stoves, although they had
served me well on *Cressy*, are not the safest forms of lighting
and heating where babies or small children are concerned, so it
was a stroke of luck when the mains electricity at last came to
Stanley Pontlarge very soon after we had moved in. An early
Talyllyn volunteer named John Rapley, who at that time ran a
one-man electrical business known as the Hydropower Company in the wilds of Cardiganshire, wired the house with me as
mate. What unknown pitfalls lie in wait for those with the
temerity to bring such new-fangled devices into medieval
houses! One example will suffice. 'Good', said John, when we
had rolled up the carpet on the first-floor landing and noticed
that the floor-boards ran lengthwise along the corridor, 'We'll
take a run along here'. But when we had, with difficulty,
prised up a floor-board, it was only to find that there was a
second set of boards below the first but running cross-wise.
This, as we subsequently discovered from our old builder, was
the practice known as 'casing'. It meant that when one set of
floor-boards wore hollow, you simply nailed another set across
them. We were also lucky enough to get a telephone pretty
soon. With such mod cons as electric light and telephone my
mother would have no truck; she moved into her new house

with her old wick lamps and her old stove, both of which she was still using at the time of writing, with the effect that pristine walls and ceilings soon became appropriately blackened. But she had to have piped water and drainage. The former was no problem; it simply meant coupling her up to our supply which was spring water piped from a point sufficiently high on the hillside above to run into the roof tanks by gravity.

Providing the new house with a drainage system was a very different story. In theory it should have been an equally simple matter, for the line of the main sewer from the old house to a septic tank at the bottom of our orchard ran within twenty feet of the new one. Yet the orchard resembled the scene of some desperate search for treasure trove before we finally located that sewer pipe at a depth of eight feet. This, despite the efforts of Sonia (who fancied herself at the art) to locate the pipe by walking to and fro with her divining rod while we had every tap in the house running. We came eroniously to the conclusion that such rods don't respond to piped water.

Most of Sonia's belongings, including a large quantity of books, lay mouldering in a tiny condemned cottage which she had rented as a store at Buckby Wharf beside the Grand Union Canal in Northamptonshire. Most helpfully, John Rapley lent us his lorry to go and fetch these. When Sonia's books were added to mine they made a formidable pile even after the duplicates had been weeded out. New bookshelves were therefore a high priority, but the difficulty was that timber was still in short supply. Here again the ever resourceful John saved the day. Apparently, in the village with a long and unpronounceable name where he lived in darkest Cardigan, the bureaucratic writ concerning timber licences did not run, for one day he turned up from Wales with a load of planks from which I constructed the first of many sets of bookshelves. These first ones occupy the whole of one end wall of our drawing room. The other do-it-yourself job I did at this time was to create a small writing room-cum-business office on the first floor. This I did by partitioning off a small portion of the very large bedroom which my mother had used and which occupied the whole south end of the medieval part of the house. This bedroom had four windows, two facing south and the others east and west respectively. My new office took away an east and a south window and still left us with a large, light bedroom.

Much as I enjoyed working with my hands, all this do-it-yourself activity was undertaken because I could not afford to employ anyone else. For our coming to Stanley Pontlarge had coincided precisely with the moment when my financial affairs had touched rock bottom and when, for the first time, I began to entertain serious doubts of my ability to earn a living by writing. To the cumulative effect of the past two summers I had spent at Towyn with not a word written was added the unpalatable fact that the last two books I had produced had turned out financial failures. A third book, which I had completed while we were at Clun, was due to appear in the spring of 1954 and was to be the most monumental failure of my whole literary career. I shall expand upon these literary disasters later; the operative fact here is that by the time this final heavy blow fell in 1954, its effect upon me was mercifully cushioned because I had obtained another lucrative and interesting, albeit temporary, job through the good offices of my old pre-war friends in the Vintage Sports Car Club.

3
On Vintage Motoring

For obvious reasons, the VSCC had suspended its activities
during the war years and I had dropped out of touch with all
the friends I had made at Phoenix Green where the Club was
born in the mid-1930s. When the war ended the Club was one
of the first motoring organizations to become active again and
its membership began to grow rapidly, as it has continued to
do ever since. But although I continued to use one or other of
my two 12/50 Alvises for every-day motoring and to pay my
Club subscription, I was slow to pick up this particular thread
in my many-stranded life owing to my almost total involve-
ment in the affairs of the IWA. Indeed, so detached had I
become from the world of motor cars, that when I received a
letter from Alan Southon, my successor at the Phoenix Green
Garage, saying that he had my 1903 Humber there and what
should he do with it, I had instructed him without hesitation
to get it into running order (it had been in store since 1939)
and then sell it for what it would fetch. I reflected that as I had
only paid two pounds for the old car and it had given me an
immense amount of pleasure, it certainly did not owe me
anything and I was therefore perfectly satisfied with Alan's
cheque   for   £35   which   was   the   net   result   of   this
correspondence.

Of my two vintage Alvises, the 1924 'duck's back' two-seater
which I acquired in 1935 and the 1925 model four-seater
which I inherited from my father, I greatly preferred the
former, not merely because it had been in my ownership for so
long but because I considered its handling qualities vastly
superior to those of the later car. With its light, whippy chassis

and brakes only on the rear wheels, with the exception of the engine it was virtually an Edwardian design, and cars of that epoch are always a delight to drive. They reveal how much was lost when chassis became stiffer, when tyres came to resemble doughnuts and when the first, not particularly effective front wheel brakes, added unsprung weight and ruined the precision of the steering. One drives a car of this Edwardian type through the seat of one's pants. In other words, it communicates knowledge of varying road conditions and of its own power of adhesion to the driver in the most subtle manner. As cars became gradually more sophisticated and refined, so this *rapport* between car and driver has been almost lost. It was for this reason that, while I lost no time in getting my own car onto the road again after the war, my father's old car continued to slumber in its garage at Stanley Pontlarge until 1949.

In the spring of that year my own car, XU 362, broke a connecting rod which came out through the side of the crankcase. This meant a major rebuild of the engine which could not be hurried and as I needed road transport I went over to Stanley Pontlarge with Jim Russell and Bill Trinder, got my father's car off its blocks, and towed it back to Banbury where I restored it to running condition. This is how it came about that during the summers of 1949 and 1950 it was the 4-seater Alvis that acted as tender car to *Cressy*. It was partly the fact that this car was running very well at the time and partly some sixth sense which knew that my life afloat was coming to an end that made me decide, in August 1949, while *Cressy* lay at Pont Cysyllte and Angela was in Italy, that I would enter for the Vintage Sports Car Club annual hill climb at Prescott. I was thus brought into personal contact again with many old friends of pre-war days who had thought me lost forever to the canals. This renewal of my links with the VSCC was to stand me in good stead later although I little realized it at the time.

During the winter of 1953/54, the British Travel & Holidays Association (BTHA), with the object of attracting American

tourists to England, thought up the notion of holding a
competitive car rally between equally-matched teams of
American and English vintage cars. The Association there-
upon approached the committee of the VSCC to ask if it
considered the idea feasible and, if so, whether the Club
would be prepared to organize such an event, to take place
early in the following September. The Club committee
thought it a splendid idea and, early in 1954, I was asked if I
was prepared to organize it by acting both as Secretary of the
Meeting and Clerk of the Course. On signifying my agreement
in principle, I was bidden to a joint meeting of the Association
and the Club in the former's offices in St James's where my
appointment was officially blessed. It carried with it a handsome salary, plus all expenses, to be paid by the Association.
Thus, thanks to the VSCC I had obtained, at one stroke, an
assignment that promised a most rewarding experience and a
welcome financial boost that could not have been more timely.

At first it was mainly a matter of desk-work for there were
innumerable arrangements to be made and details to be settled
between the VSCC, its opposite number, The Veteran Car
Club of America; with the R.A.C.; with the police and with
Shell-Mex & B.P., the latter company having agreed to give
competing cars and those of travelling marshals free petrol at
selected garages along the route. It had been suggested that
this route should be from Edinburgh to Chichester where final
tests might be carried out on the nearby Goodwood Circuit.
The BTHA felt that for the benefit of the visiting team, the
rally should pass through, and preferably stop at, as many
historic towns as possible; also places of particular American
historic interest such as Boston and Sulgrave Manor. But the
route could not be finally fixed until hotel and meal arrangements had been made. Britain's hotel and catering industry
had not then got into its post-war stride and it was no easy
matter to find accommodation for sixty-five people and
twenty-nine cars, figures that include reserves and travelling
officials. Very fortunately for me, the BTHA undertook to
deal with this problem and in the spring I set off to drive along

the line of route with A.M. McNab, representing the BTHA. It was McNab's thankless task to arrange luncheon stops and book suitable overnight accommodation for this large party, sometimes spread over two or more adjoining hotels but preferably in one. To some extent his search was limited by my judgement as to the suitability of the route and the desirable length of each morning and afternoon stage; also on the availability of suitably supervised car-parking space at midday stops and covered garaging at night.

We headed north through Lancashire, for the Americans and their cars would be disembarking at Liverpool some days before the start of the event, and the idea was that I should meet them at the landing stage and subsequently pilot them by easy stages up to Edinburgh. For this preliminary canter we arranged a first night stop at Grange-over-Sands, followed by lunch in Keswick, so that our guests could see the Lake District, before going on to Carlisle for the second night. On the third day the drive would be from Carlisle to Edinburgh via Moffat and the Beeftub Pass. Because both teams would be arriving in Edinburgh during Festival Week, hotel reservations there were particularly important. In Scotland, however, McNab's writ did not run; protocol demanded that the Scottish Tourist Board should be responsible for the Edinburgh bookings – with embarrassing results as things turned out.

With the Edinburgh arrangements in capable hands, or so we thought, we set out to plan the long rally route southwards. We considered the White Swan at Alnwick, our projected first night stop, and quite the best hotel on the entire programme, but unfortunately it was small and we were obliged to split the party by booking additional accommodation at an hotel at Alnmouth. We hoped to make our next night's stop at York, but this proved to be quite impossible and we had to make Harrogate our destination instead, visiting York the next morning. However, these were the only two cases where hotel problems enforced a change of plan. When I was able to finalize the route it read like this: (see page 56)

Day	Start	Time	Lunch Stop	Tea Stop	Finish	Time
1	Edinburgh Castle	10.00 a.m.	11.00–1.45	Dirleton	–	Alnwick Castle	4.45
2	Alnwick, White Swan	10.00 a.m.	12.30–1.45	Durham	–	Harrogate	5.40
3	Harrogate	10.15 a.m.	11.15–1.30	York	–	Boston, Lincs.	5.30
4	Boston	10.30 a.m.	12.30–3.00	Ely	–	Cambridge	5.00
5	Cambridge Backs	9.30 a.m.	12.20–1.30	Sulgrave	Oxford	Leamington	6.30
6	Leamington	10.00 a.m.	12.30–3.00	Stratford	Prescott Hill	Cheltenham	6.30
7	Cheltenham	10.00 a.m.	12.–1.45	Savernake	Winchester	Chichester	6.15
8	Chichester	10.00 a.m.	to Goodwood Circuit for final tests.				

There then followed much correspondence with both the competing Clubs about the selection of their teams. In each team there were to be five Edwardian cars (i.e. cars built before 1915) and five vintage cars built between 1915 and 1926. I have to admit that I brought a lot of pressure to bear on the American Club to include a Stanley steam car in their team. This they very sportingly agreed to do, but although the steamer created more public interest than any other competing car, it lost the Americans a great many points in the competition. The moguls of Shell seemed quite foxed by the news that a steam car was coming over and asked me what fuel it would require. But when I replied 'lamp oil', from my experience of a Stanley at Evesham many years before, Shell at once put me in my place by saying that surely I must mean TVO. I did not argue further; after all they should know.

When the two teams had been picked they consisted of the following: (see pages 58–9). The American Team was also allowed two reserves which would accompany it throughout the event. These were a 1916 Stutz 'Bearcat' driven by Tony Koveleski and McKelvie's 1929 Dusenberg roadster.

It is worth noticing that the American cars were older than ours but that their engines were of considerably larger capacity, thus reflecting that big car tradition in America which has persisted to this day. Besides these twenty competing cars and the two reserves, there were those of the members of the VSCC who would accompany them as stewards or marshals. These included Sam Clutton's 1908 Itala, Forrest Lycett's famous 8 litre Bentley, Kent Karslake in a Hispano Suiza, Laurence Pomeroy, most appropriately driving a 'Prince Henry' Vauxhall of his father's design, and Arthur Jeddere-Fisher in an Edwardian Lancia 'Theta' coupe. Finally, there were the two Alvises of John Morley and myself, his a 12/60 'beetle back' and mine the 1924 'duck's back' which had been back on the road again since 1951.

That summer, McNab and I had a second run over the course to ensure that everything was planned down to the last detail. The route had been arranged to enable the Americans

America

Car No.	Date	Make	Type	Litres or hp	Driver
1	1906	Ford	Model K Speedster	6 cyl. 40 hp	Elmer W. Bemis
2	1906	Stanley	Gentleman's Speedy Roadster	20 hp	Paul J. Tusek
3	1913	Lozier	'Toy Tonneau'	6 cyl. 51 hp (9,030cc)	Rod Blood
4	1914	Mercer	Raceabout	4 cyl. 5 litres	Ralph T. Buckley
5	1914	Simplex	Series F	4 cyl. $9\frac{3}{4}$ litres	Sam E. Baily
*6	1916	Pierce-Arrow	Raceabout	6 cyl. 13 litres	H. Austin Clark, Jun.
7	1918	Biddle	Model K Speedway Spl.	4 cyl. $5\frac{1}{2}$ litres	Ed S. Hansen
8	1919	Stutz	'Bulldog' Tourer	4 cyl. 5,900cc	Clarence Kay
9	1923	Kissel	Speedster	6 cyl. 61 hp	A.C. Baker
10	1921	Mercer	Raceabout	4 cyl. 5 litres	Roswell Moore

England Car No.	Date	Make	Type	Litres or hp	Driver
1	1908	Wolseley	4 str Tourer	4 cyl. $3\frac{3}{4}$ litres	Douglas FitzPatrick
2	1914	Vauxhall	Prince Henry	4 cyl. 4 litres	Ronald Barker
3	1910	Rolls-Royce	Silver Ghost	6 cyl. $7\frac{1}{2}$ litres	S.J. Skinner
4	1913	Sunbeam	4 str Tourer	4 cyl. 3 litres	D. Denne
5	1913	Lanchester	4 str Tourer	6 cyl. 38 hp (rated)	F. Hutton-Stott
*6	1920	Vauxhall	E Type 30/98	4 cyl. $4\frac{1}{2}$ litres	T.W. Carson
7	1935	Alvis	TE 4 str Tourer	4 cyl. 1,686 cc	A.J. Clarke
8	1926	Sunbeam	4 str Sports	6 cyl. 3 litres	A.S. Heal
9	1928	Frazer Nash	3 str Sports	4 cyl. $1\frac{1}{2}$ litres	A.T. Pugh
10	1928	Bentley	4 str Sports	4 cul. $4\frac{1}{2}$ litres	T.P. Breen

* Denotes Team Captain

to see something of our historic towns and buildings, but although an allowance of seven days to cover a total of 768 miles may sound like a very leisurely tour, in fact it was quite a tough assignment for elderly motor cars. On each stage they were expected to average not less than 25 and not more than 30 mph. Each team was credited at the start with 2,500 marks and individual cars lost one mark for each minute's late arrival at the finishing controls. On the other hand, a competitor averaging more than 35 mph between controls would lose thirty marks for his team. Besides the final tests on the Goodwood Circuit, there were four special tests which I located at various points along the rally route: a slow-fast test on a straight and level stretch of bye-road near Cambridge; a starting test in which each driver had to start his car from cold against a stop watch – this was arranged at Leamington as the hotel there had a large garage and yard at the rear which was very suitable; a speed hill climb at Prescott where each competitor would be allowed one practice and two competitive runs; and finally, on the last stage of all, a stop and restart test on the steepest section of South Harting, a hill on the Chichester road out of the village of that name which is well known in motoring history as the scene of many hill climb meetings in the early days. Each car failing to restart in this test would cost his team forty marks.

So, with all the arrangements made, in the last week of August Sonia and I set off from Stanley Pontlarge with our small son in the Alvis, our destination being Sonia's aunt's house at Roehampton where we had arranged to leave Richard in charge of a nanny for the duration of the rally. After a night in Roehampton we headed for Liverpool where the American team was due to arrive the following morning. For the first thirty miles or so of that journey I remember feeling very uneasy, imagining I heard every kind of ominous sound from the engine. For although I had devoted such care and forethought to the motoring side of the whole event, only now did I realize with a dull thud that I had taken no account at all of what would happen in the ignominious event of my own car breaking down. Added to this realization was the fact that I had recently had to do some major work on the engine and therefore had reason to expect teething troubles. But as we left London behind and the roads became clearer I ceased to worry for the old Alvis was running like a watch – as indeed, it continued to do throughout the event which, for us, meant well over 1,000 miles of motoring during which I never had occasion to lift the front seat and get out my tool roll.

Soon we were diving through the Mersey Tunnel to arrive at the Adelphi Hotel garage where we were pleased and relieved to see the Lancia 'Theta' parked. We met Arthur Jeddere-Fisher and his wife Marcia in the hotel. Over the next four days they were towers of strength to us in the task of shepherding the American team up to Edinburgh and in making them feel at home. This social side of things became progressively easier as the event went on and we came to know the Americans better; also, on the rally itself, there were many more of us around to play host. Anyway, by the end of it all the fact that they had shared in such a large slice of experience acted as a bond between the two teams. It was a case of hands across the sea with a vengeance because we all became firm friends who might have known each other for years. However, our first encounter with the American team in Liverpool was somewhat embarrassing.

The ship, the small Cunarder *Media*, came alongside the landing stage and we duly greeted the Americans as they filed down the gangway. Then we all stood around talking while we awaited the unloading of their precious cars. Eventually the hatches were off and the ship's derricks were lowered into the holds. From the for'ard hold there presently emerged, not a motor car as we expected but an outsized and very expensive-looking refrigerator. This had been lifted fully and was in process of being swung overside towards the quayside when it suddenly slipped from its slings and fell, hitting the edge of the quay wall. It burst asunder on impact, releasing coils of pipe, wires and suchlike complex technological intestines, some of which remained behind on the quay to remind us of

its passing after it had toppled into the opaque waters of the
Mersey. Between those responsible this episode occasioned
some profanity, though no more than would have occurred if
one had accidentally nudged and spilt a drop of the other's
pint of beer, but its effect upon the Americans was understandably traumatic. Putting a brave face on it, Arthur and I
argued cheerfully that the fate of the refrigerator was bound to
act as an Awful Warning and that their cars would be handled
with extra care in consequence. And so it proved, although as
each car was landed safely the sighs of relief were almost
audible.

That evening our American guests and ourselves were
entertained to dinner in the Town Hall by the Lord Mayor of
Liverpool. This splendid late eighteenth-century building was
originally built, to the designs of the Woods of Bath, as the
Liverpool Exchange but was subsequently enlarged and the
interior reconstructed, following a fire, by John Foster jun., a
local architect and the son of the engineer of Liverpool's
docks, acting in collaboration with James Wyatt. It would
have been difficult to imagine any more suitable setting for the
lustrous mahogany dining table, lit by candelabra and
burdened by a dazzling display of the City's ceremonial
silverware, than a great room that represented the apogee of
the Age of Reason. This scene was the subject of mixed
feelings on my part. Although my reason knew that it was all a
charade, an elaborate piece of municipal flim-flummery staged
at the request of the British Travel & Holidays Association in
order to impress our visitors and so help to earn dollars for
Britain, nevertheless I must confess to being impressed in
spite of myself. I could not help feeling proud of the fact that
the Americans, many of whom had never crossed the Atlantic
before, were being given a welcome to this country which they
were unlikely ever to forget. Before the rally was over it would
be made an occasion of a number of municipal junketings of
one kind or another, but for sheer stately magnificence none
surpassed that staged by the City of Liverpool.

Next morning we were provided with a police escort as far

as the city boundary. This was a relief to Arthur and myself since neither of us could guarantee to find our way out of the Liverpool labyrinth without hesitation, and I could imagine nothing more humiliating than to lead our flock into some cul-de-sac. We had agreed that I should head the procession while Arthur followed in the Lancia to round up any stragglers and render assistance where necessary. Apart from some slight difficulty over parking at the lunch stop at Garstang, this first day's run went pretty smoothly so far as I was concerned. I turned into the drive of the hotel at Grange – a huge place dedicated to conferences – right on schedule and then counted nine American cars safely home, but of the tenth, the Stanley steamer, there was no sign. When Arthur eventually put in an appearance in the Lancia, I was as alarmed as he was surprised. He assured me that he had not seen the Stanley and had naturally assumed that all ten cars were ahead of him. He very nobly volunteered to go back over the route and look for the lost sheep and very soon returned again, accompanied, to my intense relief, by the Stanley, puffing as heartily as ever.

It transpired that the proud owner-driver of the Stanley, Paul Tusek, had only had the car two years and was as yet unversed in the vagaries of steamers. Knowing this, the American Club had nominated as his passenger/mechanic one Ed Battison who was reputed to be one of the foremost American authorities on the steam car. Ed was a tall, loose-limbed New Englander with a long face and a lantern jaw. His was a delightfully dry wit, there was a humorous twinkle in his eye and he was immensely knowledgeable, not only about steam cars but also on horology, and on archaeology generally, particularly that branch of it which is now termed industrial. We took an immediate liking to Ed but it soon became clear that all was not as it should be between him and the pilot of the Stanley. Paul's motto appeared to be 'don't talk to the man at the wheel' for he persistently ignored Ed's sage advice while driving, yet whenever he paid the penalty for this ignorance, he relied upon Ed to get him out of trouble. The chief cause of dissension was Paul's failure to stop in time to replenish his water tank. Because they exhaust freely to atmosphere, early Stanleys such as his have a far brisker performance than the later condensing models, such as I had known in my youth at Pitchill, where the engine has to fight against back-pressure on the exhaust side due to the inadequacy of the condenser. But this superior performance of the older cars is offset by the need to refill the water tank every 30 to 35 miles or so. Once at the wheel, however, Paul seemed to become so intoxicated by his car's effortless performance that he would ignore all his mechanic's entreaties to stop and take on more water. It was just as well that the crew were equipped with a generous supply of spare fusible plugs. On this first occasion, however, they had not actually 'dropped the plug' although the situation had become so desperate that Ed had eventually prevailed upon Paul to turn aside up a track to a farmhouse. What the stolid occupants of that farm thought of the sudden arrival of two Americans riding a strange machine trailing a cloud of steam behind it and crying 'Water! Water!' is not recorded.

I seldom sleep well during a first night in a strange bed especially when, as on this occasion, I feel tense and excited, my mind preoccupied with details of days past and to come. Perhaps I was too concerned that the event should prove a success, yet I could not escape the fact that success depended very heavily on me. Consequently I had missed out on a great deal of sleep by the time the rally came to an end. Somehow the recollection of this first night at Grange has remained vividly with me whereas so much else has gone beyond recall. I remember how I awoke very early in the morning and, finding further sleep impossible, crept stealthily out of bed so as not to disturb Sonia. The window was wide open at the bottom for the night had been balmy and still considering how far north we had come. I knelt behind the curtains with my elbows resting on the sill, chin propped on forearm, and watched the dawn break over Morecambe Bay. It was low tide and a great expanse of sand stretched southward down the Lancashire coast in the direction of Heysham. The still air was filled with the crying and piping of innumerable sea birds and, directly below my window, dozens of small waders were hurrying to and fro on delicate feet as though walking over perilously thin ice. Before the railway age, travellers on foot, and even by coach it is said, used to avoid the long detour between Lancashire and Furness by crossing these sands. This looked an improbably daring exercise to me and I am not surprised that there should be so many legends, probably exaggerated or apocryphal, of people sinking in quicksands or overwhelmed by the tide.

While we were lunching in Keswick next day, Ed Battison suddenly turned to me and announced that he did not want to leave the town without seeing the Castlerigge stone circle. I felt thoroughly ashamed to admit that I was unaware of what he assured me was the finest stone circle in England, Stonehenge apart. It was arranged there and then that while I took Ed up to Castlerigge in the Alvis, Sonia would accompany Paul on the Stanley to Carlisle. Castlerigge was certainly well worth seeing. The circle of stones is almost complete and, set as it is on the summit of a green knoll, it is surrounded by a magnificent panorama of the Cumberland Fells, looking over Derwentwater towards the jaws of Borrowdale. Nevertheless, I confess that at this moment machines took priority over landscape in my mind. How I envied Sonia her journey to Carlisle on the Stanley! The run from Keswick was just within the steamer's tank capacity so there were no more water crises and, according to her account, the Stanley fairly ate up the miles to Carlisle, bowling along with effortless ease and silence. As things turned out, I never did succeed in having a ride on that Stanley thus my jealousy has never been appeased.

What happened next morning on the stage from Carlisle to Tweedsmuir is best told by quoting from my account of the Liverpool–Edinburgh run which I wrote for the VSCC *Bulletin* when the scenes it describes were still fresh in my mind:

Two days on the road had revealed one oversight in our itinerary due to our native inability to cater adequately for the needs of long-distance motorists. Whereas our womenfolk have become resigned to climbing field gates and disappearing behind hedges in pouring rain, every American 'Gas Station' worthy of the name provides what is euphemistically called a 'Ladies' Powder Room'. Not unnaturally, our lady visitors had expected to find the same amenity provided at our filling stations and had suffered considerable discomfort as a result. This being so, I had made a tactful announcement that on this day's run the cars would make a mid-morning stop in the square at Moffat so that those who wished could take coffee at the adjoining hotel. At the same time I had impressed upon Paul Tusek that he must stop and fill the Stanley's water tank at Moffat because he would find no water at all on the long climb over the Tweedsmuir Hills to Tweedsmuir by the Beeftub Pass.

We left Carlisle in pouring rain, but nine cars arrived in good time at Moffat after an uneventful run. Needless to add, the missing tenth was the Stanley. Arthur Jeddere-Fisher arrived to report that the car had been seen leaving Carlisle in the direction of Keswick, that it had been retrieved and headed back with some difficulty, but had since disappeared. Meanwhile I had sought local help in laying on a convenient watering arrangement for the Stanley if it arrived. This consisted of a length of hose attached to a tap inside the Public Lavatory. One by one the cars moved off in the direction of the lunch stop at the Crook Inn at Tweedsmuir, and soon I was left alone in the rain-swept square. Where *was* the Stanley? Perhaps Paul had missed the Moffat turning at Beattock and was well on the way to Glasgow by now.

But no – suddenly above the roof of an approaching car I caught sight of two cowled heads and a cloud of steam. But relief turned instantly to dismay as Paul drove rapidly through the square and vanished up the road.

Jumping into my car, I managed to head him off and shepherd him back to the Public Lavatory where, before a large audience, the tank-filling operation was smoothly and swiftly carried out. For me this was the most memorable scene of the whole event and I bitterly regret that no pictorial record was made of it.

Fortunately the weather improved as the day went on and by the time we reached the Edinburgh city boundary, where we were met by a motorcycle police escort, it was quite dry though still overcast. At first it seemed to us that the Scottish Tourist Board had made their arrangements with great efficiency. The police led us to a single large garage where all the cars were to be parked until the start of the event on Saturday. On arrival, each competitor was handed a duplicated sheet indicating at which hotel in the city he and his passenger had been booked in. Furthermore, a row of taxis stood ready and waiting outside the garage to ferry us to these hotels. Within minutes of our arrival Sonia and I found ourselves in a comfortable bedroom at the very top of the North British Hotel. This room had curious little *Oeil-de-Boeuf* windows in the angles of the room which framed Waverley station and Princes Street as in a pair of vignettes. I could see to my delight, far below, Gresley Pacifics coasting majestically into the station or, southbound, vomiting clouds of smoke and steam as they pulled away with that characteristic three-cylinder beat that sounds so strange and syncopated to ears accustomed to the locomotives of the Great Western.

We were delighted with this accommodation, but, on glancing down the list, we were a little puzzled to know why we should be the only members of our cavalcade to be booked into this very large hotel. I also noticed that Arthur and Marcia Jeddere-Fisher had alone been booked into a hotel which, on referring to my AA book, I found was even more liberally endowed with stars than our own. I decided to ring Arthur and enquire after his welfare. 'Fine!', was the answer, 'This hotel couldn't be better, why don't you two come over and dine with us?' We thought this an admirable suggestion so we walked over and were rewarded by a meal which, coming so soon after post-war austerity, seemed quite outstanding. With the journey from Liverpool safely accomplished by all concerned, we were in a mood to celebrate and it was not until we were feeling thoroughly mellow after a second glass of port that we decided it might be a good and hospitable idea to visit our American guests and see how they were faring. A glance at our duplicated sheet had shown that most of them were quartered in the same hotel: obviously some large caravanserai designed to impress overseas visitors, we thought; but when the four of us had piled into Arthur's Lancia, it did strike us as a little odd that no one, from the doorman of Arthur's hotel to strolling policemen, appeared to have the faintest idea where this hotel was to be found. We spent a lot of time cruising round Edinburgh before we finally ran it to earth in one of those suburbs which have seen better days but which, by a superhuman effort, have contrived to remain precariously respectable. The hotel consisted of a number of terrace houses run together so that it possessed no depth but considerable length. The façade was not impressive, however. Through an uncurtained window, immediately to the right of the front door, we glimpsed a scene that instantly overwhelmed us with embarrassment. We found ourselves looking into what had obviously been in palmier days a 'front room' but had been thriftily converted into a bedroom by the insertion of two double beds which took up most of the floor space. There was, of course, no fitted wash basin let alone the private bath which most transatlantic visitors expect. Sitting or sprawling on the two beds were our American friends and their wives eating fish and chips out of paper bags by the light of a naked bulb overhead. They were delighted to see us and very cheerful under the circumstances, but we doubted if they would have been so forebearing had they known the standard of their hosts' accommodation. We gave the only explanation possible under the circumstances – difficulty of booking rooms during Festival Week – apologies for sub-standard temporary accommodation and an assurance that they would be moving to more appropriate quarters the next day.

If the worst came to the worst we were perfectly prepared to exchange rooms with our guests. That would at least have made two couples happy, but in the event this sacrifice proved unnecessary. By reading the riot act to the Scottish Tourist Board next morning, the individual responsible for the bookings contrived, heaven knows how, to move all the Americans to better hotels forthwith. Why in the first place he should have housed us in luxury while he relegated our American guests to what was virtually a doss-house is something I have never been able to fathom. Either he must have been preternaturally stupid or else he concealed a positive phobia about Americans. Anyway, he was responsible for the only really embarrassing few hours we experienced during the whole event.

A high proportion of the English team railed their cars up to Edinburgh and these arrived in covered vans ahead of their owners. I have pleasant recollections of driving the 'Prince Henry' Vauxhall through the streets of the city early one morning en route for the garage where the rival team was housed. It had a very brisk performance for a car of 1914, reminding me of its derivations, the famous 30/98 Vauxhall with which I had become so familiar in my days at the Phoenix Green Garage before the war.

The morning of the start was fine and sunny as the two teams lined up together for the first time on the Castle Esplanade at Edinburgh. The competitors were arranged in numerical order which meant that the oldest cars were at the front with Sam Clutton's Itala and my Alvis heading the columns as pilot cars. With polished brass and nickel plate twinkling in the morning sunlight, the two columns of cars made a brave sight as the Lord Provost officially started us on our way and into the first hazard. This consisted of driving between ranks of pipers who, dressed in full fig, piped us such a deafening farewell salute that it quite drowned the noise of our engines, which were not of the quietest.

I do not intend at this distance of time to give a blow-by-blow account of the days which followed, but only to mention certain incidents which spring vividly to mind whenever I recall this memorable event in my life. The first day's run was smooth and uneventful, but towards the end of Sunday's long stage from Alnwick to Harrogate it became obvious that all was not well in the American camp. First, we sighted the Stanley stopped beside the road amid a haze of smoke and a strong smell of burning paint, its crew standing regardant on the grass verge. The burner beneath the Stanley's boiler, which operates upon the primus principle, had suddenly ceased to vaporise with the effect that yellow flames and thick black smoke began to belch from every cranny of the car. Ed had promptly released the tank pressure so that by the time we arrived upon the scene the fire was out and Ed was regarding the car with calm amusement, particularly the yellow paint on top of the snub bonnet which had risen in one enormous blister. 'Looks like a mighty fine omelet', was Ed's laconic remark. Ed seemed satisfied that he could cope with the situation so we went on our way and soon overtook the Lozier limping slowly along emitting a horrible clanking noise from its nether regions.

At the Harrogate hotel, Sonia and I were allotted a most spacious and luxurious bedroom complete with private bath but, tantalizingly, I saw practically nothing of these creature comforts because I spent practically the whole night working on these two American lame ducks which had managed to crawl into the Harrogate garage. Because it was a Sunday evening, no mechanics were available, yet the cars must be ready for the road by the morning if it was humanly possible. The Stanley's trouble, which had made its burner increasingly temperamental ever since the car left Liverpool, proved to be that the vaporiser tube was almost blocked solid with carbon. So solid was it, in fact, that the in-situ steel wire 'pull-through' provided for cleaning the tube was so firmly embedded that it was impossible to extract it. The burner had to be removed and the offending tube drilled out. The reason for this excessive carbonization, the like of which Ed Battison had never seen before, was undoubtedly the use of TVO. For shortly after this when, characteristically, Paul Tusek ran out of fuel in a small village miles from anywhere, they were obliged to refuel at a village shop which only stocked lamp oil. There was no more trouble in the Stanley's steam-raising department from then on, much to the delight of her crew. So the boffins of Shell had been wrong in recommending TVO and my hunch had been right after all. And while on this subject of fuel, I fear that the Shell Company and their filling station managers were somewhat downcast to discover members of both teams queuing up for the BP Commercial pump and leaving the more exotic Shell brands severely alone. We were not looking any gift horses in the mouth; it was simply that, as our American friends knew as well as we did, modern high octane fuels make an unsuitable diet for elderly, low compression engines.

The trouble with the Lozier proved even more intractable than the Stanley's choked vaporiser. Indeed the car had been lucky to reach Harrogate at all for its front universal was in an advanced stage of disintegration. At this stage I have to say that, compared with English practice of equivalent date, the American cars were archaic in design and crude in execution. The side-valve L head engine of the 'Prince Henry' Vauxhall might seem archaic by modern standards, but it was highly efficient compared with the contemporary T head side-valve American power unit as this rally revealed. The Lozier was particularly agricultural in its engineering, the offending universal being the most primitive type of Hooke joint. I spent a long time flat on my back under the car dismantling it, only to find that part of the joint needed welding and re-machining before it could be assembled again. By this time I was almost asleep on my feet, but I have dim recollections of knocking up a general machinist, to whom I had been recommended, in the early hours of the morning and of holding converse with him as he leaned out of his bedroom. I can't think why he did not throw a jug of water over me and slam the window shut, but instead that stout Yorkshireman dressed, opened up his little workshop and did the job. Then I had to reassemble the car and it was broad daylight before it was ready for the road.

It was an overcast morning and although it remained fine during the prolonged midday stop in York, when the time came round for starting the long timed section to Boston it began to rain relentlessly and continued to do so all the way to Boston. Nevertheless, when I think of the rally it is this afternoon's run that I recall more clearly than any other. For some reason which I cannot now remember, having timed the competing cars away from York it was essential that I arrived at Boston in time to clock them in at the finish control. Although the cars were forbidden to exceed a 35 mph average on pain of penalty, to overtake all of them meant some pretty hard driving, particularly as it was wet and the greater part of the route consisted of narrow 'B' class roads through flat, fenny country where occasional long straights alternated with sharp corners and twisting sections dictated by the dikes and drains bordering the road. As a result of press and radio reporting we found that the rally was attracting an increasing amount of interest as we progressed. Undeterred by the rain, there seemed to be little groups of people gathered in each village and at most road intersections to watch the cars go by. To a man they were evidently convinced that they were watching a long distance road race and, because I was driving noticeably faster than the others, I found myself repeatedly greeted with cheers, wavings on and shouts of 'Come on England!' Obviously they were under the impression that, having been delayed in the earlier stages, I was, despite the bad conditions, making a determined bid for the lead. Although it was misplaced, I became infected by this enthusiasm and had a most enjoyable drive, arriving at the point I had selected for the finish control on the outskirts of Boston well before the first competitor came into sight. Granted that I had been indulging in a piece of exhibitionism, but nevertheless that afternoon I came neaerer to experiencing what it must have felt like to drive in one of the great trans-continental road races of the Edwardian era than I shall ever do again.

The next memorable event for me was the lengthy and leisurely lunch stop at Sulgrave Manor. Most of our previous stops had been in towns where crowds swarmed round the cars like wasps round a honey jar so that they had to be cordoned off and protected by the local police. But at Sulgrave there were no crowds and there was plenty of time to stroll about in the sunshine and examine each other's cars, something we had not had time to do before. Apart from the Stanley, which was in a class of its own, I thought the most covetable car in the American team was Ralph Buckley's magnificent 1914 Mercer 'Raceabout' and at Sulgrave I was privileged to take this rakish, splendidly restored open two-seater out for a short run with the owner in the passenger seat. My opinion of early American cars went up many points for I found it handled with beautiful sensitivity and accuracy, while with 5 litres of engine in a light chassis and a 2.5 to 1 top gear ratio, it displayed that kind of effortless performance only to be found in Edwardian cars of the highest class. No wonder this car ran perfectly throughout the event. Although otherwise starkly functional, the Mercer displayed one piece of typically American bravura in the guise of what was described as a 'monocle windshield' clipped to its long steering column. This left the mechanic to face the full rigours of the cold blast, deprived of even this minimal protection, yet Mary Buckley accompanied Ralph throughout the entire event apparently feeling, and certainly looking, none the worse for it.

It was on the afternoon's run from Sulgrave to Oxford that we sighted Ed Battison standing beside the road. There was no sign of the Stanley or its driver. Our hearts sank. Had there been some unimaginable disaster? If the Stanley had exploded leaving not a wrack behind, why was Ed still with us? It transpired that after a more than usually temper-trying argument, Ed had declared that he intended to wash his hands of the whole affair and demanded to be set down. Though we had no room for Ed, he was picked up by a more spacious following car and by the next day the crew of the Stanley were reunited, both having agreed to bury the hatchet.

At the start of the penultimate day's run from Leamington
to Cheltenham via Prescott, disaster struck Elmer Bemis's
beautiful 1906 six-cylinder Ford Model A, which shared with
the Stanley the distinction of being the oldest car in the event.
The Ford broke the driving pinion of its differential, yet, by
some miracle, the local Ford agents managed to repair it and
have the big white car on the road again within twenty-four
hours so that it was able to rejoin us at Cheltenham next
morning. This unlucky breakdown compelled the American
team captain, Austin Clark, to call in his first reserve and so it
was the Stutz 'Bearcat' which replaced the Ford on this day's
run and at the hillclimb at Prescott.

In the latter event, each competitor was allowed two
practice runs followed by two timed runs, the best time to
count. Fastest time of the day went to Ronald Barker driving
the 'Prince Henry' Vauxhall in 61.56 seconds but, considering
they so seldom drive their veteran motor cars in anger in their
own country, the American drivers performed very creditably
indeed. Captain Clark did very well to get his immense
Pierce-Arrow up the hill in 67.54 seconds considering that it
was so long it could hardly get round one hairpin bend without
a shunt. Another outstanding performer was Paul Tusek on
the Stanley who ascended the hill in almost total silence to
become the outright winner on handicap with a time of 72.04
seconds. From near the top of the hill, I watched the Stanley
coming up swiftly towards me between the trees, buoyed up,
it seemed, by its white cloud of exhaust steam. Passing closely
by me as it accelerated away towards the top of the hill its
exhaust sounded like the quick panting of some over-eager
dog, a subdued and gentlemanly sound compared with the
raucous hubbub and mechanical commotion of its successor.
No wonder that steam engineers round about 1900 considered
it engineering indecency to cause anything so violent as an
explosion to take place in a closed cylinder for the purpose of
propelling a piston. This was certainly the first time a steam
car has made the ascent of Prescott and it is probably the last.

The performance of the Stanley at Prescott, coupled with

the happy solution of its vaporiser problems, seemed to have inspired in Paul Tusek an over-optimistic faith in the capacity of his car which ignored its advanced age, and this brought about the Stanley's sad downfall on the very last stage of the rally. After performing brilliantly in the stop and restart test on South Harting Hill, Paul Tusek turned his car round and returned to the foot of the hill to collect his passenger. Cars were allowed to shed their passengers for this test and arrangements had been made to ferry them to the top so this was quite unnecessary and was evidently undertaken, not out of consideration for Ed Battison but in order to impress the bystanders with the hill climbing powers of the Stanley by making a second climb, this time non-stop. Starting with a full head of steam and opening the throttle wide, he charged the hill at a fine pace until, when he was nearly at the top, the normal healthy panting sound of the Stanley's exhaust suddenly expired in a hissing sigh of steam as the car rolled to a stop. It was evident that the valve gear had become seriously deranged and the car had to be conveyed by lorry over the last few miles to the garage in Chichester where the cars were to be stabled prior to the final tests at Goodwood.

I felt it was vitally important that the Stanley should run at Goodwood on the morrow and so, immediately I arrived in Chichester, I telephoned my friend David Curwen at Devizes to invoke his aid. I knew that he had recently overhauled the only Doble steam car left in England and that if he could not put the Stanley to rights nobody could. Like the good friend that he was, David responded to this SOS immediately and together we laboured for most of the night in the Chichester garage. Having got the engine out of the Stanley chassis we could see that repair would be a comparatively simple operation provided we could remove a steam chest cover in order to get at the slide valve and its spindle. This was our undoing. This cover was not held on by studs as is the usual steam practice but was a large circular cast-iron plate threaded directly into the cylinder and steam-chest casting; a somewhat dubious piece of mechanical engineering design, we thought.

As we struggled to get this cover off, it became obvious that it had never been removed during the car's restoration; indeed from the look of the engine as a whole, David and I judged that this must have been no more than a superficial face-lift.

When at last we succeeded in getting the cover off, its threads proved to be so hopelessly rusted and corroded away that there was no hope of making the cover hold against full steam-chest pressure. So, tantalizingly, although the original defect could now easily be put right, our necessary surgery had immobilized the patient until a replacement part could be fitted. This would be difficult and quite impossible in the time available because the female threads in the steam-chest itself did not look too good either. There was nothing we could do but put the existing cover back as well as we could, using plenty of gasket 'goo' on the threads and to tell Paul that provided he used only a whisper of steam he might be able to coax the car to Goodwood and perhaps make a couple of slow demonstration laps of the circuit which, in the event, he just succeeded in doing.

Goodwood was, as was our intention, the climax of the rally and the owners of some 290 vintage and veteran cars had assembled at the circuit to welcome the two teams and to watch the final tests from the grandstand. By far the most spectacular of these was euphemistically called a 'Stamina Test' whereby, to avoid loss of marks, competitors had to complete a minimum of fifteen laps of the circuit in forty minutes. While the American team understandably decided to play it cool by concentrating on completing the fifteen laps in the specified time, the Englishmen who, it is apparent, do not treat their elderly machinery in the kid-glove fashion notable elsewhere, decided that the test was a glorious excuse for a final flat-out blind. Ronald Barker driving the 'Prince Henry' Vauxhall set the pace by lapping consistently at just over a mile-a-minute which is not bad going for a 1914 motor car. Also impressively fast was Anthony Heal's 3 litre Sunbeam despite the fact that, unknown to the driver, its hood had become unfurled and was billowing out behind like a parachute brake. Meanwhile Jimmy Skinner's Rolls-Royce and Francis Hutton-Stott in his Lanchester 'forty' continued to fight a relatively slow and silent yet grim and hotly contested battle from start to finish, their two stately carriages exchanging the lead on almost every lap, the Lanchester keeling over on its cantilever springs on the corners in a most unstately manner. Everyone completed the required number of laps except the unfortunate Tony Koveleski's Stutz 'Bearcat' which developed undisclosed engine maladies. Having at last been given a chance to show his car's paces by the failure of the Stanley, this was a bitter disappointment for Tony and a sad blow for the prospects of the American team.

By way of a grand finale and 'goodbye' to our friends from America, I had planned that all 290 of the attending vintage and veteran cars should debouch from their parks onto the circuit and process round for two laps in line ahead before dispersing. As anyone with any experience of organizing such events will know, where the number of cars is so great such an apparently simple exercise is easily ordered but difficult to perform successfully. It was greatly to the credit of the Vintage Sports Car Club's team of marshals that this final event went off splendidly so that, as the last car left the circuit, I was able to breathe a final deep sigh of relief, not unmixed with sadness. It was all over now except for the announcement of the results at a final party at Goodwood House where it transpired that the English team had won by the embarrassingly large margin of 1,333 marks and Tim Carson, our team captain, was presented with a trophy of appropriate size by the Duke of Richmond and Gordon. In fact, of course, the visiting team is always at a grave disadvantage in an event such as this as the Americans were to prove when they turned the tables on us in a return match in America two years later to make the score one all. There has yet to be a decider. The award for the best overall performance of any car in the rally went, to my surprise and delight, to John Clarke's 12/50 Alvis, the touring equivalent of my father's car. What also pleased me was the fact that the three Alvises which had been round the rally course, John Clarke's, John Morley's and my own, had each performed faultlessly throughout although their combined ages added up to eighty-one years.

Now that one of the most memorable events in my life was suddenly all over my feelings were a curious blend of sadness and relief; sadness because that unique feeling of camaraderie that had possessed us all while the rally was on now instantly dissolved leaving only an empty feeling of anti-climax behind it; relief at the thought that now there was nothing that could go wrong and with the realization that there was nothing left to worry about came a great relaxation. I felt as though I could sleep for a week.

The success of this first Anglo-American rally led to two jobs of a similar kind though nothing like so onerous, the first being exactly a year later – the twenty-first birthday party of the Vintage Sports Car Club which was celebrated at Goodwood on 10 September 1955. In spite of the gulf of the war years, to one who remembered so vividly the Club's small beginnings at Phoenix Green it was difficult to believe that so many years had passed, and I felt suitably honoured when I was asked if I would organize the motoring side of the celebrations. Someone had had the happy notion of inviting, as guests of the Club, those whose names had become famous in motoring history either as drivers or designers or both. After being entertained to luncheon by the Club in a marquee, these distinguished visitors emerged, each to make a *tour d'honneur* of the Goodwood Circuit in a motor car appropriate to his achievements. In most cases this motor car was provided by a member of the Club, but a notable exception was H.R. Godfrey (the 'G' of G.N.) who drove down to Goodwood from London with his wife in his own beautifully-preserved 1922 G.N. in which he duly lapped the circuit. As readers of the first part of this autobiography will know, my first two cars were G.N.'s, while I knew that when Godfrey and Nash were building their first car before the Great War, both were young apprentices at the Willans Works at Rugby. So I was not going to let this occasion pass without making the acquaintance of this particular celebrity, and as he is now no longer with us I am extremely glad that I did so. I found him a humorous, charming and completely natural and unassuming individual; in fact I was soon swapping jokes with him about our experiences of the car's foibles, roaring with laughter at the recollection of bygone mechanical misfortunes and entirely forgetful of the fact that he had designed it. Had my duties as Clerk of the Course permitted, I could have talked to him all the afternoon. It was what might be called a star-studded day. Sir Harry Ricardo had designed the engine of the 14/40 Vauxhall and, sure enough, there he was being driven round in a 14/40. Georges Roesch of Talbot fame was there and so was George Lanchester, then a lively octogenarian who drove a 36 hp Lanchester round the course. Of the drivers, there was H. Kensington-Moir at the wheel of a 4½ Bentley to represent 'the Bentley boys', Sir Francis Samuelson, who had won his first race at Brooklands in 1910, driving his own 3-litre 'T'T' Sunbeam, while our host, the Duke of Richmond, with Lord Essendon beside him, circulated in a 30/98 Vauxhall; both had been well known in motor racing circles before the war as the Earl of March and the Hon. Brian Lewis. But the personality who made the greatest impression upon me was that incorrigible old character Lord Brabazon of Tara.

'Brab' was down to drive the Austin which he had first driven in the French Grand Prix of 1908. Herbert Austin had built four of these cars for the race of that year of which three were driven in the event at Dieppe by Moore-Brabazon, Dario Resta and Wright. They were not conspicuously successful to put it mildly and 'Brab', in fifteenth place, was the first of the team to finish. For this he was presented with a special cup by a grateful Herbert Austin. No doubt he richly deserved it. Now, a survivor of these four cars, beautifully polished and prepared, had been brought down from Longbridge in a transporter attended by numerous white-overalled mechanics for his lordship to drive. In the process of unloading in the paddock, this equipage attracted the attention of an admiring crowd. At that moment 'Brab' arrived. He bounced into the

Clerk of the Course's office at the opposite end of the paddock exclaiming brusquely: 'Now then, where's this damned car I'm supposed to be driving?' I offered to lead him to it and we strode off up the paddock road together. At our approach the crowd parted respectfully and then stood hushed while the great man, legs apart, hands clasped behind his back, stood silently contemplating a car which in all probability he had not set eyes on since he had raced it in 1908. Finally he exclaimed in a loud voice 'Hmm! – it always was a bloody awful car', turned on his heel and walked away leaving mechanics and spectators dumbfounded. However, no matter what he might think of the car he certainly had not forgotten how to drive it. Indeed his verve as he propelled it out of the paddock was almost frightening, and what was even more alarming was that on reaching the course he turned left instead of right and roared round the circuit in the wrong direction completely ignoring the agitated signals of the marshals. 'Brab' was the kind of man who could get away with murder.

The day's celebrations ended with another 'Grand Parade' consisting this time of 250 vintage cars proceeding round the circuit headed by four Presidential cars: 'Prince Henry' Vauxhall, 8 litre Bentley, Hispano and, needless to say, the Itala. It was an impressive and appropriate finale and it sounds a fairly simple thing to organize. But ask anyone who has ever marshalled at a motoring event what it takes to extract drivers and cars out of paddock and car parks and formed up into an orderly queue and then, when it is all over, to disperse them again in an equally orderly manner.

This problem of dealing with numbers arose in the biggest possible way in the last motoring event which I was asked to organize – the 4th International Veteran & Vintage Car Rally at Brighton in May 1963. International interest in early cars grew so rapidly during the 1950s that an International Federation of Veteran Car Clubs was formed, its main object being to organize a rally in a member country each year. It was Britain's turn to be host to this rally and a joint committee consisting of members of the VSCC and the VCC was set up to organize it, Brighton being chosen as the starting point owing to its associations as the finishing point of the original 'emancipation day' run of 1896. In the autumn of 1962 I was asked if I would organize this event and act as Clerk of the Course. The rally was planned to last two days. On the first, the cars would start from the Madeira Drive at Brighton and take part in a road run, with a midday stop for lunch. In this the cars would have to maintain a certain average speed and there would be secret checks to ensure that they did so. On the following day competitors would converge on the Goodwood Circuit – with which I was by now becoming very familiar – where they would be called upon to carry out special driving tests against the watch. This sounded a simple enough programme until I was told that the committee was expecting 300 entries. In the event, there were 312 cars which meant that, allowing for the fact that some drivers might bring two or even three passengers and that there would be the crews of official cars in addition, there were likely to be over a thousand people to be bedded down and catered for.

Given sufficient notice, accommodation in Brighton the night before the event was relatively easy. But how were all these cars to be got away promptly from the Madeira Drive without causing, and being bogged down by, hopeless traffic congestion in the morning rush hour? Where could one halt such an army for lunch? Where could they park their cars together and sleep for two nights? Cars varied widely in date; car number one was a wheezing one-lunger of 1896, while at the opposite end of the scale were some of the fastest cars of 1930: a Speed-Six Bentley, a 38/250 supercharged Mercedes and a Type 43 blown Bugatti. To select one road course to suit everyone was obviously out of the question and I eventually decided to plan three routes each distinguished by colours on road signs and car numbers: a green route for veteran cars, a blue route for Edwardian cars and a red route for the vintage boys. Ideally, these would diverge at Brighton, converge for a communal lunch stop and then diverge once more to meet again at the night stop.

It was quite obvious that no hotel in Sussex could cope with such a lunchtime invasion, so I wrote to the National Trust asking if we might have the use of Petworth Park, and, somewhat to my surprise, the Trust agreed. It was arranged with a Brighton caterer that on arriving at Madeira Drive for the start, each driver and passenger would be handed a boxed picnic lunch while an enterprising local man at Petworth agreed to set up a small marquee in the Park from which he would dispense hot coffee and tea. As to the problem of night accommodation, the committee suggested that this would be solved by our taking over Butlin's Holiday Camp at Bognor for two nights, which was why the rally was timed to take place early in May just before the Camp was due to open and receive its first contingents of happy inmates. I had never been inside one of these camps in my life, but from what I had heard about them I confess I felt some misgivings about this part of the proceedings. Nevertheless, with ordnance maps of Sussex spread all over the drawing room carpet at Stanley Pontlarge, I began to plan my three routes between Brighton, Petworth and Bognor and was eventually able to work out what I believed to be a workable scheme.

Only the veteran cars would leave Brighton by the London road, turning left as soon as they had crossed the South Downs to pass through Poynings, Bramber, Steyning and Storrington to Petworth. The Edwardian and vintage cars would also make for Poynings, but by going straight along the sea front to Hove where they would turn righthanded and cross the Downs by the steep road that passes the Devil's Dyke. At Poynings the Edwardian and vintage cars would part company, the former following a zig-zag route through Partridge Green, Ashurst, Ashington and Wisborough Green, while the vintage cars travelled much further north, covering three sides of a square whose topmost corners were Staplefield and Loxwood.

After lunch at Petworth, the veteran cars would drive directly to Bognor, facing their biggest trial of the day in the inevitable climb over the South Downs. Many of them faced this annually at Pycombe on the Brighton Run, but this time they would have to tackle the Downs at Bury Hill which was longer and steeper. The Edwardian and vintage cars would take different routes which converged so that both could tackle South Harting Hill. Then they diverged once more, the Edwardians passing to the north of Chichester while the vintage cars took a longer route to the south of that city, by way of North Mundham. This meant that the cars would approach Bognor from three different directions which, I hoped, would ease congestion.

It was just as well that I was able to do so much advance planning on our drawing room carpet because it may be recalled that the winter of 1962/63 was the severest within living memory. It began to snow heavily in Gloucestershire on the afternoon of Christmas day, and frost and snow did not relax their grip until mid-February. Our signpost, bearing the legend 'Stanley Pontlarge No through road', almost disappeared from sight beneath a mountainous snow drift. But thanks to the fact that we were running two vintage cars, both with very good ground clearance, we were never quite snowbound. It was, of course, essential to verify the suitability of the three rally routes I had planned, and to record times and mileage, by driving round them, and I had arranged to do this accompanied by two members of the rally committee on 28 January, but the weather made such an exercise quite out of the question, so, hopefully, we put the date forward a fortnight to 18 February. Even then, some of the minor Sussex roads were only just passable and the bare Downs roundabout Devil's Dyke seemed a very fair imitation of Siberia. Nevertheless, we were able to confirm that, with only very minor variations, the routes I had chosen would be suitable and length and time about right. I was also able to determine sites for six secret time checkpoints, two on each route, and also note down certain traffic intersections where, on the day of the event, control would be desirable either by the police or by RAC patrols. But whether the event could be held in May as planned seemed very doubtful, so severe was the havoc wrought by the intense frost to the Sussex roads on many sections of the course. At the top of South Harting Hill, for example, the tarmac surface of the road looked as though it had been lifted by a scarifier. In the event, however, the West Sussex Highways Department did a splendid job and had all the rally routes repaired in time.

Very soon after this I paid a second trip to Sussex in the Alvis to confer with the local police, with the officials responsible for Goodwood Circuit and to pay a visit to Butlin's Camp at Bognor. By now the thaw had set in and all the roads were passable but there was still a great deal of snow lying around, the weather was overcast and the wind very 'peart', as country people say, particularly when confronted in an open motor car. Under such conditions, to look a holiday camp in the face is an experience calculated to daunt the stoutest heart. A monochrome setting of grey skies, melting snows and cold, grey seas made the crude primary colours in which the camp was tricked out seem more than usually tawdry and depressing. The high, unclimbable wire ring fence with which the camp was surrounded to ensure that its inmates had their good time at Butlin's and nowhere else, made me think of concentration camps and the Berlin Wall. 'Abandon hope all ye who enter here', I muttered gloomily as I swung the car in, drew up outside the camp offices and stated my business. I was shown in to the office of the Camp Commandant who, with a broken nose and a jutting jaw looked like everyone's idea of a heavyweight boxer. Perhaps this occupation was an essential qualification for the post, I speculated. What we were asking of Butlins was two nights bed and breakfast plus dinner after arrival on the Friday night plus, on the Saturday, a packed lunch to take to Goodwood and finally a buffet supper to accompany the presentation of the awards and the inevitable speechifying which marks such a farewell occasion. Because a number of guests were to be invited on this second evening, I estimated that the buffet would have to cater for at least 1,500 people and I doubted whether Butlins could cope with such a situation, bearing in mind that the taste of the guests would be somewhat more exacting than the average holiday camper. I voiced my doubt as tactfully as I could to the Commandant, whereupon he replied 'I'll send for my Catering Manager' and pressed a bell.

There presently shambled into the room an individual who looked as though he might have come straight from taking the money on the dodgem cars at an autumn mop fair. He was swarthy, hirsute and unshaven and he was wearing a dark overcoat that descended almost to his ankles. He held the lighted end of a cigarette cupped within the palm of his right hand and, every now and again, he would take a deep and sibilant drag from the yellow butt that protruded from between his fingers. At sight of him I had a sudden horrific vision of a long table groaning under the burden of golden mountains of fish and chips garnished with pink candy floss. 'Bert', said the Commandant, 'This is Mr Rolt who's organizing the car rally; he'd like to know what you're going to give them for the buffet supper on the Saturday night.' Bert looked at me speculatively for a moment before replying. Then with a shrug of his padded shoulders he replied; 'You can 'ave whatever yer wants guv – smoked salmon, the lot' Despite my private doubts, there was nothing I could do but take his word for it and in the event Bert did not let me down. He produced the largest and most sumptuous cold buffet table I have ever seen at which white-hatted chefs deftly sliced up enough smoked salmon to stock a fair-sized river.

The only snag about Butlin's Camp was that there was nowhere to put the cars under cover during their owners' two nights stay. There was no security risk, but competitors might well complain bitterly if their precious cars had to be parked in the open on that exposed site near the sea. So at great expense and difficulty it was arranged between Butlins and a local tenting contractor that a series of huge marquees sufficient to house all the 312 motor cars should be erected on the camp site. All in vain. On the day of the event the wind blew so boisterously off the sea that the contractor was obliged to strike his marquees before they were struck for him.

Consequently, when the competitors arrived at Bognor it was to find no shelter for their cars but only grim-faced men engaged in desperate conflict with yards of wildly flapping canvas. But, much to my surprise and relief, there were no complaints.

Apart from this failure over the marquees, the event on the Friday passed off with a clockwork regularity which surprised me considering that the drivers included so many strangers from overseas. There were entrants from America, Belgium, Eire, Germany, Holland, Italy, New Zealand and Norway of whom only the Italian team of Alfa Romeos, led by Count Johnnie Lurani, lent a characteristic touch of light comedy to the proceedings by arriving at speed only just in time for the start to the accompaniment of much shouting and gesticulation. Like Paul Tusek and his steamer, these Italians were apt to cause consternation by making sudden appearances travelling rapidly in the wrong direction. Because the veterans taking the green route through Brighton were heavily outnumbered by the entrants in the Edwardian and vintage classes who would be going out through Hove, I made a last minute decision to make the number of cars using the two routes exactly equal by sending some of the older and smaller Edwardian and vintage cars out with the veterans as far as Poynings where they could rejoin their proper routes. This meant that the cars could be lined up for the start in two columns and despatched from the end of Madeira Drive in pairs, those in the right hand column turning right onto the London road. In this way the drive was cleared of all 312 cars in less than half an hour.

When the entry list was complete I had been surprised and pleased to see that they included four steam cars. These were: No. 2, the Soame 'Steam Cart', a one-off job of 1897 from Norfolk of such archaic form that it might have been thirty years older: No. 50, also from Norfolk, a Gardner Serpollet of 1904; No. 106, a 1911 non-condensing Stanley, and finally No. 215, a 1920 condensing Stanley, said to have been the demonstration car sent over to the English distributors by the Stanley brothers just after the Great War. Four steam cars in one event was something so unusual that, on the spur of the moment, I decided to offer a special award for the best performance by a steam car.

The somewhat complex arrangements at Petworth went almost miraculously to plan, the cars converging on the park by their several routes and then diverging once more after they had lunched. Some of the crews from overseas found time to visit the state rooms at Petworth House. As they were walking across the Park the 1911 Stanley panted quietly past them heading for the lake. Descending to the water's edge it extended a delicate copper-tipped proboscis into the lake and took a deep draught. Steam cars have an endearing animal quality about them such as no petrol car however characterful can ever display. In this case the Stanley's master showed a very proper concern for the thirst of his steed and was rewarded for his consideration by winning my award.

Competitors had a series of four driving tests ahead of them at Goodwood next morning and, as this would have been a very slow proceeding and difficult to organize if 312 cars had taken each test separately, the tests were laid out consecutively in front of the grandstand in such a way that, once he had been started, a competitor drove through all four tests, the average time taken to complete them being little over a minute so that we had got through them by early afternoon. I had looked forward to staging another 'Stamina Test', that thinly disguised long distance race that had provided such an appropriate conclusion to the Anglo-American Rally but, alas, it was not to be. Since 1954 the general competition regulations of the RAC had multiplied exceedingly and this 1963 International Rally was described on its RAC Permit as a 'Touring Assembly' at which racing of any kind was stricty *verboten*. Nevertheless, I did stage a series of two lap 'Demonstration Runs' by successive pairs of carefully selected cars whose performance was, in theory at least, strictly comparable. This produced some interesting results. One of these match events was between the two Stanleys, surely the only 'race' between steam cars to be staged in this country since the earliest years of this century. This proved to my satisfaction my belief in the superiority of the earlier, non-condensing car. By the time they had entered their second lap, all that the driver of the 1920 car could see of his rival was a little white cloud of steam in the distance.

It was at the conclusion of these interesting, if slightly irregular proceedings that I made my one serious error of judgement. Remembering how successful and impressive a finale it had been at the last two events I had organized at Goodwood, I decided to round off the day with another Grand Parade round the circuit. But, whereas previously 250 or so vintage cars had taken part, this time there were 312 cars of vastly wider date range and consequently variation in performance and, as I soon discovered to my cost, this was more than could be managed. To put the oldest cars in front seemed to be asking for trouble because no self-respecting Bentley or Bugatti could fairly be expected to adapt its gait to that of the Soame Steam Cart which could hardly have kept pace with a funeral procession. When assembled, the line of cars seemed to stretch almost half way round the circuit. From my position at the head of the procession I could just see over the roofs of the pits a thin column of smoke rising from the chimney of the Steam Cart half way down the Lavant straight. As we moved off I became acutely conscious of the powerful machinery that was impatiently breathing down the back of my neck, but I continued to crawl along in bottom gear hoping that in this way I could prevent the procession from eating its tail so that at least the spectators in the stand would see all the cars pass once in reverse number order even if chaos broke out later. But evidently those behind me failed to appreciate the reason for this slow motion exercise and were determined not to waste the opportunity by such snail-like progress. With a snarl a Bugatti tore past me in a fierce burst of acceleration closely followed by a Mercedes emitting an eldritch scream from its blower, and hotly pursued in its turn by three thunderous Bentleys. The floodgates had been unloosed and there was nothing whatever I could do about it. The surprised and startled owner of the Steam Cart had not even opened his regulator before he saw a melée of fast cars bearing down on him. Chaos ensued. I don't now what it looked like from the stands, but to me it seemed almost as hazardous as the notorious Paris–Madrid, an organizer's nightmare in fact. Providentially there was no accident and somehow the anxious marshals managed to slow the cars down and shepherd them off the circuit and on to the road for Bognor.

And so back to Butlins and Bert's fabulous buffet supper. I think any English competitor would say that our stay at Butlins was the most memorable feature of the event. I do not believe that anyone had seen the inside of a Holiday Camp before, so that to do so was a wholly novel and interesting experience. The beds in the chalets were comfortable, the appointments adequate and instead of the canned music or the cheerful 'Wakey, wakey!' over the public address system, which I had dreaded, there was only a discreet feminine voice informing us that it was 8 a.m. Altogether the service could not have been better or less obtrusive. Most of us spent the first evening wandering about the camp discovering, with fascinated interest, how the other half of the world spent its holidays. The Camp seemed to have a curious mixed ancestry, part show-biz, and part fairground. In one hall we looked through a glass wall into a swimming pool as though into some monstrous goldfish tank. In one of the many bars we were treated to a representation of a tropical thunderstorm every hour. We were fascinated, too, by the calculated efficiency with which the bars were run. As soon as the till takings in a bar fell below some pre-determined figure, when it was judged no longer economic to keep it open, out went the lights and the customers were forced to move on. As a result, by 11 p.m. all the bars had closed save one into which all the more hardened drinkers had perforce gravitated. I heard of only one disappointed customer, a lady passenger who, having come to the seaside, understandably wished to see the sea and even, perhaps, dabble her toes in it. She was disappointed and angry when she found herself barred from the sea by the Camp's perimeter fence. She did not appreciate that, unlike the amusements provided inside the Camp, the sea was for free and therefore represented unfair commercial compeititon.

These three events in 1954, 1955 and 1963 did a great deal to enliven and enrich, in both senses of the word, my early years as a father and a householder. After all, I might have 'gone on the bank', in other words 'settled down' at last, but I had no intention of becoming a vegetable. In his speech at the birthday party luncheon at Goodwood my friend, the late Laurence Pomeroy, pointed out that there was nothing common or mean about vintage cars and that in this way they resembled their designers and their drivers, for they continued to attract people of character and personality. This may sound snobbish but I have proved it to be true. Of the different worlds in which I had moved over the years, it is in this world of vintage motoring that I have found kindred spirits and most of those whom I regard as my truest and oldest friends ever ready to come to my rescue in time of trouble and difficulty.

4

Irish Interludes

My three months voyage over the Irish inland waterways in 1946 which I describe in *Green and Silver* enabled me, as it were, to get under the skin of Ireland in a way that I do not believe I could have achieved by any other means, not even by tramping the roads. For a boat seems to stimulate talk as no other vehicle can, especially when, as ours did, it puts in an unexpected appearance on such a disused waterway as the Royal Canal which pursues its lonely way through the midland bogs between Dublin and the Shannon. In the course of that voyage not only did I get under the skin of the country but the country got under mine, so much so that as the years passed I felt an increasing desire to go back. This magnetic attraction might be explained by the few genes I inherit from my Anglo-Irish great-grandfather in County Cork, yet I think it was due in much greater measure to the fact that in rural Ireland I was irresistibly reminded of the simpler, more natural world of my childhood on the Welsh border. The sheep and cattle fairs in the streets of the small towns with men leaning on sticks earnestly assessing quality or striking each other's palms to seal a bargain; the small, crowded bars and the individual shops where nothing was hygienically packaged; the paucity of motor vehicles and, in their place the creaking and click-clack of carts; here was the scent of turf fires instead of the wood smoke of Wales but the smells which mingled with it were the same; homely, natural smells of animals or of dust and dung upon the roads; above all perhaps the sheer luxury of breathing such soft, bland unpolluted country air, the blessed quiet of it all and the lack of feverish hurry. All these things brought memories of childhood welling up from a world that no longer existed on the other side of St George's Channel.

My first return to Ireland was only a flying visit to Dublin in 1949 where I had been invited to speak to the Royal Dublin Society on the subject of canals. My lecture was in the afternoon, and before it I was entertained (literally) to luncheon by members of the Society in an upstairs room in a certain famous Dublin Hotel that is frequented solely by Irishmen. I felt tremendously honoured and conversation scintillated as it always does on such occasions in Dublin. My immediate companion was a charming, witty, wizened, white-haired little man who, he told me, owned an old established photograhic and optician's business in Dame Street. But my day was made when I discovered to my delight that his name was none other than Thomas H. Mason, author of *The Islands of Ireland*, one of the select few books that I had carried around England in *Cressy's* bookshelves. I cannot at this distance recall one word of our conversation, but I know I found the talk of this delightful old man as spellbinding as his book which so perfectly distils the magic of the Irish islands. Not only did Thomas Mason write the book, but he also took the superb collection of photographs with which it is illustrated. Both text and pictures are manifestly the product of a life-long love affair with the islands of Ireland and a deep understanding of their peoples. The author writes about them not coldly as an anthropologist or sociologist would do, but as his fellow countrymen and his friends. For this reason the book positively exudes that particular combination of beauty and sorrow, comedy and tragedy that is the very stuff of life in the islands of the west.

That day in Dublin has become memorable for another reason – it has gone down to history as the day on which my tongue was loosed. The great British public appears to assume, quite wrongly, that because a man succeeds in mastering the very private and solitary art of the written word he should also be master of the publicly spoken word as well.

This was another professional hazard which I failed to take into account when I decided to take up authorship, so when the first invitations to lecture came in, I was not only surprised but terrified by the prospect of having to speak in public. Consequently, the first few occasions when I was forced to do so are best forgotten, so acutely embarrassing were they. I totally lacked self-confidence and started with the fatal assumption that my audience knew far more than I did on the subject they had asked me to speak about. Yet on this particular afternoon in Dublin my Irish audience displayed such warmth and were so obviously sympathetic towards me, so eagerly responsive, that I found my tongue, and from that day to this I have never again found myself at a loss or been daunted by an audience.

My next visit to Ireland was in the early spring of 1952 and was of longer duration. The purpose this time was to gather material for the Irish chapter of a book called *Lines of Character* which was to describe a selection of the more characterful railways in England, Scotland, Wales and Ireland. In Ireland as elsewhere, most of the lines we travelled over have vanished without trace. So has the steam locomotive so far as commercial service is concerned, whereas in 1952 its continuing existence was taken for granted. As a consequence the book has become an historic document together with the pictures which were specially taken for it by Pat Whitehouse, the Hon. Secretary of the Talyllyn Railway Preservation Society.

On what was to be a sort of unofficial honeymoon, Sonia and I crossed by sea from Fishguard to Cork, about ten days before we were due at Towyn to take up our duties on the Talyllyn Railway. Our first objective was the Tralee & Dingle Light Railway in remote West Kerry. It was this craziest and most characterful of all narrow gauge railways which had determined the timetable of our expedition, for the line operated only on the occasion of the monthly cattle fairs in Dingle. I had obtained footplate passes for us and we aimed to board one of the empty cattle trains which left Tralee westbound on the Friday afternoon, and returned from Dingle with their freight on the following afternoon when the fair was over.

It was the first time I had made the Cork crossing and, as we steamed slowly up the lovely estuary of the Lee in the cold, clear light of that early spring morning, I thought there was no better way of approaching Ireland. Because we had arranged to stay in Cork that night, later in the day we went exploring along the north shore of the estuary having taken a train to a little station on the Cork–Youghal line. We discovered a long-ruined 'demesne', a sad relic of 'the troubles' no doubt, and walked in the pale sunshine through what had once been a large garden sloping down to the reedy margin of the Lee. It was a magical place that we had stumbled upon, reminding me of *The Secret Garden* which was one of my childhood's favourite books. For in this mild climate of southern-most Ireland, this forgotten garden had become a dense jungle which, even so early in the year, presented a spectacle of almost tropical splendour. Camellias had reached the stature of tall trees and their shapes of glossy green were starred with blossoms, crimson, pink and white. Curiously enough, I only discovered later that this ruined house may have been once the home of my Cork ancestors.

Next morning we changed trains at Mallow Junction and so commenced a slow journey into the west along that seemingly interminable single line that follows the Blackwater to its source and then strikes across the bogs to Killarney and so on to Tralee. I have seldom enjoyed a railway journey more. When we got to Mallow we had been surprised to discover that the train included a restaurant car, something one does not expect to see on a stopping branch line train, but then the English visitor is apt to forget that Irish branch lines can be so long and Irish country stations so few and far between. Unlike England where hundreds of stations have been closed and demolished, Irish stations have always been sparse, particu-larly in the west, simply because the population is so small and scattered. At this time, just before the railway systems of both countries began seriously to shrivel, branch line travel was a special pleasure but a totally different experience in Ireland. In England, the frequent wayside stations became the chief source of satisfaction and of a curiosity that increased the more deeply rural the stations became. As soon as my train had jerked to a standstill I would be on my feet and looking out of the window to see what the station building looked like and what manner of folk – if anyone – were leaving or boarding the train at such a remote spot; also to admire the stolid quality of the station staff, the rich country burr of their accents and their bright flowers – and even sometimes the topiary work – on the station platform. At each such stop one could capture something of the flavour of the place: its scents and sounds, the smell of new-mown hay or the church clock striking the hour; perhaps even a glimpse of a village street or of a spire rising above elm trees. But such scenes of cosy domesticity are much rarer in Ireland.

Almost alone in the dining car, we ate the usual Irish tea consisting of fresh soda bread, delicious butter and anonymous red jam while we chatted to the steward who, lacking company, was in a mood to talk. All the while the train trundled sedately along on its undulating way across the bogs and, through the wide windows on our left hand, there began to loom up the majestic blue shapes of Maccgillycuddys Reeks beyond Killarney, their peaks outlined against the westering sun. There was little sign of habitation beyond the occasional white-washed cabin on the green rim of the tawny bogland and the only sign of life we saw was when the train ran over one of the rare ungated level crossings and we would catch a glimpse, brief as the opening of a camera shutter, down the perspective of one of those long, white, and dusty roads that are laid straight as a ruler over the plains of Ireland. Here we would see for an instant, dwarfed to the size of insects by the scale of the landscape, tiny, crawling black figures: two women with shawls over their heads perhaps, a boy trotting on an ass with panniers, or a man carting turf. A slender spiral of blue smoke, rising far away, probably showed where the turf cutters were brewing up a dish of tea. I thought to myself then that branch line travel in Ireland is much more closely akin to a slow sea voyage or a journey by desert caravan. The infrequent stations are the small ports or the welcome oases. This simile is made the more apt by the inhabitants who, in the more remote parts of the west, line the platform of their local station simply for the pleasure of seeing the train come in, just as on some remote island of the Pacific, the quay is crowded to greet the monthly mail boat.

We were feeling a bit gummy-eyed and the worse for wear as we hurried through the streets of Tralee next morning on our way to what had once been the passenger station of the Tralee & Dingle Light Railway: for we had had little sleep. When we arrived in Tralee the previous evening we saw form the bill-boards that a grand Ceilidh was to be held that night in a local hall so we resolved to go. We were dazzled and enchanted, wondering what other town of equivalent size could produce such an array of talent. The only trouble with the show was that it was far too long. It was nearly midnight when we got back to our hotel only to find that the extensive re-construction of the interior, in readiness for the forth-coming summer season, was still in full swing. The hammering, or what sounded like the sudden dropping of heavy planks from a great height, went on all night long. Who says the Irish are a lazy and shiftless race?

Dingle is the northern-most of the five peninsulas, two in Kerry and three in Cork, that southern Ireland thrusts out into the Atlantic. It is a wild and savage coast. Each of these five fingers is mailed with rock and cliff and engaged in a perpetual combat with the Atlantic surges. Each has a high backbone which, in the case of the three northern-most, achieves the stature of mountains. It is because the land between the mountains and the sea is of particularly good quality that the Dingle peninsula has become celebrated as a cattle raising district, while it was thanks to this richness that it weathered the great famine much better than other areas of the west. It is rare to see a ruined farm on Dingle, whereas if you follow the south-west coast of Cork from Skibbereen to Mizen Head, the fact that three out of four farms are ruined still bears grim witness to the famine. I find no romance in such ruins but prefer a prosperous countryside which is why I prefer Dingle.

The Tralee & Dingle Railway ran (for alas I am compelled to write of it in the past tense) for three-quarters of the length of the peninsula. Having perambulated half way round the town of Tralee it headed west along the shore of Tralee Bay as far as Castlegregory Junction where, having thrown off a branch to the town of that name, the main line swung inland and set out to climb the mountainous spine of the peninsula to reach the south coast. Dingle is on this south coast, but even if it were not, it would have been impracticable to carry the railway much further along the north side because the formidable massif of Brandon juts out into the Atlantic to form an almost impassable barrier. One of the peaks of Brandon, Masatiompan, sweeps steeply down to the sea from a height of 2,500 ft to make an obstacle daunting even to the optimistic engineer of the Tralee & Dingle. He, therefore, chose to scale the central ridge by way of the Glenagalt pass, the railway clinging to the side of the Glen and clawing its way upward on a seemingly interminable gradient of 1 in 29. No wonder the train of empty cattle wagons that awaited us at Tralee was double-headed. Behind us there was to follow a second and much shorter train hauled by the third surviving example of the railway's motive power.

I mounted the footplate of the pilot engine and Sonia that of the train engine, the guard squeezed into what little space was left to him in a bogie brake-van largely given over to cattle-carrying, and we were off. I wrote a full account of this journey by rail to Dingle in *Lines of Character*, so I will not repeat it here. What I did not record in that book, however, was the much more eventful journey back, loaded with cattle, to Tralee on the following day. The shape of the book decreed that I leave this out. Although we subsequently journeyed northwards from Tralee, first to Sligo and then into Donegal, travelling on other odd lines which are now no more, such as the Sligo, Leitrim & Northern Counties, the County Donegal and the Londonderry & Lough Swilly, I decided to describe these at the beginning of the book and to end with our arrival at Dingle. As Dingle has the distinction of being the most westerly town in Europe, Dingle station with its monthly train service had become a kind of railway ultima Thule and the artistic appropriateness of ending the story there made anti-climactic any account of the journey back to Tralee the following day.

The monthly cattle fair at Dingle was over by noon and by one o'clock or soon after, we pulled out with a train packed from end to end with cattle. As on the outward journey, a second, shorter train was due to follow us. All went well until we were pounding up a steep bank between Anascaul and Emalough. We had reached a point where the line had climbed out of Gleann an Scail, where Cuchulainn is supposed to have fought one of his legendary battles, and were crossing a desolate stretch of bogland on the high flank of a mountain known as Brickany, when I happened to glance back from the footplate at the long train snaking along behind us and noticed that the roof of one of the wagons in the centre of the train was heaving up and down and rocking from side to side in a most alarming manner. 'Hey!' I shouted above the tumult of the labouring locomotive, 'We've got one off.' The driver leaned over my shoulder, 'The devil we have!' he confirmed. He whistled and gesticulated to the driver of the train engine, snapped his regulator shut and then cautiously applied the vacuum brake.

We all climbed down for the inquest: the two drivers and their firemen, the guard and ourselves. The cattle wagon was certainly well and truly off the road with all four wheels and the wonder of it was that it had not made matters worse by turning over. At that time there were only three plate-layers employed on the thirty-one miles of line so a mishap of this kind was not surprising. It had been sunny when we left Dingle but now clouds had rolled up the sky driven by a

north-east wind and there were occasional scuds of hail or
sleet. It was bitterly cold out there on the open mountain and I
felt very small indeed in that vast, sombre landscape of
mountains and hurrying clouds as I listened to the animated
debate between the five Irishmen as to how best to deal with
the situation. First, two urgent telephone calls had to be
made; one to Tralee to summon a breakdown gang to come
out by road, the other to Anascaul to hold the following train
and to ask the driver to detach his locomotive, come forward
to pick up the rear portion of the train and return with it to
Anascaul. Meanwhile our two locomotives would take the
front portion of the train over the pass and down to Castlegregory Junction where the pilot would be detached and come
back to Anascaul to assist the now heavier second train. It was
hoped that by this time the breakdown gang would have got
the derailed vehicle onto the road again so that the pilot engine
could propel it to Anascaul.

So we went forward once more and when we eventually
came to a grinding halt at Castlegregory we were given the
choice of continuing with the train engine to Tralee or going
back over Glenagalt with the pilot. Because this was certainly
the last opportunity we would ever have to travel on this
remarkable railway it was a case of in for a penny, in for a
pound, so we were soon clanking over the pass once more, our
light engine making easy work of the gradient. As we
descended the far side we could see across the open bog that
the breakdown gang had played their part. The wagon was
back on the rails; we could also see a little knot of men
sheltering from the wind in its lee and their lorry standing on
the road nearby. We were taking all this in when we were
momentarily startled out of our wits by the sudden loud
explosion of detonators under our wheels. Although the errant
wagon had been visible at least half a mile before we reached it, it
was awesome to think that the writ of the railway rule book ran
even on this semi-derelict outpost of the furthest west.

We propelled the re-railed wagon before us back to Anascaul where a certain amount of shunting was necessary before

a long train of cattle wagons with two engines at their head was
once more ready to depart. Two chimneys vomited steam and
black smoke and for the second time that day we began the
climb to Emalough. As we approached the scene of the
derailment we saw that the breakdown gang had remained
behind to watch us pass. It was just as well that they had done
so, for, right in front of their noses, a wagon in the middle of
the train jumped the rails in precisely the same fashion as
before. We began to wonder if we should ever see our hotel
beds in Tralee that night. And what of the unfortunate cattle,
crammed for hours into those small vans? However, the gang
with their re-railing equipment to aid them soon had the train
under way once more. But there was one more hazard ahead of
us, a hazard of an improbable kind such as one could only
encounter in Ireland. It was nearly dark when we stopped for
water at the crane at Castlegregory. Our driver looked at his
turnip watch by the light from the firehole, shook his head and
muttered with dire foreboding that he feared the 'tide would
be makin''. We failed to see the relevance of this remark until
he patiently explained the situation to us. The banks of the
estuary of the river Lee which empties into the head of Tralee
Bay have been raised in time past to prevent flooding, but
these flood-banks fell into neglect and have now been breached
in many places. One effect of this neglect is that high spring
tides flood over the track of the Tralee & Dingle as it
approaches Tralee, to a sufficient depth to extinguish the fires
of the locomotives, or so we were told. At any rate our drivers
evidently believed it, for the two locomotives, shooting
sparks into the night air, their flailing side-rods clanking like
a runaway steam roller, fairly ate up the remaining level
miles to Dingle, the long train of cattle wagons snaking
crazily behind them. I never thought I should find myself on
a train racing to beat the tide and I found it a truly
dream-like experience – like much else that can happen to
one in Ireland.

In the event, all was well. We found the tide just lapping the
tracks; it was over the sleepers but not over the rails so the

train passed and, whistling madly at each unprotected crossing, circled round the outskirts of the town and drew to a final stop in the station from which we had departed – could it only have been yesterday morning? It seemed half a lifetime ago. We bade farewell to our engine crews while a number of drovers, who had been waiting for us for hours, set about unloading their beasts. Then we made all speed to our hotel, for we were madly hungry, and were soon consuming an enormous Irish 'tea' consisting of steak and chips upon a vast scale followed by the inevitable soda bread, butter and red jam.* We realized then that we had seen the last of the Tralee & Dingle Railway – even in Ireland it obviously had no future – but Dingle itself had cast a spell over us and we knew that one day we should return.

We did go back to Dingle, travelling by the same route and staying in the same hotels, but only after nine years had gone by and it was May 1961. There was no dining car any more on the train from Mallow to Tralee and of the Tralee & Dingle Railway there was practically no trace at all. A stranger to Dingle would have been surprised to hear that there had ever been a railway; but there were forlorn and dilapidated remains to be seen if, as we did, you knew where to look. Otherwise, little had changed in the space of nine years. In fact, so little of note had happened in these nine years that we were welcomed back to Dingle as 'those two English people who were on the little train the day they had the derailment'. It is this relatively slow pace of change which, for us, made a visit to Ireland such a solace.

In Ireland I found I could relax and recover from an overdose of rebuilding, redevelopment, re-structuring, re-organizing, reorientation and rationalization. We booked a

---

* At this time a few provincial Irish hotels offered 'Dinner' as a concession to English tourists which we soon learnt to avoid. For twice the price of 'Irish Tea' one got the same steak and chips but with tinned soup and tinned fruit salad instead of the unlimited and delicious fresh soda bread with jam and butter.

room in Dingle for a week and hired two bicycles from a shop just round the corner. Each morning we were awakened by the sound of creaking carts as their owners queued up in the street outside while waiting to deliver their churns of milk to the dairy. After their turn had come and gone they would disappear into an adjacent bar to fortify themselves for the return journey with pints of porter, leaving their horses or asses standing outside, heads a-droop, with long-accustomed patience. Bearing in mind the amount of time consumed in travelling to and fro, it seemed a very tedious and costly way of delivering a few gallons of milk each morning. Would not collection by dairy lorry from the farm be much more economical? But at this point I reminded myself that this was Ireland where no one asked such coldly logical and calculating questions simply because other considerations, tradition, custom, old habits, the imponderable things that make up the quality of life and give it savour even for the poorest, properly took priority over mere efficiency.

On our first day out from Dingle we had an easy but spectacular ride along the deserted coast road that rounds Slea Head, the furthest tip of the peninsula. For most of the way the road clings to a ledge cut in the lower slopes of Mount Eagle which here stoop steeply down to the sea. On this wild western rim of the old world, craggy, treeless and storm-swept, where one is very much alone and there are no sounds other than the thunder of breakers, the booming of the wind and the cries of sea birds gliding and swooping on up-currents of air, the sense of the force of an ancient and elemental world is overwhelming. It is a very salutary experience because it cuts a man down to size. One is also made aware that very slowly but none the less surely, stubborn rock is losing the battle with the sea, for the advance guards have already been overwhelmed. Like so many armed knights, cut off but still fighting on against desperate odds, the western islands began to come into view as we rounded Slea Head, rocks ringed about with white water: Inishtooskert, Beginish, the Great Blasket, Inishnabro, Inishvickillane and, in the furthest west, invisible behind the bulk of the Great Blasket, the drowned peak of Tearaght. There were once oratories of the Celtic church on Inishtooskert and Inishvickillane, the former credited to St Brendan, although how such holy men managed to subsist at all in such wild places is past knowing. Within the memory of man, these and other smaller islands have been uninhabited or only used for summer pasturage by the people of the Great Blasket where the island village was inhabited until 1953 when its dwindling population moved with reluctance to the mainland. Such remote islands and their inhabitants are capable of casting a spell upon certain people 'from over the water' as strong as any enchantment of Prospero's making. The name of Robin Flower has become as inseparably associated with the Great Blasket as has that of J.M. Synge with the Aran Islands.

Robin Flower visited the island frequently from Cambridge over a period of twenty years beginning in 1910. He became an Irish speaker and was beloved of the islanders who called him 'Blaheen', the Little Flower. In his book, Thomas Mason describes how Flower was responsible for introducing him to the island and its people. 'Blaheen' also became a great friend of the island patriarch, Tomas O'Crohan, and he was responsible for translating into English and publishing under the title of the island patriarch, Tomas O'Crohan, and he was responsible for translating into English and publishing under the title Blasket in 1856 and had lived there all his life. He was much loved and respected in Ireland as a Gaelic scholar. Robin Flower, too, paid tribute to the island and its inhabitants in *The Western Island*, first published in 1944. In the last paragraph of this book there occur the prophetic words: 'Here, too, they will be gone in a few short years', but in fact he is referring here to the fairies who lived on only in the minds of a few old people. The book betrays no inkling that the island community he knew and loved for so many years would so soon cease to exist. Happily, he did not live to see the islanders leave.

Although, as its name denotes, the Great Blasket is by far

the largest of the group, it is little more hospitable than the smaller islands. It consists of the top of the drowned mountain of Slievedonagh whose long, narrow ridge runs from south-west to north-east and for the most part falls steeply to the sea. It is only at the north-eastern end that the slope become more gentle so that pasture and tillage become possible. There is actually one patch of near-level ground on the northern-most tip of the island and here the people would play their games, or the young folk dance to the music of a fiddle. As we approached Dunquin, the point of departure for the Blasket, this north-east face of Slievedonagh began to open up so that we could see the whitewashed cabins of the deserted village scattered down the lower slopes above the cliffs. From a distance one might think them still inhabited.

Like the island of Bardsey, the Great Blasket is a great deal less accessible than it appears at first sight. For both are separated from the mainland by a narrow but very treacherous strait, in this case Blasket Sound. It is beset on every side by cliffs and jagged rocks and its waters, even on the calmest day, seem always restless. To make the passage between the island and the mainland more difficult, the so-called harbour below the cliffs of Dunquin is exposed to the south-west, while the entrance through the rocks to the island landing place is so narrow that it is extremely difficult to make with safety when there is a strong sea running.

It was in this Blasket Sound that *Our Lady of the Rosary*, one of the finest and largest ships of Spain's Armada met her end. According to tradition, either by luck or by superb navigation, this great ship weighing 1,000 tons had success-fully passed through the narrow, rock-strewn channel between Beginish and the Great Blasket to anchor safely in the sound. With her elaborately painted and gilded upper works, one can see her riding there like some bird of exotic tropical plumage that has been blown off course into this alien and menacing world of monochrome. But this spectacle did not endure for long. As the light began to fail a south-westerly gale blew up, *Our Lady of the Rosary* began to drag her anchor and was dashed to pieces with the loss of all hands against the cliffs about Dunquin.

This particular visit to Ireland was made especially memorable because I achieved at one stroke two ambitions: to land on the Great Blasket and to ride in an Irish curragh. As the owner of one of Harry Rogers' Severn coracles, I was naturally very interested in the various forms of curragh which we saw in the course of our journeyings in the west. What was most fascinating to me was the discovery that from an ancient, wattle-framed original covered in cow hide, both Severn coracle and Irish curragh had developed on precisely the same lines as regards the materials used and the methods of construction employed, although it seems highly improbable that there has been any connection between the two for centuries. Both use sawn ash laths for the frame and cover it with white cotton duck coated with tar. They even appear to paint the inside of the ash frame with the identical shade of green paint!

The story of the curragh in Ireland goes back to those legendary days of the Celtic church when St Brendan and other holy men set out in their skin-covered craft in search of Hy Brasil, that island of the blest which, men said, could occasionally be seen from the cliffs of western Ireland as a shadowy shape in the path of the setting sun. Brendan is said to have sailed as far as the Everglades of Florida in quest of this holy land of lost Atlantis. Such sea-going curraghs were considerably larger than anything known today. The modern forms of the curragh still to be found along the west coast of Ireland are intensely localized. Their construction and use appears to have spread very slowly southward down the coast from the primitive little tub – no more than a slightly elongated coracle – used by the Tory islanders off the coast of Donegal to the latest and finest flowering of the curragh-maker's art – the Kerry or Dingle curragh which, it is said, did not exist before 1850. Moreover, Tomas O'Crohan in his autobiography says that in his youth on the Great Blasket all the islanders used wooden boats until two of them went off to

Dingle Fair and purchased a curragh or 'canoe' as the islanders called it. When they proudly appeared in Blasket Sound with their purchase, their craft looked so frail compared with the wooden boats that the island women, anticipating their imminent demise, began keening. Nevertheless, the islanders soon became wedded to the Dingle curragh.

This is how James Hornell, in his fundamental and definitive study of this subject*, describes the Dingle curragh:

> The curraghs that go fishing from the many little harbours in this district are the largest, the most elegant, the most beautifully proportioned and the most carefully made of all surviving types. Every part harmonises; they ride the water more lightly than the sea-fowl yet are strong enough to battle successfully with the wild Atlantic gales that torment this coast in winter.

It took something very special to make this otherwise sober researcher wax almost poetic. The nearest relative to the Dingle curragh is the type used – perhaps for centuries – by the Aran islanders; it is certainly the nearest to it in size and lines. Most Irish curraghs have a bow sheer so pronounced that when lightly laden the bows ride high above the water. In the case of the Aran curragh, as on other types, this is achieved by an ugly angular break in the line of the gunwale which gives the impression that the otherwise straight gunwale has been bent upward as an afterthought. On the Dingle curragh there is not only a smooth sheer on the bow but on the stern also, the gunwale describing one supremely graceful arc from stem to delicately in-curving and up-tilted stern. No wonder the Blasket islanders called their curraghs canoes. They were 25 ft long with a maximum beam of 4 ft 6 in and they were fitted with four rowing thwarts although three oarsmen were the

* 'The Curraghs of Ireland' from *The Mariner's Mirror*, the Quarterly Journal of the Society for Nautical Research, Vols XXIII, XXIV, 1937–8.

usual complement. They were also equipped with a fifth thwart right for'ard in which a small mast for a lug sail could be stepped. There are plenty of references to these Dingle curraghs sailing, but it is not a sight I have seen myself. When Hornell was in the area in 1936 he reckoned tht Michael FitzGerald of Ballydavid on the northern rim of Smerwick Harbour, which lies to the north of the Blaskets, was Kerry's, and therefore Ireland's master curragh-maker.

The balance of probability is that the curragh in which I voyaged to the Great Blasket was one of FitzGerald's making, but I could not be certain of this because of difficulties of communication. For the three islandmen who rowed us over to the Blasket were all Gaelic speakers and had not a word of English between them. We had met one of them in the little bar at Dunquin and, although we could only communicate with him through a bilingual third party, we thought we had managed to establish a satisfactory relationship with him and to secure an undertaking that he would row us out to the Great Blasket next Sunday at noon. We had made it clear that there would then be four of us because on the Saturday two of our vintage car friends, John and Paul, would be flying out to join us for the whole of the following week. What we did not realize as we pedalled our way back to Dingle by another route was that the intermediary concerned was mistrusted by the islanders and that our friend had taken our expressed desire to visit the Blasket with a very large pinch of salt. So, when Sunday came round, it was Sonia who had to seek out our 'captain' and, without the aid of words, so convince him of our bona fides that he relented, summoned two of his fellows and beckoned us to follow him down the steep cliff path to the harbour where, upon the narrow shore above the tides, several curraghs lay bottom up looking like small stranded whales. The selected whale soon resembled some strange six-legged monster as the three dark-suited men lifted it over their heads and then bore it aloft down to a grey but silver-shining sea. As it rode lightly as a leaf beside the little quay it seemed absurdly fragile. How could such a cockle-shell possibly bear its crew of three plus four passengers? The question answered itself as we stepped gingerly on board and I found myself balancing as I used to do in my coracle. I remembered an Irishwoman referring to the clumsy clinker-built rowing boat we had towed around with us on our *Green & Silver* expedition as 'a very giddy boat'. I wondered what she would think of this one.

As an engineer, I found myself thinking of similar structures in which all superfluous material must be pared away to leave a sparse rib-cage, where each member is precisely suited to its purpose so that the whole achieves the goal of supreme lightness and great strength. I thought first of the frame of a big rigid airship and then, becoming more up to date, of the space-frame of a modern racing car. But then I realized that these were objects of scientific calculation and therefore not analogous with FitzGerald's beautiful curragh frame because the latter was perfected by intuition and not by calculation; by that mysterious gift which inspires the hand of the craftsman. The mud-wattled nest of a bird seemed a more fitting analogy than a space-frame.

The three islanders took their places on the thwarts, pushed off, and then struck out to a lovely rhythm with their long, thin-bladed oars. No doubt it was calm to them, but to us the Sound seemed decidedly choppy, its surface corrugated by short steep little seas. Now I understood why, in the last century, the Blasket islanders had been so speedily converted from their wooden boats. Seated in the bow as I was, I should very soon have been drenched under such conditions had this been a wooden boat, burying her nose into each wave. But like a practised steeplechaser to a jump, this curragh lifted lightly and effortlessly to whatever obstacle the sea cast in her path so that throughout our entire trip, out and home, she never shipped a drop of water. She was like some wild thing, reacting instinctively to her element and, in this this respect, totally unlike any form of boat which I have experienced either before or since. It was all most exhilarating.

By contrast, the island was a sad place. The once obviously well-used track that led from the landing place and climbed up between the terraced cabins now wore a neglected air, being obviously only rarely used. The reason why the village looked so deceptively habitable from the mainland was now made plain – the dilapidation of their old homes was being held in check by these men. They frequently visited the island to shoot rabbits, or in the course of fishing expeditions, and used their cabins for shelter or storage. The captain of our curragh kept chickens on his little holding and we found a hen sitting on a clutch of eggs. It became clear to us that although Dunquin was only the breadth of a narrow sound away it represented exile to these men as surely as would the antipodes. Hence the chickens and the brave attempts to check the effects of wind and weather on their island homes which I found extremely moving. It made me realize that the spell cast by islands cannot be dismissed as a mere modern romantic dream of the simple life; of getting away from it all. God knows these men knew all there was to be known about the hardships of life on this speck of land on the wild westernmost rim of Europe, yet the Great Blasket still had them by the heart and would do so till their dying day. I not only felt moved but also embarrassed. These men would have been justified if they had refused a passage to four English people to whom a deserted island was merely an object of curiosity to wile away a Sunday afternoon. I felt like some stranger who comes to a wake merely for the morbid pleasure of staring at the corpse. So, while the men busied themselves in the village and caught rabbits, we strolled on the slopes above until they signalled us that it was time to return to the landing place.

The other highlight of this week's stay in Dingle, and certainly our most energetic day, was our ascent of Brandon Mountain, at 3,127 ft the second highest peak in Ireland. We set off on our bicycles, following the road that cuts due north from Dingle across the peninsula until it ends at the little fishing harbour of Brandon Creek. It was hard slogging. The long straight road led us continuously upward, alternately riding and walking. On either hand our way was lined by great bushes of fuchsias in full crimson blossom which were growing on top of the typical celtic hedge-banks. To this austere and treeless landscape the fuchsias that grow in such profusion not only bring welcome colour but a certain tropical luxuriance that seems almost bizarre in such a context. A native of the rainforests of Central and South America, the fuchsia was not brought to England until 1788, to presumably we have 'the old ascendancy' to thank for its introduction to western Ireland.

Our immediate objective was a farm named Ballybrack that lay up a steep little lane to our right just before the gradient eased and the road began to drop towards Brandon Creek. Ballybrack had seemed, from my inch-to-the-mile map, to be the best starting point for the ascent because a path marked 'The Saint's Road' appeared to lead thence directly to the summit. What I had failed to notice was that the map, which I had ordered specially from the Irish Ordnance Survey Office, had last been revised in 1899. When afterwards I checked this against a more modern half-inch map I found that the ominous words (site of) appeared below the Saint's Road. I should have realized from my previous experience of climbing Ben Gower, one of the Twelve Pins of Connemara, that the ascent of Brandon might be difficult. It is not that Irish mountains call for rock climbing or any do-or-die expertise of that kind, but they do have a habit of surrounding themselves with treacherous wet bogs in which he who was so foolish as to plod on would presumably gradually disappear from sight. And where there is not wet bog, the mountain flanks are fleeced so luxuriantly with tough-rooted ling or gorse that walking is at best extremely arduous, and at its worst impossible. Beneath such a dense miniature jungle there was no trace whatever of the Saint's Road. Nor was there even a sheep track to help us through the undergrowth, for the good reason that sheep seem to be a rarity on such Irish mountains as I have seen, presumably owing to the bogs and the sheer lack of nutritious bite. Nevertheless, we struggled on towards the summit, consoling ourselves with the thought at at least the weather was favouring us. For in this mild and humid maritime climate, Brandon Mountain, like Snae Fell in the Isle of Man, is lost in mists and cloud more often than not. But today it was clear and sunny and we could see the peak plainly before us.

By two o'clock we had reached the fragmented ruin on the summit which is presumably all that remains of St Brendan's oratory. The view was breath-taking. The mountain is the highest point of a ridge that extends from Brandon Peak in the south to the northern coast where Masatiompan sweeps superbly to the sea. To the west we could see far below the little inlet of Brandon Creek, while to the east we looked down the valley of the Owennafeana river to the waters of Brandon Bay and beyond to that strange little archipelago, the Seven Hogs or Magharee Islands that lie off Rough Point on the further side of the bay. But we were only just in time to see this wild landscape in all its splendour, for we had not finished our sandwiches before the sun, which had been blazing down out of a clear sky, suddenly lost its power. No clouds were to be seen but, on jumping up, we noticed that the sea, which had hitherto been visible to the horizon, had now become shadowy and indistinct, veiled by mist like the waters of some inland lake in an autumn dawn. Although we did not fear rain, we plunged back down the mountain, not wishing to be lost in the mist. We eventually reached Ballybrack without mishap and looking back, saw that Brandon had already withdrawn itself from sight.

At intervals during this rigorous day we had thought how delightfully refreshing was the prospect of a six-mile free-wheel back to Dingle as soon as we regained the hard road. Alas, it was not to be. I was leading and we had only gone a hundred yards or so when I heard behind me a sharp report like the crack of a .22 rifle. No, we had not been ambushed by wild Kerrymen; it was the sound of Sonia's back tyre exploding. Sonia was stoically prepared to face a six-mile tramp back to Dingle, but I would have none of it and set off free-wheeling in search of rescue with her useless bicycle, clasped by its steering head, towing alongside. It was characteristic of

Irish hospitality and friendliness that, on hearing of our plight, the proprietress of our hotel in Dingle, without a moment's hesitation, offered me the use of her small Austin car. So, thanks to her we were spared a wearisome anti-climax to what had been another memorable day.

On the Monday after our voyage to the Great Blasket we left Dingle with Paul and John to explore by road the so-called 'ring of Kerry' and the south coast of Cork from Skibbereen to Mizen Head. This was all new country to us and it was, therefore, a most enjoyable experience though we thought none of it the equal of Dingle. The first night we spent at Glenbeigh and after dinner walked down a bosky private drive that linked our hotel with Glenbeigh station on the broad gauge Valentia branch. From the look of things, the station might have been a private one built to serve the hotel only. But we were saddened to see a demolition train slumbering in the platform. Eastwards the metals were still intact, stretching away to their junction with the Tralee-Mallow line at Farranfore, but westwards the train had left behind it only a vacant road-bed, a thin layer of ballast which bramble and briar would very soon penetrate. It had been a spectacular railway and expensive to build, but now Cahersiveen will never again hear the sound of a railway train.

I think it was on the next day that the small but memorable episode of the ford occurred. I do not recall the precise wherabouts, but all four of us lay sprawled on a little grassy knoll, a ruined castle to the left and, running from left to right in front of us, a narrow tidal creek. Between us and the castle a white road led down to a ford across this creek. Came a crunch of cart wheels and we saw, coming down this road towards us, a typical Irish two-wheeled cart drawn by an elderly and tired looking horse. Its driver looked equally tired as he lolled, swaying slightly, a-top of a miniature mountain of sacks piled on the flat platform of the cart. We were thinking how typical the whole scene was of rural Ireland – it could have made an Irish Tourist Board photograph – until the cart rolled down to the ford and the scene became quite untypical. Without slackening pace or any sign of animation on the part of its conductor, the whole equipage went deeper and deeper into the water until nothing whatever remained visible except the horse's head and the driver. We got to our feet, expecting in our innocence to see the horse begin to struggle and plunge or the whole outfit begin to float away. Not at all. At the same pace the horse and cart emerged from the ford, ascended the slope opposite and presently disappeared. At least we understood the reason for that pile of sacks.

In 1963 I paid my latest visit to Ireland. We resisted a strong pull from Dingle and decided to break new ground by exploring Donegal, making our base at Killybegs. That small fishing port was the western-most terminus of the County Donegal narrow gauge railway system so that we had spent an hour or so in the town during our rail tour in 1952 and to go back there, after the lapse of over a decade, was a railway experience as sad as our return to Dingle. Killybegs is one of the most thriving fishing ports on the whole west coast, but its rail connection, like Dingle's, has disappeared almost without trace. I recognized the shed where the fish crates were loaded into railway wagons, but now it stood silent and shuttered at the head of the quay, a couple of rusting rail-ends protruding from beneath its bolted doors.

I shall remember the week we spent in Donegal for two things: Slieve League and the little deserted village and harbour of Port. Slieve League is a mountain almost 2,000 ft high which rears itself from the very brink of the sea. To climb it from inland as we did and, on reaching the summit, suddenly to see beneath one's feet the waves crawling far, far below over a steely grey sea like a shimmer of shot silk, or a fishing boat reduced to the size of a water boatman, was a breath-taking experience. On the landward side the mountain falls away equally steeply to a small lough, held like a drop of dew in a green hollow between its knees. Consequently, the summit of Slieve League consists simply of a straight and narrow ridge that appears razor sharp from a distance yet, in fact, contains just room enough for a narrow path known as the 'One Man's Pass'. The seaward flank is claimed by some to be the highest cliff in Europe, but whether this stands or not depends on your definiton of a cliff. To be truthful, Slieve League's fall to the sea is not vertical except for the last few hundred feet. Nevertheless, I am glad it was a fine, calm day when we walked the One Man's Pass, for the slopes are extremely steep and I would certainly fight shy of such a place in a high wind.

Port is on the west coast, north of Glencolumbkille and it is sheltered from the north by a great cliff called Port Hill. We reached it from Meenacross by one of those seemingly endless bog roads. This one swooped away westward, following the gentle lift and fall of the bog, until it could go no further and there was Port, a little huddle of empty cabins under the lee of the headland to our right, the small, disused quay straight ahead. The cliffs of the headland and the vertiginous stacks which had broken away from them were all pink-capped with sea thrift, among which hundreds of tern and kittywakes, were either nesting or resting. There was no sound but the slump and fret of the waves against the cliffs, the roar of wind in one's ears and, of course, the crying of seabirds. It seemed to me that until the last trump sounded these elemental voices alone would be heard here, for I thought Port one of the loneliest places I have ever visited, the deserted village on the Blasket not excepted. Lonely and sad, but not in the least awe-inspiring, sinister or frightening. It was sad because here was yet another point of intimate contact with the natural world that man had forsaken and each such withdrawal can only be made at the price of spiritual loss.

This visit was the reverse of our previous one in that our friends, John and Paul, joined us for this first week in Donegal, but then had to fly home leaving us with a second week on our own. We had come out without any clear idea what we should do with ourselves, but I now decided with Sonia's agreement that we would do our best to visit the Aran islands and so fulfil another long-standing ambition of mine. So I booked us a hotel room in Galway and our friends agreed to drop us off there before heading east to Dublin. We stopped once en route from Killybegs to Galway – to pay homage to Yeats in Drumcliff churchyard. They had not brought the poet back to Ireland when first I visited Drumcliff in 1946. I had known the epitaph he had composed for himself for years:

> Cast a cold eye
> On life, on death.
> Horseman, pass by!

Read off the page the words compose a tyically proud and gnomic Yeatsian utterance, but to read them from the graven stone in this wild place with majestic Ben Bulben towering above the little churchyard was a very different experience. It made the hair on my head stir, as the poet no doubt intended it should, as I saw in imagination a rider on a great white horse sweeping past on the road to Sligo.

As a preliminary to our 1946 voyage, we had visited Galway and I described in *Green and Silver* how we watched the Aran steamer, the *Dun Aengus*, come into the harbour and how the islandmen wore suits of home-spun 'bawneen' which were held up at the waist with gaily coloured belts (*crios*) which I had likened to the 'spider-web' belts once worn by the boatmen of the English canals. Circumstanced as we were then, a visit to the islands which had been made real for me by the writings of J.M. Synge was not possible, but now it seemed that the moment had come at last.

We learned in Galway that the island steamer, now the *Naomh Eanna*, was due to dock on the evening of our arrival so, after an early dinner at our hotel, we walked down to the harbour to watch her come in. Asking where we could stay on Aran, a friendly member of her crew gave us an address and telephone number at Kilmurvy on Aranmore and we took action accordingly. After the long sea passage and the times of sailing had been allowed for, we reckoned we could only spare two nights on Aranmore and would have no opportunity to visit the other two islands where landing is more difficult,

Aranmore possessing the only deep-water quay. But at least we should have seen Aran with our own eyes.

Aranmore is by far the largest of the three islands; it spreads its length of eight miles west to east in the approaches to Galway Bay. It is never more than two miles wide and in section it is wedge-shaped, the formidable cliffs of its southern shore tapering down to golden strands divided by little broken rock promontories on the northern coast that looks toward Connemara and the Twelve Pins. For seven of these eight miles the island's one main road wanders along this northern coast. It runs from Killeany, through the island capital of Killronan where the steamer calls, to the tiny hamlet of Bungowla near the western tip of the land. At intervals along this road one comes upon strange rectangular pillars of stone topped by crosses and bearing inscribed entablatures. They are memorials to bygone generations of islanders, but when I first saw them I speculated whether their bones might not be immured within the pillars, for Aran is a place where anything is believable.

The house where we stayed at Kilmurvy lay toward the western end of this road. It was not actually on the road, but a little to the south of it, sheltering under the lee of the rising ground from the prevailing south-westerlies. Behind the house the rocky ground rises to the terrific climax of Dun Aengus, the mightiest pre-historic stronghold I have ever seen or am likely to see. The central citadel was originally protected from the north (the direction from which we approached it) by four successive stone ramparts, semi-circular in plan. The outer two have been almost quarried away, but the inner pair still stand almost unbelievably intact in all their forbidding grandeur, 18 ft high and 13 ft thick with an inner platform for the patrolling defenders, themselves protected by a menacing *chevaux de frise* of jagged stones which would effectually prevent any mass assault. Each of these surviving lines of fortification is pierced by a single low and tunnel-like sally port, the one offset from the other. Doubtless the outer fortifications were similarly equipped.

Some believe that the fortress was originally circular and that the southern half has been washed away by the sea. I do not think that this is so because the inner citadel is protected on the seaward side by cliffs which here form the most formidable natural barrier that man could conceive. Although of puny height in comparison with towering Slieve League, these cliffs are infinitely more vertiginous and awe-inspiring for they have actually been undercut by the sea. I crawled forward on all fours to a cliff verge, as sharp as the edge of a wall, and found myself gazing directly down 300 ft to a swirling confusion of dark waters marbled with veins of foam. In such situations the Aran islander would sit line fishing by the hour, legs nonchalantly dangling in space, the line descending between his thighs or fixed to his toe. I have a fairly good head for heights, but such feats are not for me; I withdrew my head and crawled slowly backward from that dreadful edge. Dun Aengus certainly needed no man-made defences on its seaward side.

Throughout the history of Western Europe the flow of successive colonizations has always been from east to west. Newcomers have always pushed the older race before them until, on the rocky coasts of the Atlantic, they could go no further but could only stand and turn to meet their adversaries. Sometimes there was no adversary because in much of the west the land was too poor to be covetable, but in the case of the Belgic Celts, the Firbolgs, the Tuatha de Danaan, or whoever were responsible for Dun Aengus they must have had some peculiarly relentless foe to force them to build so impregnably here on the rocky rim of the known world.

Our brief visit to Aran was favoured by quite exceptionally fine weather and it was a wonderful evening, calm and still, with the Twelve Pins standing up roseate in the distance across Galway Bay, as we set out to stroll westwards along the island road as far as the hamlet of Onaght where I had noticed the words 'Seven Churches' marked on my map. Presumably the number seven held some mystical significance for the saints and scholars of the celtic church, for in Ireland they are

always number seven, no more and no less, the most famous
being the seven churches of Clonmacnoise beside the Shannon. Here on Aranmore the seven were on a much more
modest scale being each no larger than an oratory intended for
private prayer. Whereas the white-washed cabins of the
hamlet were at the roadside, these little ruined holy places lay
huddled below road level and midway between it and the
strand. Dusk was beginning to fall by now and so intent were
we in tracing the walls of the churches that we did not notice a
woman come out from the cabin opposite and stroll towards us
until she accosted us in her soft Irish voice. It was not long
before she had introduced herself. She was Maggie Dirrane,
star of that great Flaherty film *Man of Aran* which I had seen
many years before and never forgotten. She was no longer the
slip of a girl she was when that film was made in the early
1930s, but her calm, unlined face was still beautiful and her
voice would have soothed an insomniac to slumber. When we
told her we had both seen the film she was delighted and
talked on into the deepening dusk about it and how she had
come to London for the première. It was clear that this
episode had been the one great event of her life, but she was
content to treasure the memory of a now almost incredible
happening as an astronaut might recall a past landing on the
moon. Unlike so many others, she had remained untouched
by the tinsel glitter of an urban world but had returned to her
island birthplace with no unsatisfied cravings. When we told
her we intended to walk to the western-most tip of the island
next day she invited us to call in at her cabin as we were
passing. We did so and stepped into an interior of stone flags
and gleaming white walls that was scrupulously clean and
spotless. But the seven churches below could not have displayed a healthier disregard for material comforts or possessions than did Maggie Dirrane's cottage.

On no island but Aranmore have I been given so strong a
feeling that I had come to the end, or the beginning, of the
world and this sense of elemental simplicity and austerity is
particularly strong as one reaches its western end at Bungowla.

Towyn Wharf Station as it was in 1951 (*P.B. Whitehouse*)

Talyllyn Railway 1951: Helping David Curwen (on footplate of *Dolgoch*) to marshal a train at Towyn Wharf Station (*P.B. Whitehouse*)

Centenary Celebrations 1965. John Betjeman, first member of the Society, unveils a plaque to mark the completion of improvements to the Wharf Station (*John Adams*)

Standing on the footplate of the Kerr Stuart 90 hp diesel locomotive (ex-Eskdale Railway) which I had helped to build forty years before and had not seen since (*Brian Morgan*)

A train arrives at Towyn Pendre after a successful trial run in May 1951
(*D.W. Harvey*)

Trying out Ralph Buckley's Mercer with its monocle windshield at
Sulgrave, Anglo-American Rally 1954

International Rally 1963; the start of the Grand Parade at Goodwood that later got out of hand (*Autocar*)

Embarking in a Dingle curragh at Dunquin for Great Blasket Island, 1961

Talking to Maggie Dirane outside her cottage on Aranmore, 1963

The figurehead of the *Emily Burnyeat* on the quay wall at Whitehaven
(*Burnyeat Ltd*)

The Mangla Mole at Wallasey ready to begin its first drive under the Mersey
(*Mersey Tunnel Joint Committee*)

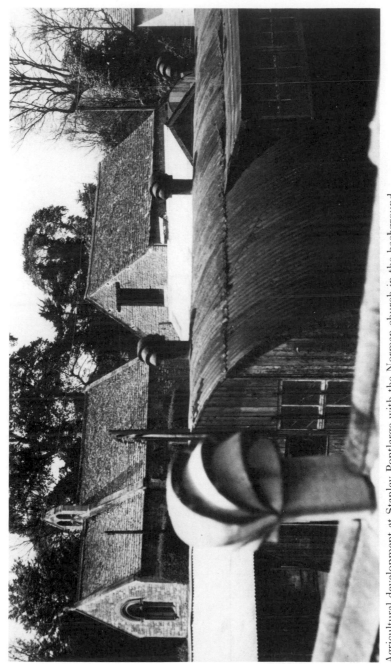

Agricultural development at Stanley Pontlarge with the Norman church in the background

Stanley Pontlarge: the west front

Stanley Pontlarge: the east front with family party, 1957 (*Jim Russell*)

The Claverdon Pumps, since restored (*Brian Morgan*)

The Walker Fan Engine, Severn Tunnel Pumping Station, Sudbrook, since destroyed (*J.L.E. Smith*)

Portrait of the author

The Great Steam Fair, Shottesbrooke, 1964: general view from the roof of the house

Taking the money on the Bioscope (*David Farrell*)

Driving the Alvis at the 35th Anniversary Meeting at Prescott, 1973 (*Michael Charity*)

It is not only that the islanders lack all those main services which we now consider essential to civilized living, for they share this deprivation with many other island communities. What makes Aran unique is that there is no fuel on the islands* and precious little soil either. The only element which is present in abundance and of which one is made ever conscious is stone. Wherever naked rocks will permit, the whole surface of Aranmore is parcelled into minute plots of 'gardens' by an intricate network of stone walls, not the neat dry walls to which we are accustomed but merely boulder piled precariously upon boulder so that when seen against the sky they frequently appear translucent like a pile of cannon-balls. There are no gates because there is no timber. When an Aran man puts a beast out to pasture he takes the wall down to let it in and builds it up again behind it. But many of these tiny walled enclosures contain no soil at all, only huge flat plates of fissured limestone. When we were on Aran in June, the only natural feature to soften the harsh, almost sinister, face of this stoney landscape were the brilliant wild flowers growing in profusion in the fissures of the limestone.

It is in these small stone fields that the potatoes are grown. First the fissures in the rock are plugged as well as may be with small stones; then a series of broad ridges consisting of alternate layers of sand and seaweed are built upon the rock and in these the potatoes are planted. In *Man of Aran* we are shown Maggie Dirrane cutting seaweed on the strand and then carrying it up to the fields in a pannier on her back. We saw Maggie Dirrane's successor coming up from the sea with her harvest of seaweed, the only difference being that she carried her pannier on donkey-back. Life does not change much on Aran. Yet change there is, none the less. Despite lavish financial aid from the Irish Government, the population of Aran continues to dwindle. It is increasingly a population of the old and the very young; the able-bodied have emigrated to

* Turf has to be imported by sea from Connemara as there are no bogs on the islands.

England or to America. The fish, they will tell you, no longer come to the shores of the island so that one of Aran's traditional trades and staple foods has gone. I suppose the growth of tourism to some extent compensates for the loss, but this is a humiliating trade. It seemed to me that the shabby men, who brought their side-cars down the pier at Kilronan to meet the steamer and jostled each other for the custom of the few tourists who landed, looked very different from those figures in homespun clothing and bright belts I had seen coming ashore from the old *Dun Aengus* in Galway only seventeen years before.

Yet the most remarkable thing about Aran is that a small country, so arid and inhospitable to life despite its beauty, should have supported through so many centuries a self-sufficient community whose rich life could be an inspiration to an artist like J.M. Synge. This ancient life continued here generation after generation undisturbed for the very simple reason, I imagine, that the land, if such it can be called, was much too poor to attract absentee landlords. Naked rock is not a marketable commodity. If the sad day should come when Aran, like the Great Blasket, is depopulated, then future visitors to this lonely bastion of rock in Galway Bay will surely marvel that man was ever able to wrest a living from such a desert. That he did so and brought to fruit so fine a human flowering gives food for thought. I am glad I was able to visit Aran when I did; it is a salutary example to over-civilized man.

5
The Truth about Authorship

Beyond retailing how my initial debut as a writer came about, earlier chapters of these volumes have had so little to say about my life as a writer that the reader could be forgiven for suspecting that the new career which I had embraced so enthusiastically in 1939 soon began to pall. Or, to put it in another way, that forcing a passage up some derelict canal, injecting new life into a moribund railway or organizing a rally for vintage cars were all much more exciting occupations than sitting at a desk. It is certainly true that it was only after I had made the decision to become a writer that I realized that I was a man of action and not a contemplative or an intellectual. Although I have always enjoyed writing, I soon discovered that the writer's study could too easily become a place of retreat, a convenient escape from the harsh world outside into a smaller, cosier world of the writer's own ordering or creation. A writer may delude himself that by thinking great thoughts onto paper he is thereby enlarging himself, yet by so confining himself to his study he is diminishing his wholeness as a person as surely as if he were to spend all his daylight hours hewing coal underground. For this reason I have never made writing a nine to five job. Self discipline, yes, but rigid routine, no. Moreover, no matter how pressed I have been financially I have never dropped my outside interests. In any event I am sure it would have been a mistake so to do, so closely were these interests identified with my writing.

Nevertheless, when all this has been said, a great and increasing slice of my life, particularly in the years after I settled in Gloucestershire, has been devoted to writing. That this does not emerge from the preceding pages is due to the simple fact that outside interests are likely to be more interesting to read about. There is not much to be written about the hours one has spent in the study, although in my case they were absolutely vital because I possessed no other source of income. It is true that my salary as a car rally organizer helped me out at a particularly difficult period, but this was exceptional. That I have succeeded in keeping a wife, bringing up and privately educating two sons, assisting an impoverished mother and maintaining an ancient Gloucestershire house, all solely upon my literary earnings is a source of pardonable pride to me. It was not an easy achievement. It involved great self-discipline and long hours of work seven days a week.

In the palmy days before the last war, successful and lifelong 'marriages' between author and publisher were the rule rather than the exception. Then as now, most publishers' contracts contained an 'option clause' giving them first refusal of the author's next book. Provided the author was sufficiently eminent and the quality and subject matter of his output predictable, then there was very little reason why either side should wish to break this option clause. If a writer did appear under a number of different imprints, it was generally held in the trade to indicate that he was a difficult character. I estimate that my books have appeared under no less than fifteen different imprints, a figure which excluded paperbacks and foreign editions, so by the standards of yesterday I would be judged a very awkward customer indeed. But times have changed. The rewards are relatively lower and the pace hotter; so much so that it is no longer possible, as it was in more spacious days, for a successful author to earn a living from one publisher. Hence, when a publisher has offered to commission me to write a book on a certain subject, the holder of the option on my future work has raised no objection.

Two other factors tend to militate against long or exclusive author/publisher relations and one is the conservatism of publishers. Though they would have you believe that they are past masters at spotting new talent or exploiting new literary pastures, their bias is always in favour of the known talent working in a familiar field. Hence the tendency of writers to become as type-cast as actors. Thus the author of a definitive history of lightships who follows it up with a study of the uses of sealing wax or a complete natural history of the cabbage is unlikely to have his option clause invoked. From the publisher's point of view such an attitude is understandable for, having decided to accept a book his great problem is to decide how many copies to print of the first edition. This decision is much more easily made if there is some safe precedent to guide him. From the point of view of the professional author (by which I mean full-time) this pressure from publishers for 'the mixture as before' may prove disastrous in the long term when he suddenly realizes that he has run out of mixture. It was the realization of this danger at an early stage, coupled with an innate dislike of specialism, that led me to ring the changes on subject with the result that I found myself fluttering from publisher to publisher. As I have said, because Eyre & Spottiswoode published my first book, I felt in honour bound to offer them my next, yet they were obviously disconcerted when *High Horse Riderless** fell upon their desk for they declined it. In the light of subsequent events, I think they were mistaken, for George Allen & Unwin, who accepted the book as a sprat to catch a mackerel, landed as a result *Green and Silver* and *Inland Waterways of England* both of which were successful, the latter extremely so, and are still in print at the time of writing.

Why then did I not remain an Allen & Unwin author? I should have liked to do so. I got along famously with Philip Unwin and I have always thought that *Green and Silver* and *Inland Waterways of England* were the most handsomely

* [*High Horse Riderless* was re-issued by Green Books in 1988.]

produced of any books of mine. But, alas, this marriage was soon dissolved. Philip Unwin was keenly interested in railways, and this was reflected in the firm's list. So naturally I offered them my next book *Lines of Character*. However, unlike the two previous titles where the illustrative material had been supplied gratis by Angela, this new railway book was illustrated by Pat Whitehouse who, not unnaturally, expected his fair share of the proceeds. But the policy of that dynamic little man, Sir Stanley Unwin,* who ruled the firm, was to take care of the pence and to leave the pounds to look after themselves. He considered that Pat Whitehouse's fair share was too much and the book was rejected. So, for the sake of a trivial sum my relationship with Allen & Unwin was broken to our mutual loss.

Lines of Character was subsequently offered to and accepted by Constable who published it with conspicuous lack of success. And this brings me to the third and final reason why a writer tends to change publishers. It is that for some mysterious and unfathomable reason certain author/publisher relationships tend to be unfruitful. Although my relations with Michael Sadleir and Ralph Arnold of Constable were very happy and they appeared to be prepared to publish any book I was prepared to give them the big snag was that they could not sell them. My association with the firm began when my agent (the same who attempted to interfere with the publication of *Inland Waterways of England*) placed with them my little book of ghost stories, *Sleep No More*, which could be held to represent my earliest literary effort since it included the three stories I had written for magazine publication before the war.† Michael Sadleir's reception of this modest collection of stories was so extravagant that it quite went to my head. He hailed me as the successor to M.R. James,

---

* Author of *The Truth about Publishing* from which the title of this chapter is unashamedly derived.

† See *Landscape with Machines*, p. 218.

whose *Ghost Stories of an Antiquary* I first read at the age of eight and at five-yearly intervals ever since. He further insisted that we find an illustrator for *Sleep No More* of the calibre of the artist who was responsible for so splendidly illustrating James's first collection of stories before his untimely death. Somehow, I cannot now remember in what way, a young artist named Joanna Dowling was discovered and proceeded to produce some really excellent illustrations for my stories. Poor Joanna, she looked upon this commission as her big breakthrough, yet for some reason that was never really clear to me, Constable, having commissioned her, decided in the end to use only one of her pictures, and that the least satisfactory, as a jacket illustration. It was a little slim mouse of a book that eventually appeared in 1950, a book whose inferior paper soon yellowed. It was never reprinted although some of the stories were subsequently anthologized and others read over the radio.* So ended my only venture into fiction.

Had not my hopes been raised by Michael Sadleir, I should have expected little from *Sleep No More*, but I confess I expected a great deal from *Horseless Carriage*, my first literary expression of my vintage car enthusiasm, which was likewise published by Constable. I sensed that interest in this subject was expanding rapidly and hoped that this would be reflected in sales, but I was disappointed. The book when it appeared in 1950 was unattractive; it wore an unfortunate jacket and the publishing style was stolid but uninspiring. Although it won good notices, particularly in the motoring press, sales wholly failed to come up to my expectations. It was left to my old friend Sam Clutton to prove beyond dispute that my hunch was correct when, in collaboration with John Stanford, he published from Batsford *The Vintage Motor-car* in 1954. This book was an immediate best seller and it went on selling for years, being the undoubted precursor of the spate of motoring

---

* [*Sleep No More* was reprinted by Harvester Press, 1975 and the ghost stories continue to appear in anthologies, most recently in the *Oxford Book of English Ghost Stories*.]

books that marked the later fifties and sixties. There is no sour grapes about this because I would be the first to acknowledge that *The Vintage Motor-car* is a vastly better and more entertaining book than *Horseless Carriage*. Nevertheless, the success of the former makes me certain that in other hands my own book could have sold a great deal better than it did.

The failure of *Horseless Carriage* was only the first of a series of progressively heavier blows whose cumulative effect, apart from being financially disastrous, made me, for the first time, doubt my capacity as a writer. First, *Lines of Character* appeared in 1952 and straightaway sank without trace beneath an incoming flood-tide of railway books. Next came *Railway Adventure*, the story of my experience of running the Talyllyn Railway in 1951 and 1952. I set great store by this book. I saw it as the railway equivalent of *Narrow Boat* and felt confident that it would retrieve my fallen fortunes. I even designed a jacket for it which would make clear its affinity with *Narrow Boat* and persuaded John Betjeman to write a foreword for the book. All to no purpose. When it was published in 1953 the hush that greeted it was positively deafening and soon the book had sunk like its immediate predecessors – or so I thought at the time. However, *Railway Adventure* was subsequently successfully revived by David & Charles in hardback and by Pan Books in paperback, thus proving the moral of this sad tale.*

There was to be one final crowning disaster. While Sonia and I were living in Laurel Cottage, the little furnished house we took at Clun, I conceived the idea of concentrating a number of actual historical happenings in the English Midlands upon one imaginary industrial town. The book would present the story of the growth of this archetypal town and the fortunes of its chief families from the days of the first monastic mill on the river to the present day when the presence of an atomic research establishment on the outskirts of a huge blackened town struck a new apocalpytic note. The book

*   [It has continued in print and in 1992 is about to be re-issued again.]

ended with the bewilderment of the town's 'labour' inhabitants on finding that, despite the fact that their elected representatives had nationalized the basic industries, the gap between wages and prices had continued to widen until the prospect of starvation became very real.

It had always struck me that, despite its overwhelming importance in the story of mankind, far too little attention had been paid to the Industrial Revolution in the worlds of literature and art. I was resolved, in my small way, to remedy this deficiency, my object being, not to glorify but to explain and to awaken understanding. It seemed to me that with this book I had hit upon an ideal vehicle to give the whole course of the Revolution a concise and dramatic shape. I called my imaginary town, and the book about it, Winterstoke. I invented the name because I felt it had a suitably dour and foredoomed ring to it; it was only subsequently that I discovered there was a real Winterstoke in Somerset, near Taunton, but no matter. I began by drawing two maps (which eventually appeared as endpapers) of Winterstoke, one c. 1790 and the other modern. I lived with those maps for six months and during that time Winterstoke, which was in fact an amalgam of Stoke-on-Trent and Coalbrookdale with bits of Wolverhampton and Derby thrown in, became intensely real to me. I walked its shabby streets, the towpaths of its blackened canals or the bank of its stinking river, the Wendle. I smelt its acrid polluted air, I knew its pretentious Victorian buildings and statuary, and was equally familiar with its every colliery, ironworks and factory. I hoped I could make my readers share this knowledge with me and see Winterstoke for the terrifying urban monster it was, typifying what English history over the past three hundred years had all been about. But such hopes proved vain. For although I thought, and still think, that the book rang wholly true and that what I wanted to say could not have been said in any other way, the fact remains that it fell between every kind of stool, being neither fact nor fiction. As the reviewer in the *Daily Telegraph* justly observed:

> Fictionalised history is ninety-nine times out of a hundred productive of fallacy; either by the subordination of fact to the requirements of the plot, or by over-simplification, or by gross partisanship on the side of the hero. But *Winterstoke*, by L.T.C. Rolt, is the hundredth case.

This was very nicely put, but unfortunately the hundredth case only went to prove the rule. I had not any great expectations, for although I knew that *Winterstoke* was one of the best things I would ever write, I also knew that it would be a difficult book to sell. But I was unprepared for the catastrophic result. Sales were so minimal that they did not even cover the paltry £100 advance on royalties which I had received. I do not believe that the book was even remaindered; I think it was mercifully pulped into oblivion, a kindlier fate for an author's brain-child in such circumstances. I was later told that the book had been short-listed for a well-known literary award but a miss is as good as a mile and this was cold comfort. The happiest outcome of this melancholy publishing episode was that *Winterstoke* brought me my best friend in the world of publishing, John Guest of Longmans. John wrote me a genuine fan letter when he had read the book, suggesting a meeting in London. I write 'genuine' advisedly and with emphasis because letters from publishers' readers are often designed, by flattery or otherwise, to attract new authors to their publisher's list. In John's case this was not so, although he had cast bread upon promising waters, for it would not be long before I should beat a path to Longmans' door.

Winterstoke was published in 1954, the year of the Anglo-American Car Rally, so the providential nature of the latter assignment can now be more fully appreciated. In retrospect, the remarkable thing about this unfortunate period in my literary career is that Constable, in spite of repeated failures, should have continued eagerly to accept any book I cared to offer them. Indeed, in the end it was I and not they who was forced to break their option on my future books. It is the only time I have done such a thing. I received an extremely pained letter from Ralph Arnold to which I replied that the break was due to no personal reason whatsoever but was purely financial, in other words if I continued our association any longer I should be stoney broke. I confess that at this nadir of my fortunes I began to question my future as a writer. After all, over the past four years Constable had published no less than five of my books covering a very wide range of subject but had failed to make a success of any of them. But was this their fault or mine? Very fortunately I was soon to be reassured on this point because my luck was about to turn.

By no means all ideas for books originate with their authors. It frequently happens that a publisher or his reader may have a promising idea for a new book, think of the most suitable author to tackle it, and approach him with their scheme even though they may have had no dealings with him before. If the author likes the idea too, the result is a commissioned book. My next three books, *Red for Danger*, *A Picture History of Motoring* and my biography of Brunel, all originated in this way although the last book, in the event, was not commissioned by its originator.

It was *Red for Danger* that first revived both my morale and my sagging bank balance. The idea for a book about railway accidents was put up to me by Richard Hough, who was at that time with the Bodley Head in Little Russell Street, and it immediately struck me as an extremely promising one. I realized also that I was unusually well placed to write such a book because my two summers on the Talyllyn Railway had brought me into contact with the Railways Inspectorate, the government department responsible for investigating all railway accidents. The then Chief Inspecting Officer, Colonel G.R.S. Wilson, not only gave me the freedom of all their records and reports but placed a room at my disposal so that I could study them undisturbed. This was the first book I had tackled which entailed research and I soon found myself suffering from too much source material rather than too little. Moreover, the evidence of eye-witnesses at the accident inquiries, the patient efforts to establish the true cause and to

ensure that such a thing could never happen again, all this was
intensely dramatic, and I felt I should be a poor hack indeed if
I could not use such material to good account. But the sheer
volume of it alarmed me. It covered a period of more than one
hundred years and most of the accidents reported upon were
of a very minor kind. What I really needed were some kind of
guide-lines on which to work. Then I remembered that an old
copy of the *Railway Year Book* which I had on my shelves
included a table of major railway accidents in chronological
order. This gave brief details of the cause in a final column
headed 'Remarks'. It was from this list that I was able to make
my preliminary choice of accidents to be described in the book
and, thanks to that last column, I was able to group them into
categories for chapter purposes. Armed with this 'scenario' I
was able to attack the reports in a much more purposeful
manner. The fascination of these reports in most cases fully
justified my selection, though occasionally my studies in
London uncovered some unexpected nugget which I either
substituted or added. I am aware that some of the drier (or
should I saw more classical?) railways writers condemn *Red
for Danger* as over-dramatic and sensational. To this I would
reply that they must level the same criticism at the transcript
of the inquiries, for it is all there and is not my invention.

When *Red for Danger* was published by the Bodley Head in
1955 I would not allow myself any expectation of success, for
my hopes had been dashed too often. Nevertheless, it soon
became clear that this book, at any rate, was going to sell. It
quite quickly went through two Bodley Head impressions and
was also published by Pan Books, my first title to appear in
paperback format. This brings me to one of the mysteries of
the trade which still eludes me: What governs a publisher's
decision to let a title go out of print or 'o.p.'? I eventually
began to receive letters from my readers complaining that *Red
for Danger* was unobtainable, so I wrote to the Bodley Head
asking if it was their intention to reprint. No, it was not, they
replied, and would I like all rights to revert to me? To this
question they received a very prompt 'yes please' for, knowing

that publishers move in a mysterious way, I was already negotiating with David & Charles to produce another edition of the book with an additional chapter at the end to bring it more up to date. What I never anticipated was that there would be another Pan edition. In my ignorance of paperback publishing I regarded paperbacks as almost as ephemeral as magazines, so that after one large edition had been sold out a title would be forgotten. Yet not more than a fortnight after my acquisition of the rights, the Bodley Head forwarded to me a letter to them from Pan Books in which the latter announced their desire to print a further edition.

At this point I should explain that one of the most contentious clauses in the hardback publisher's 'standard' form of contract is that whereby he lays claim to no less than 50 per cent of the proceeds of a paperback edition. He justifies this by arguing that whereas he incurs a considerable financial risk in undertaking first publication of a title, by picking the plums from his list the paperback publisher is betting on a certainty. His 50 per cent share of the proceeds therefore represents a fair return for this risk. To this the writer replies that although this argument may be valid in the case of a first novel, it certainly should not apply to the work of an established author. Under such a clause, half the proceeds of the first Pan edition of *Red for Danger* had gone to the Bodley Head, but their renunciation of rights meant that the whole of the proceeds of the second edition would come to me. At this time I badly needed such a stroke of good fortune. In the event, the new hardback and paperback editions of *Red for Danger* were published simultaneously and, mysteriously, neither seemed to inhibit the other for both have gone on selling briskly through further impressions. But why, oh why, one wonders, did the original publishers, whose idea it was in the first place, decide to drop the book?

One unexpected side-effect of *Red for Danger* was that I succeeded in persuading the Bodley Head to accept a little book consisting of four inter-related essays called *The Clouded Mirror*. This book, like *High Horse Riderless*, was an expression of the spiritual side of my nature; a self engaged upon a different journey through life than the physical and temporal self who chiefly holds the stage in this autobiography. These two selves, the one introverted, inquiring, humble, contemplative, sustained and sometimes moved to ecstasy by mysterious intimations of ineffable bliss, and the other extrovert, outgoing, restless and impatient, ever seeking some new field to explore with passionate enthusiasm; these two went their separate ways through life yet influenced each other at many points. This first self was a shy and reticent creature reluctant to set pen to paper except under the influence of some strange, over-mastering compulsion which was fortunately of rare occurrence because his writings proved virtually unsaleable. *The Clouded Mirror* was a case in point. The theme or themes of the book are complex, so I will not attempt to describe it, but it was triggered off in the first place, by my reaction to the atomic bomb and atomic power generally, something that had not existed when *High Horse Riderless* was written. The book was written very quickly and at high pressure during the early spring of 1953. It was begun in Roehampton and finished in that little writing room I have described at Aller Park in North Devon where, as from some low-flying aircraft, I looked straight down into that deep valley where gulls wheeled in a deep void of ocean air. Even Constable turned down the result, so I count myself very lucky to have persuaded Richard Hough to publish it. *The Clouded Mirror* also appeared in 1955 and sank without trace.

The second successful book I mentioned, *A Picture History of Motoring* needs only a brief mention. It was one of a series planned by Edward Hulton, at a time when his magazine empire was still at its zenith, with the idea of making use of the big Picture Post Library of Photographs* which he had established off Fleet Street. It was published by the Hulton

---

* It was subseqently taken over by the BBC and was moved to Marylebone where it is known as the Radio Times Hulton Picture Library. [Now The Hulton Picture Company.]

Press, did well in this country and was extremely popular in America. In case this should conjure up visions of showers of golden dollars falling into my lucky lap, I should explain that in a transaction of this sort, particularly where such lavishly illustrated books are concerned, the American publisher buys the sheets of the book from England which he then has cut and bound in America. Such a deal is the subject of very hard bargaining, which usually results in the American publisher getting the sheets at a knock-down price, and all the unfortunate author receives is a small percentage of this price.

It was David Cape who first conceived the notion of a biography of the Victorian engineer, Isambard Kingdom Brunel. Like all brilliant ideas it seemed obvious. Why had I not thought of it before? I had been a lifelong admirer of the Great Western Railway and its famous engineer whose powerful and extraordinary personality made him a plum subject for a biography. Yet no biography of him had been written since 1870. I suppose the idea did not occur to me simply because I had never thought of trying my hand at biography. Yet I intended to try now and try with a vengeance for here was a book which could scarcely fail. In the event, however, few books can have had a stormier passage before it was eventually published.

David Cape had recently come out of the army and joined his father's firm. He mentioned his idea to Frank Rudman, a mutual friend in the publishing world who very kindly suggested me as the only possible author. Frank then wrote to me with the effect that, one lunch-time, the three of us met together in a London pub to discuss the project. It transpired that David had not yet broached the idea to his father and he appeared to be rather shy about taking this hurdle for a reason with which I was later able fully to sympathize. However, now that he had found his author he said he would certainly do so and that I might expect a letter from his father within the next few weeks.

Sure enough I did receive a letter from Jonathan Cape suggesting an appointment and in due time I visited No. 30,

Bedford Square and was ushered into the sanctum of this doyen of publishers with his impressive mane of white hair. I have never had a less satisfactory interview with any publisher. So far from being at pains to put me at my ease, he seemed more concerned to impress me with his own eminence. It was clear that David's idea had not raised a spark of enthusiasm; also that old Jonathan had never previously heard of Brunel. He obviously looked upon me as a complete novice whom his son had picked up somewhere, for he talked of the submission of a synopsis and a specimen chapter for approval prior to signature of contract. Although I am not a vain man, this surprised me because I had always assumed that on occasions such as this an astute publisher would make it his business to find out something of the background of the author he was going to interview. In my case this would have involved Jonathan in the minimum of trouble for I noticed there was the inevitable volume of *Who's Who* in the bookshelf behind his head. However, he finally said grudgingly that he would send me a contract. I left.

I wish now that I had kept and framed that contract instead of sending it straight back accompanied by a stiff note saying exactly what I thought of it. It was quite the worst contract I have ever seen. It contained every clause that the tyro author is warned to beware of when dealing with the big bad wolves of the publishing world. At the same time I wrote a personal letter to David Cape explaining why I had had to turn the contract down, how sad I was about it and that, as the idea of the books was his, I wanted him to feel free to pursue it elsewhere. To this David replied that he made me a gift of the idea because he was sure I was the man to write the book and that he intended to give me what help he could to find another publisher. Shortly after, David left the family business. To what an extent this row over the book was responsible I never discovered.

David strongly recommended me to place matters in the hands of a good literary agent and offered to introduce me to one of his acquaintance. My past experience of agents made me feel extremely doubtful about the wisdom of this course but, under the circumstances, it would have been most churlish of me to reject, out of hand, David's counsel and offer. So I was introduced to an agent of the greatest eminence and repute who, having heard our story, unhesitatingly recommended Collins. If we wished he would do his best to interest them in the project. This he certainly succeeded in doing, for he came back to me with a very fair contract which included an advance against royalties larger than anything I had been offered before. On the strength of this I began work on the book in very good heart.

My knowledge of Brunel at this time had been largely gleaned from E.T. MacDermot's masterly *History of the Great Western Railway* which I had acquired when it was first published between 1927 and 1931, so it was obvious that if my biography was to stake any claim to be definitive there was a great deal of research to be done. I had never embarked upon such a piece of detective work before, searching here and there for clues and stray facts until, like the pieces of some scattered jig-saw puzzle, they fitted together and a picture began to emerge. That picture was a portrait of Brunel and, unlike most heroes of one's childhood, as I added fact to fact so he was not diminished but rather grew in stature. Not literally, for Brunel was a small man, but in the sheer overwhelming magnetism and force of personality. From his granddaughter's house in Royal Crescent at Bath with its furniture and pictures rescued from the sale of his vanished house in Westminster; from the coffin-like box of original documents, including all his exquisite sketch books, in the library of the University of Bristol; to Walwick Hall, the home of his great-grandson, Sir Humphrey Noble, high on the line of the Roman Wall in Northumberland, I followed him, and to evoke his shade I stood before the great sulphureous southern portal of Box Tunnel, on the dizzy height of the Clifton suspension bridge and, at midnight, in the dark depths of the Thames Tunnel, the silence there so profound that the churning of the screws of passing river craft could be heard overhead. Just as Brunel's handwriting became more easily decipherable the longer I studied it, so the man himself seemed to become more substantial. I could almost smell the smoke of his cigars.

The happiest outcome of this particular quest was my friendship with Sir Humphrey Noble and his wife Celia. Sir Humphrey was enthusiastic about my project and invited me to stay at Walwick while I studied such original material as he had there. I found that this consisted of copy letter books, original diaries of Brunel's father, Sir Marc Brunel, dating from the Thames Tunnel period and, greatest prize of all, two volumes of a journal kept by Brunel between 1830 and 1834 with occasional entries to 1840. These last I was permitted to bear away with me so that I might have them at my elbow as I wrote the book and they proved to be the richest treasure trove, making me feel closer to the man himself than anything else. No research could have been carried out in more congenial surroundings and never was researcher more hospitably entertained. For life at Walwick was lived in a style that reminded me of the Edwardian days of my remote childhood and which I had thought quite extinct.

The house stood precisely on the line of the Roman Wall at the point where, coming from the west, it begins to sweep steeply down in order to cross the valley of the North Tyne. By lifting a trap door in the polished floor of Sir Humphrey's library, one could descend a short vertical ladder and actually stand on the Roman paving below. The drive gates opened onto that splendid Roman road that parallels the Wall on its southern side, arrow straight for most of its course, but lifting and falling continuously as it cuts across the rolling green waves of the Northumbrian uplands. Apart from occasional journeys either by rail or road through Newcastle by the east coast route, I knew Northumberland not at all and I was at once struck, by the spaciousness and the heroic scale of the landscape. These views over miles of moorland, forest and fell conveyed a sense of freedom by contrast with which the small hills of a typical southern landscape seemed miniscule and claustrophobic. To a visitor from the south there seemed far less people about and far less traffic on the roads.

From the terrace at Walwick, in clear weather, one could look across the valley of the South Tyne and over the upland miles of Alston Moor to the dark heights of Cross Fell and Milburn Forest sharp against the skyline. Somehow the fact that it stood alone and that it commanded such a wild sweep of landscape made me appreciate the comforts of Walwick the more. The range of outbuildings that enclosed a courtyard had been converted into comfortable self-contained flats which housed the domestic staff whose sole function it was to maintain the rhythm of country house life with smooth and unobtrusive efficiency. There consistently came into my mind when staying at Walwick that saying of the aesthetic Villiers de l'Isle Adam which Yeats was fond of quoting: 'As for living, our servants will do that for us.' From morning till night there was nothing whatever to do except to obey the discreet signals of the deep-toned gong summoning one to luncheon or warning one that it was time to take a bath and dress for dinner. The elderly butler, Tod, would double the role of valet when any male guest was staying in the house, unpacking the luggage and laying out whichever clothes he considered suitable. Personally, I hated this last service. I felt self-conscious about my clothes, imagining Tod curling his lip at a darned sock or a shirt cuff just beginning to fray. When unpacking it seemed to me that the old man took a perverse pleasure in stowing things in the most unlikely places, for it often entailed a most protracted search to discover their whereabouts. In return, I took an equally perverse pleasure in asserting my independence by not wearing what Tod had decreed I should wear, changing a green tie for a red, or putting on the other pair of trousers.

The popularity of spas and their cures before the First World War was, in great measure, due to the fact that the Edwardian rich ate too much and, in this respect also, Walwick maintained the true Edwardian tradition. It was a diet that even an agricultural labourer would have found more than adequate, so it made me, who was doing only sedentary work poring over papers in the library, feel like a Strasbourg goose. This daily marathon began with breakfast which was a purely male affair; ladies took breakfast in their rooms and were not expected on the scene until mid-morning at the earliest. Often only Sir Humphrey and myself appeared for this meal. We would together confront an array of silver covers standing upon the largest hot plate I have ever seen and concealing beneath them every variation upon the theme of breakfast that the mind could conceive. Even had we been tramping the high fells since dawn, the two of us could have made little impression upon such a prodigal mountain of food and I used to wonder what became of it all. Were the servants gathered in the servants' hall waiting impatiently until we had finished? To a zealous research worker, time passes swiftly, so that it seemed that I was constantly interrupted by some fresh assault on my digestive tract. Hardly had I got breakfast below my belt before dry sherry and salt biscuits appeared in the library as a warning that the luncheon gong would sound in half an hour's time. When it came it was no light meal but one which, in ordinary circumstances, would have set me up for the rest of the day. And, of course, it was followed by the time-consuming ritual of coffee, taken either in the drawing room or the library. It seemed as though the taste of that coffee had scarcely left my tongue before a delicious tea was served before the fire in the library. If one lingered over this as I was tempted to do, the next thing one knew was that the first warning dressing gong was sounding from the hall.

Dinner at Walwick was more than a meal, it was a ritual and a very protracted one at that. My host and hostess invariably dressed for the occasion no matter whether there were guests or no. Whereas at luncheon the wines were the responsibility of Tod, before dressing for dinner it was Sir Humphrey's custom to descend to his cellar to select the wines himself. To the right of his chair at dinner stood a small revolving dumb-waiter upon which, among other things, resposed his wine book, a diary of successive dinners in which he would note down all particulars of the wines drunk and then, pencil poised, invite the comments of his guests upon them. My knowledge of wine was practically nil. Before the war I had never been able to afford to drink it, while during the war it had been unobtainable. So my embarrassment may be imagined when my host turned inquiringly towards me, notebook in hand, and asked for my considered judgement on the claret. Dinner ended with the retirement of the ladies to the drawing room while the men resumed their seats at the dining table and a cut glass decanter of port was circulated, its contents glowing in the light from the branched candelabra. It was at this stage of the ritual that I once committed a most tremendous gaffe by lighting up a cigar. In the more depraved circles in which I normally moved, cigars went with port as naturally as Guinness with oysters or chips with fish, but not so at Walwick. My rashness earned me a stern whispered reproof from my host which did not escape the fellow guests who had been invited to dinner to meet me. Wishing the ground would open and swallow me up, I somehow managed to stub out the thing and surreptitiously replace it in my cigar case. It was an inflexible rule of the household that so long as the port decanter was circulating there would be no smoking and, as Sir Humphrey was apt to linger long over his port, and as I was at this period a compulsive smoker, I found this the one deprivation of life at Walwick. When, after taking coffee in the drawing room, I finally tottered up to bed it was to find a large plate of fruit and a tin full of assorted biscuits on my bedside table, just in case I should suffer an attack of night starvation, presumably.

If the Noble family sound unusual descendants for a Victorian engineer to have, I should perhaps explain that Isambard Brunel, unlike some of his contemporaries, was no horny-handed, self-made and self-taught prodigy but a man of taste and sensibility who would have fitted effortlessly into the *milieu* of Walwick Hall – except that, knowing his forceful personality, I very much doubt whether even his great-grandson could have dissuaded him from lighting up one of his favourite cigars after dinner. Here, as elsewhere the impress of that strong, perfectionist personality made itself manifest. In the hall hung the superb regulator clock which had once swung its slow pendulum in the engineer's office at 18 Duke Street and which still kept perfect time. Treasured in the library were a beautiful set of ivory-mounted drawing instruments and a great leather-covered cigar case, with a separate cedar wood compartment for each cigar, which Isambard used to carry with him on his interminable journeys of inspection. Sir Humphrey showed me these and other things with intense pleasure and pride, not only because they were relics of his ancestor but also because he shared with him the same discriminating taste and love of well-made things. They also shared a certain physical resemblance. Both were small in stature with the same dark eyes and heavy brows. Sir Humphrey's hair was white, but had Brunel lived into his sixties and himself become white-haired, the resemblance might have been even more striking.

I was interested to discover that Sir Humphrey was linked to engineering history through both sides of his family. His grandfather, Sir Andrew, held a commission in the army and became a ballistics expert of considerable repute who was sent to Newcastle by the War Office to test Sir William Armstrong's new breach-loading gun. Armstrong formed so high an opinion of Andrew Noble's ability that he persuaded him to become his partner. There is one curious sidelight on this story which I did not discover until much later. Sir Andrew Noble brought to the north with him, as tutor for his sons, a certain Oxford scholar, a palaeographer and student of liturgies named John Meade Falkner (1858–1932). This strange man, who seemed predestined for an academic career, became, first secretary and then Managing Director of Armstrong Whitworth & Company, travelling widely and negotiating contracts with foreign governments. He then retired from business life and returned to Durham where he became Librarian to the Dean and Chapter of the Cathedral and the chief authority on its rites and music. He is best remembered today for his three works of fiction: *The Lost Stradivarius**, *Moonfleet*, and that strange novel, *The Nebuly Coat*. Those who have read *The Nebuly Coat* can scarcely fail to deplore the fact that a man of such remarkable literary talent allowed himself to be persuaded, presumably by Sir Andrew Noble, into the world of business. Nevertheless, that he was such a success in that world surely reveals his unusual, many-sided character. Falkner is a man whose biography I would like to write, but unfortunately the books I would most enjoy writing are seldom those that bring the money into the till.

I am often asked how much work a particular book involved. This is a difficult question to answer because I am usually finishing one book at the same time as I am doing research for the next. Nevertheless, I would estimate that the research and the writing of my Brunel biography took me eighteen months. If this does not seem much for a book of 120,000 words containing much original material, I would only reply that authors cannot afford to work a forty-hour week. Also, that I have learnt by experience that the whole art of research is knowing when to stop. As the work of adding fact to fact goes on, so the writer must constantly sift the inchoate mass of material so acquired until a pattern of order either emerges or is by him imposed upon it. It is at this juncture, when the shape of the book becomes clear in his mind, that the author can afford to stop research and start writing. Without this vision of order, research into any subject can easily become obsessional, the pursuit of facts never ending, and the projected master work either never written or unreadable. Because my work has never been assisted by any

---

*   My attention was first drawn to Meade Falkner by a friend of mine who pointed out that the last ghost story in *Sleep No More*, 'Music hath Charms' (I think it the best story I have written), was but a variation on the theme of *The Lost Stradivarius*. Never having heard of the latter and feeling rather piqued, I went straight off and bought No. 545 in the Oxford World Classics Series which contains the story in question and also *The Nebuly Coat*.

kind of research grant, academic or otherwise, I could not in any case afford to carry on in such a fashion.

'What book are you working on now, if I may ask?'
'A book about Brunel.'
'Brunel? Who's he?'

Interchanges of this kind had occurred with depressing frequency during the past eighteen months so that when I submitted the finished typescript to George Hardinge at Collins, although I was confident that I had made a good job of it, I did not feel so optimistic about the book's future. Biographies of little-known characters are usually foredoomed to failure; in my enthusiasm I had assumed that Brunel's name was a household word and was discouraged to find that this was by no means the case.

However, George Hardinge was enthusiastic about the book and all seemed set fair when I received a mysterious message from Collins to the effect that Mr Milton Waldman wished to see me and would I please arrange an early appointment. Mr Waldman, it transpired, had but lately returned to the Collins fold from America where he had acquired some ideas about publishing. When I was shown into his office he was seated at a table leafing through my Brunel typescript. He slapped the palm of his hand down on the book and pronounced: 'We've got the makings of a best-seller here' and then went on to tell me just how this desirable goal could be achieved. It was a simple recipe which consisted of lifting the more dramatic incidents out of the book like so many plums out of a pie, stringing them together and throwing the rest away. This, I realized, was American publishing philosophy which holds that no book is incapable of improvement and employs a team of editors to do the improving, grooming books for best-sellerdom as Hollywood starlets used to be groomed for stardom. As these editors have to justify their salaries few books, unless they are by some acknowledged master, escape their attention, the end product being almost as mediocre and lacking in individuality as that American horror, the abridged or condensed novel. I explained that it was the object of my exercise to write a definitive biography of Brunel, not to produce a hypothetical best-seller. Even if it failed to sell widely, at least the former would possess a certain permanent value, whereas a failed best-seller is a worthless thing. In any case it was never my ambition to write a runaway best-seller as such a thing can be a financial embarrassment to an author, earning him far too much money in too short a period with the result that he falls prey to the tax inspector.*

It was obvious that our meeting had reached a complete impasse since we both held fast to our respective opinions. One side or the other had to make a token submission so I concluded our uncomfortable session by agreeing to take the typescript home with me and mull the idea over. I was a very worried man when I got home that night. It is a bold author who backs his own judgement against that of an experienced publisher if only because it is difficult to assess the merits of his own brain-child coolly and objectively. And yet I felt in my bones that I was right and that it would be madness to tamper with the text in the way that had been proposed. Suddenly I made up my mind – I would send off the text to my friend John Guest of Longmans first thing in the morning. John received the book on a Friday and, as he told me afterwards, he spent the whole weekend reading it because a decision was obviously of some urgency. That decision was quickly made and gratified me exceedingly; Longmans would publish the book as it stood and would repay Collins the amount of the advance they had already paid me. So, after many vicissitudes my Brunel biography was finally 'put to bed'. It was published in 1956. A month or two after these events I walked into

---

* To mitigate this injustice a meagre tax concession was made whereby an author is allowed to 'spread back' his earnings on a book over the previous three years. I once tried this. By the time claims for back tax had been settled and my accountants' extra charges paid (for additional correspondence) I found I was exactly £15 to the good.

Longmans offices in Clifford Street and was very surprised to see George Hardinge; he had moved over with Brunel.

Longmans netted from Collins not one book but three. I had become so enthralled with Brunel that long before I had finished his biography I began to see myself as a kind of latter-day Samuel Smiles, producing a whole series of engineer biographies. The considerations governing the choice of subject were that they should be well-known names about whom there was something new to be said, for there is no point in writing a serious biography unless it can shed some fresh light on its subject. James Brindley, Thomas Telford and the two Stephensons were the characters I originally selected but I eventually decided to drop Brindley because there seemed to be insufficient material to add to what Smiles had already written about him.

Research and field work on Telford and the Stephensons naturally took me to the north again. In the case of Telford, whose major engineering works seem invariably to be set against some of the most spectacular landscape backgrounds in Britain, I decided to combine business with pleasure. Sonia and I had a most delightful run to the north along the backbone of England by way of Buxton, Chapel-en-le-Frith, Holme Moss, Huddersfield, Halifax, Skipton, Richmond, Barnard Castle and Stanhope to Hexham. We stayed a few days with the Nobles at Walwick before leaving the Alvis and going on into Scotland by rail. We caught a train at Humshaugh station on that long-vanished branch line of the old North British that winds up the valley of the North Tyne and through the wilds of Kielder Forest. This eventually landed us at Riccarton Junction, one of those strange, completely isolated railway enclaves set in the midst of a desolate moor. Here we caught a train by the old Waverley route to Edinburgh, then north again to Inverness where I had arranged to spend some time going through the records of the Caledonian Canal in the canal offices at Clachnaharry. On completing my work there, we were lucky enough to obtain a passage through the canal in a brand new inshore fishing boat from Lossiemouth which was making her maiden voyage to the west coast fishing grounds. Her crew were kindness itself plying us with mugs of hot cocoa and the most enormous Abernethy biscuits I have ever seen.

Unless one travels through the Caledonian Canal with a knowledgeable eye, it is apt to be dwarfed by the sheer scale and grandeur of the landscape of the Great Glen. This is a false impression, for the truth, as I now discovered, is a tremendous work of civil engineering, especially bearing in mind its early date and the wild and almost trackless state of the Highlands at that time. Had such feats of engineering been carried out in England (as they later were by the railway builders) they would have been hailed as the wonder of the age, but in the Highlands of Scotland they were largely unsung except by personal friends of Telford, like the poet Robert Southey. This emphasizes the truth of one of my golden rules which is never to write about anything of which one has not had first-hand experience.

From Fort William we travelled by rail to Mallaig, by steamer to the Kyle, and so back to Inverness whence we returned to Northumberland. Picking up the Alvis, we next motored westward into Dumfries in order to visit Telford's birthplace and the country in which he grew to manhood in the neighbourhood of the village of Westerkirk and the little town of Langholm in Eskdale. Here a particularly satisfying piece of detective work was the discovery of what I am confident were the ruins of the shepherd's cottage in which Telford was born. This was done by comparing the actual lie of the land with the somewhat romanticized steel engraving of the birthplace in Smiles' *Life of Telford*. The ruins appeared just where we expected them to be, but as this was in the midst of a new Forestry Commission plantation, by now either they will be hidden beneath funereal spruce or they will have been digested by some monstrous stone-crushing machine such as the commission use to provide road material.

Before *Brunel* was published, an advance copy was sent to the panel of literary experts who select the Book Society choices and also award 'recommends' to the also-rans. *Brunel* was not even among these also-rans, a fact which was not in the least surprising, for how could a book about an engineer possibly qualify as literature? In other words I was a victim of Sir Charles Snow's 'two cultures'. So I was surprised to see, when *Telford* was published, that it bore the legend 'Recommended by the Book Society' on the jacket. When I asked Longmans for some explanation of this, they advanced the theory that the Book Society panel had been so surprised by the success of *Brunel* that they had decided to play safe by bestowing a cautious laurel leaf on *Telford*. In fact, although *Telford* went on selling, it was at a lower rate than the two other volumes in this trilogy. I am sure this is because Telford the dour, reticent, solitary and single-minded Scot, is a far more difficult character to bring alive than the others. Hence there is a certain lack of human interest in the book, although to some extent this is compensated for by the magical, fairy-tale quality of Telford's great engineering works and the romantic landscapes in which they were invariably set.

In quest of the two Stephensons I again motored north, this time alone in the duck's back Alvis.* I stayed for the inside of a week at Walwick while I made pilgrimages to Wylam, Willingdon Quay, Killingworth and other sites associated with George or Robert Stephenson and then, bidding farewell to the hospitable Nobles, moved to a hotel in Darlington so that I could explore, by foot and by car, the line of the old Stockton & Darlington Railway. I was surprised to find how much evidence – stone-block sleepers, bridges, the ruins of winding-engine houses – remained to be seen.

It was on the long drive back from Darlington to Stanley Pontlarge that an amusing, in retrospect almost surrealist, incident occurred. I had just driven through Leek and I was

---

* By this date we were regularly using both Alvises, the four-seater as a family car, usually driven by Sonia and used for shopping, ferrying our two young sons to and fro to school and so on. While the duck's back, as always, remained my personal transport.

brooding sadly over the fact that on this whole long journey
out and home I had so far encountered only one fellow vintage
motorist in the shape of a rather tatty 3-litre Bentley when I
saw ahead of me an almost unbelievable sight. It was the rear
of a large blue touring car of, it appeared, late Edwardian date
with a smart brown cape-cart hood erected which prevented
me from seeing the driver or his passengers, if any. But the
most remarkable thing was that this vehicle was emitting
indubitable puffs of steam. A steam car, by heavens! Aside
from the rallies I mentioned in an earlier chapter, this was the
first and last time I have seen a steam car being driven on an
English road in the ordinary way of business. We were still in
the outskirts of Leek, so I decided to pass the steam car,
driving on until I came to a suitable stretch of road in open
country where I could park the Alvis on the verge to await the
steamer's arrival. I argued that an enthusiast would surely stop
on seeing my car. At length the steamer appeared, proceeding
at a slow and stately pace. As it approached I saw that it was
being driven with intense seriousness and concentration by a
tall, gaunt old man who looked to be at least eighty years of
age. There was no other occupant. Standing beside my car, I
beamed at him and waved, but if he saw me he did not betray
the fact, keeping his gaze fixed on the road ahead. My
curiosity now thoroughly aroused, I determined to follow him
to see whither this strange old gentleman was bound. This
meant for me a third gear crawl, but it did not last long. A
gloved hand was punctiliously extended from the steamer to
indicate that its driver was about to turn right. Automatically,
I made a similar signal, thinking we were approaching a road
junction, but then hesitated on seeing that the steamer was in
fact turning into a private drive. I pulled into the left and
slowed to a crawl. On one of the gateposts was fixed a board
bearing the legend CHEDDLETON MENTAL HOSPITAL. At
this point I considered it prudent to abandon the chase and
drive on, but I am still curious about that car and its elderly
conductor. I think the car was an Edwardian Stanley somewhat rebuilt and modified, but I cannot be certain.

With the publication of my three engineer biographies between 1956 and 1960 I found to my profound relief that the ghost of *Narrow Boat* no longer hung round my neck like an albatross. Although that first book is still in print and still selling, it has been quite eclipsed by my biographies. I was no longer introduced as 'the man who wrote *Narrow Boat*' but as the man who wrote *Brunel* or, more commonly, as the engineering historian. This did my morale an immense amount of good, banishing once and for all that gloomy notion that I might, after all, be only a one-book man. *Brunel* and its immediate successors made me a new reputation and this is why I think it is unnecessary to pursue this book-by-book account of the vicissitudes of my literary career any further. Instead I shall end this chapter with some reflections and opinions based on experience. But in case I should sound sour and embittered, I would say at once that if I could have those thirty years over again I would not do other than I have done. This is because all the hazards, the financial worries, the disappointments and frustrations have been well worth enduring for the sake of the blessed freedom I have enjoyed. Ever since 1945, when I left the Ministry of Supply, I have been my own master, free to come and to go as I please. In the modern world this is a pearl beyond price as I well know.

I have heard many an author praising his agent as though he were some kind of miracle man. This has not been my experience. Perhaps I do not write the kind of books an agent is accustomed to handle. Perhaps I am not the right kind of author. The eminent agent to whom David Cape introduced me proved no more satisfactory than his predecessors. When I transferred *Brunel* to Longmans, the contract he had won from Collins became null and void but, by an act of inconceivable stupidity, instead of using this opportunity to get away. I passively allowed him to draw up contracts with Longmans for *Brunel* and for the other two biographies. He obtained no better terms than I could have got myself, yet for this I have had to pay dearly ever since by parting with his percentage pound of flesh on every penny these three books have earned.

The reason why I finally decided that I must get rid of this agent was simple. I was commissioned to write a short text for a new educational series aimed at teenagers. Its title was *Transport and Communications* and it was tailor-made to the editor's wishes. I had just completed and submitted this book when the firm concerned sold their publishing division to Ward Lock, who said they did not intend to proceed with the new series. I obtained meagre conpensation plus the right to publish the book elsewhere. A tailor-made book of this kind is not easy to place and I had not the time to flog it around. This, I thought, is what my agent is for, so I promptly sent it off to him. After six months, nothing had happened although he assured me he was doing his best. So I asked him to return the typescript to me and within a week I had placed it with Methuen Children's Books who produced it very well and subsequently published a revised second edition.

Not surprisingly, after this experience I decided once and for all that I would have no further truck with agents. What about handling foreign rights? A question that is often asked at this point. The answer is that any publisher worth his salt can handle such rights as well as, or more efficiently than, any agent, at least that is my experience, while the author pays less away in commission because a publisher exacts his share of foreign rights whether or no the author has an agent. Conversely, the fact that the publisher has placed the foreign rights does not stop the agent drawing his commission on the proceeds from them. In my view the answer to the deficiencies of the literary agent is a simple one of £.s.d. Compared with an actor's agent, the literary agent's commission on the average author's earnings is miniscule so it is a case of the old saying: 'yer gets what yer pays for'.

To anyone engaged in any other business the accounting methods of publishers seem unbelievable. Authors' royalty accounts are made up at half-yearly, or sometimes yearly, intervals. Moreover they are not actually issued and paid until at least two months after the end of the period concerned. It is an accounting practice handed down from days when rows of clerks before stand-up desks wrote out the statements with quill pens, and it has become completely anachronistic in days when it would be perfectly feasible to settle accounts quarterly. But, of course, it does mean that the publisher has the author's money to play around with, interest free, for quite a while. The author must needs take the publisher's royalty statements entirely on trust. If he has a suspicious mind he could instruct his accountant to inspect his publisher's books, but apart from ruining author/publisher relations, few authors could afford such a course, his accountant's time being far more costly than his own. In any case such an exercise would normally be fruitless because the great majority of publishers are strictly honourable.

The injustice of the tax system where authors are concerned is not widely appreciated. For example, the copyright in my books is my capital and my royalty payments represent the annual interest on that capital. Yet if I fall into such dire financial straits that I am forced to sell the copyright in some of my books, the sum realized is taxable as income. Another example: the inland revenue cannot be made to understand why, in a period of galloping inflation, my income, along with that of other authors, is slowly but surely falling. Such a reversal of the norm simply cannot be. Consequently, 'allowing', as he puts it, 'for normal growth' my tax inspector makes regularly an absurdly high assessment of my next year's income so that I am forced to go through the annually expensive ritual of appealing against it.

Besides his never-ending running battle with the inland revenue, the unfortunate author has to tolerate, with as much patience as he may, many other difficulties or frustrations peculiar to his profession. He continually receives letters from his readers complaining that a particular title of his is out of print and asking how can they obtain a copy. This particular query recurs with such depressing frequency that I have sometimes thought it would be time-saving to have a duplicated reply to it which would read: 'the book you mention is not out of print. If you would patronise an honest bookseller instead of a chain-store, he would order you a copy.' Unfortunately, good, honest booksellers grow fewer and further between, while chain-stores, selling fewer and fewer books and more and more worthless bric-à-brac, proliferate. If it is not on their shelves, the latter simply cannot be bothered to go through the motions of ordering a single copy and so come up with the facile lie that the book is out of print. So the author has to tolerate a retail trade the majority of whom refuse to sell his books despite the fact that they get a 'cut' of $33\frac{1}{3}$ per cent compared with his own meagre royalty of 10 or 12 per cent.

Despite all the efforts that authors have made in recent years to enlighten it, the great general public remains extraordinarily – one might almost say obstinately – ill-informed about the rewards of authorship. They are unable to comprehend the fact that, alone of the professions, an author can earn a national reputation yet still remain as poor as a church mouse. My name first featured in *Who's Who* in 1953 at a time when I was sailing perilously close to the financial rocks.* From then until now the number of circular begging-letters I have received from innumerable deserving causes would fill a large cart. If those responsible for these campaigns realized that authors are in no position to dispense alms, they would save a great deal in printing and postage. But no, it is assumed that because an author has graduated to the 'establishment' he is naturally affluent. Fifty years ago, this might have been a correct inference to draw, but it is certainly not true today.

Then there is the fallacious argument that because an author's royalty is calculated on the selling price of his books, in these days of high book prices he must be sitting pretty. The law of diminishing returns begins to operate. It also disregards the fact that, owing to these high prices, the author

---

* As my name was not particularly well known in 1953, I wondered then, and still wonder now, by what means the publishers of this unique work decide who shall be numbered among the elect.

is subjected to increasing pressure from publishers to accept a lower percentage royalty. After all, such as printers and book-binders, are tightly organized in trade unions so there is only one person left to squeeze, the primary producer, the unfortunate, unorganized author.

The greatest social injustice from which the author suffers in this country is that, through the public library system, it has been taken for granted by the citizens of the Welfare State that he exists to provide them with free entertainment. If the tax man is the author's enemy number one, I would name the public librarian as enemy number two for his implacable opposition to PLR. Even when a scheme is devised which does not commit him to any extra work, his attitude does not change. What I find peculiarly odious is that the librarian likes to pose as the author's chief patron. Without library sales, his argument runs, most authors could not exist, ergo, by campaigning for public lending rights, the author is biting the hand that feeds him. Such an argument betrays a wilful ignorance of the economics of authorship. It would have been economically impossible for me to have earned my living for thirty years on the fruits of library sales alone. In fact, the boot is on the other foot and all librarians are, in the last analysis, dependent, like everyone else concerned with books, on the work of the author. Had PLR been instituted at the time I began my literary career I should by now be able to retire. As it is, I must go on working until I drop and the relief of PLR, though there are signs that it may come soon, may come too late to help me.

In preparing my annual accounts I group my sources of income under the following four headings: Royalties; Advances and Other Payments; Articles and Reviews, BBC etc.; Lectures. The phrase 'Other Payments' I shall explain later, suffice it to say here that these first two items represent my income from writing books which far outstrips the figures under the other two headings. The latter represent the odd jobs that come my way because I am known as a writer of books. As it is, I suppose I turn down about 50 per cent of the total number of requests I receive. There are several reasons for this. First, it is distracting when one is in the middle of writing a book to have to break off and bend one's mind to a magazine article or review. Secondly, there is the knowledge that one is devoting precious time to something essentially ephemeral, whereas no book can be so described. Even if a book appears to be a ghastly failure at the time of publication it has a stubborn survival value. It continues to live on the shelves and in the minds of the discerning few until suddenly, perhaps many years later, its merit is recognized and it is reprinted. Thirdly, there is the simple fact that, with rare exceptions, ephemeral writings are seldom worthwhile financially. For example, if a reviewer is conscientious, as I try to be, and actually reads the book he is sent to review, then the paltry fee he receives is an insult to his intelligence. The most I can say for reviewing is that it is a way of building up a modern library on one's subject.

I include the BBC and its independent rival in the category of unrewarding ephemera. That this should be so is certainly true. Broadcasting and television rates are so low that one is forced to conclude that they are based on the assumption that no author will be able to resist the publicity value of microphone or television camera. I find such an assumption so distasteful that, having no thirst for the kind of publicity that 'the media' purveys, I became stubborn and uncooperative at the mere mention of a possible appearance on 'the box'. The usual tactic is for the producer or his secretary to ring up and ask very deferentially if he could possibly run down to Gloucestershire to consult me about a new programme on some historical engineering topic. After wasting the whole of an afternoon of my time picking my brains, the possibility of my participating in some way in his programme is tentatively raised. To my natural question about fees he makes the routine reply that that must be left to the Contracts Department. The inference is that he is an artist and that I, like him, should be above such financial haggling. This is an invariable gambit and unless the victim is forewarned it usually pays off:

he may even find himself in the studio and taking part in a programme without having received any contract, as I very foolishly did on one occasion. The only rule is to insist upon a fee being agreed before allowing them to waste your time.

I blame the influence of television for that 'personality cult' which has invaded the press and, with rare and honourable exceptions, has pushed serious reviewing into the background. When I leaf through my old press-cutting books, the obvious shrinkage of review space and the decline in the quality of reviewing during my writing lifetime is saddening. In the place of reviewing we have interviews with writers in which the reader is regaled with their views on this and that, a pen portrait of their wife or mistress, what their literary ambitions are, their taste in food and drink and their 'life style' generally. Authors presumably endure such inquisitions, like television appearances, for the sake of the publicity, but no writer would consider a column of such trivial gossip a fair substitute for a serious and honest attempt to assess the merits or demerits of his latest book.

This is not to say that I consider that column inches of reviews are of vital importance to an author any more than I think publicity efforts on the part of the publisher are vital. Many a new author feels aggrieved when he finds, not only that his precious book is not reviewed in the 'Sundays' but that it has not been included in his publisher's advertisements either. He should not worry. No amount of rave reviews and no amount of publicity will sell a bad book, whereas a good book sells primarily on personal recommendation passed on from reader to reader. From experience, I am sure that this is true because I do not think that any author can have achieved so large a reputation and sales as I have over the years to the accompaniment of less publicity or so meagre a ration of review space. The reason is, of course, that to literary editors, the kind of subjects I write about are technical and therefore unsuitable matter for Literature (with a capital L) which should be concerned with art and not with science or technology.

Lecturing makes another very small item on my annual

balance sheet because the paltry fees offered again illustrate the popular fallacy that an established author must necessarily be well-heeled. I receive letters from innumerable local societies, or branches of national ones, inviting me to lecture at some remote town which may be in England, Scotland, or Wales. They invariably offer to reimburse my expenses but only very rarely is there any mention of a fee. So, instead of presenting me with a straight offer to be accepted or rejected, they put me to the trouble of replying and stating my fee, an invidious chore which I dislike. This disclosure of my fee is frequently the end of the matter, for these enthusiastic lecture organizers will never realize that an author's lecture fee must cover, not only the lecture itself but the time he consumes – usually the best part of two days – in travelling to and fro between his home and Leeds, Liverpool or Norwich as the case may be. If the fee does not cover this loss of time, then it means that I can earn more by sitting at my desk at home. University Extra-Mural Departments, who should know better, are among the worst offenders in this respect, offering insultingly low fees for their lecture courses.

I have found that lecturing is like acting in one respect in that one's performance is dependent on the responsiveness of the audience. I can tell in the first few minutes whether they are 'with me' or not. Strangely enough, I have found that the quality of the audience in this respect varies from county to county and town to town. I have found my most responsive audience in Leicester and my least in my local town of Cheltenham, a judgement that is based not upon one but on several experiences in each town. But my least responsive audiences of all consisted of members of the Historical Association to whom I had been asked to speak on the subject of Thomas Telford at Attingham Park in Shropshire. Their average age must have been about seventy and before returning to Attingham for dinner they had had a very long day's sight-seeing. Consequently, when they adjourned to the library for my after-dinner talk, the entire audience fell asleep as though they had been pole-axed. I talked on against a background of deep breathing and gentle snores, observing in the reflected light from the screen the rows of closed eyes and open mouths.

The other unnecessary hazard to which a lecturer is subjected arises from the inability of organizers to provide the correct equipment with which to project the slides or film strips used for illustration. This, despite the fact that I always spell out my requirements in words of one syllable. I arrive to find either the wrong projector or no projector at all, whereupon members of the audience volunteer to set out upon a frantic combing of the town in an attempt to track down the correct machine, often returning flushed and breathless after a fruitless quest. Alternatively, they have the correct projector but either the lead is not long enough to reach the nearest power point, or the plug does not suit and no alternative plug or adaptor can be found. Sometimes incidents of a more dramatic kind occur. I was about to address a packed audience in a large hall in Llandudno and as soon as I called for the projector and it was switched on, every light in the hall went out, plunging us into total darkness. I groped my way back into the little room behind the platform, felt for a chair and left them to sort it out, listening to the muffled sounds of confusion, the calls for torches and matches, from without. As no one appeared to know where the main fuses were, it was some time before order was restored.

My most memorable experience as a lecturer occurred at a large technical college in a Lancashire town not many miles from Manchester where I had been invited to deliver the annual Ramsbottom Lecture.* As he was driving me to the college after meeting me at Manchester Piccadilly station, I thought the college lecturer seemed rather ill at ease. Finally, he swallowed and said nervously that he hoped I would not be disappointed in my audience. To the question: 'Why should I be?' he explained rather lamely that, owing to a stupid oversight, a rival lecture had been arranged for the same night.

* The name is fictitious.

Proceedings began according to custom with dinner in a nearby hotel given by the current representatives of the Ramsbottom family to the lecturer and the Principal of the College. This over, we all progressed across the street to the imposing portico of the college where, in the entrance hall through the glass doors I found myself confronted by these notices:

SMALL LECTURE THEATRE: L.T.C. ROLT

LARGE LECTURE THEATRE: Dr. J. BRONOWSKI

The Principal and I turned left and walked onto the platform of the small theatre together. I was gratified to see that the auditorium was packed and that the porters were carrying in extra chairs which they were setting out in the aisles. The Principal stopped in his tracks 'Good gracious me!' he exclaimed, 'There must be some mistake.' He banged on the table for silence and announced in a loud clear voice 'This is NOT Dr Bronowski's lecture. Will those who think it is move as quickly as possible to the large theatre across the hall.' No one stirred. 'Extraordinary', he muttered, before repeating his announcement in a still louder voice. This time it provoked some faint, ironical cheers from the audience, but still no one moved. There was then nothing for the Principal to do but to introduce me, which he did perfunctorily and with a just perceptible shrug of the shoulders as if to say there is no accounting for human nature. Lancastrians are not the most tactful of men and I can well understand why they have a reputation for calling a spade a bloody shovel.

6
Writing for Industry

The 'other payments' mentioned in the last chapter represent the fees I receive for writing books for industry, usually to mark a particular company's centenary. This is a source of income I had never considered when I decided to make writing a career, yet it adds up to a very substantial sum over the years. Usually such books are produced for private publication and distribution in which case I receive an agreed outright fee payable in instalments, but occasionally a company history may be made available for sale as well as for private distribution so that I then get a small royalty additional to my fee.

Looking back over the years, I think my survival as a writer would have been far more difficult, if not impossible, had it not been for this lucrative side line. It has led me into some embarrassing situations but it has also produced some very interesting experiences which I would not on any account have missed.

This particular story began when I was at Towyn in 1951, running the Talyllyn Railway. One morning I received out of the blue a letter from a firm of publishers, whose name I had not heard of before, who described themselves as 'publishers to industry'. They asked permission to add my name to their 'panel of authors' and since there appeared to be no strings attached, I naturally consented. Months and years slipped by and I had forgotten all about the matter when, in the winter of 1954/55 I received a letter from this firm inquiring whether I would be interested in writing a centenary history for Samuel Williams & Co. of Dagenham Dock. Although I had never heard of this firm, it sounded an interesting assignment so I accepted and, in the light of after events, I am very glad that I did so.

Old Samuel Williams, the founder of the company, was a working lighterman on London River who prospered until he owned a modest fleet of lighters. By 1855 there was only one small part of the lands bordering the Thames between London and the sea which must have looked substantially the same as it had done in the days of the Roman occupation. This was the site where the celebrated Dagenham Breach had occurred in the seventeenth century. This was a serious failure of part of the embankment which protected the neighbouring flat lands from being overwhelmed by the tides. To close this breach posed an almost insuperable problem to seventeenth-century engineers and when, after years of effort, it was finally closed by the redoubtable Captain Perry, a large lake and a great area of salt marsh remained behind. Samuel Williams had the wit to realize the potential value of this marshland and he bought it for a song. He next secured a contract to dispose of all the spoil produced during the building of London's Metropolitan and District railways. This he lightered down the river and dumped on Dagenham Marsh, thus gradually reclaiming it. It is now the site of the company's busy Dagenham Docks and it is also, incidentally, the site of the Ford Factory which Samuel Williams & Co. sold to Fords, also carrying out all the preparatory works including a great deal of pioneer concrete piling.

I found this Dagenham job most interesting and enjoyable, while it was also directly responsible for providing me with a new and novel experience – an ocean voyage in a cargo ship. Although I am not particularly attracted to the sea, I had always felt a desire to make a long sea voyage just to see what it was like. But I was determined not to travel as a cossetted passenger in one of those ships designed to make her customers forget they are at sea by providing the illusion of a luxury hotel. Instead, I wanted to travel the ocean the hard way by a merchantman in which I hoped I might have the run of the ship from bridge to engine-room so that I could experience at first hand what a modern 'life on the ocean wave' was really like. Now, at Dagenham, precisely this opportunity offered itself.

One of the company's principal activities was the traditional one of shipping 'sea coal' coastwise from Tyne to Thames. This traffic was handled by a subsidiary known as the Hudson Shipping Company and shortly before I came onto the scene the decision had been taken to expand this company's activities. No longer would they be confined to coastal trade; they would also go deep-sea. To this end two new bulk carriers were ordered from Readhead's yard on the Tyne – this at a time before the bulk carrier became as popular as it is today. Considering what traffic these two new ships might profitably engage upon, the company decided that the West Indian sugar trade appeared the most promising. The raw sugar had, up to now, been carried in bags so that carriage in bulk offered substantial economies, as was quickly appreciated by Tate & Lyle who chartered both ships.

The first of these ships, the *Hudson Deep*, was commissioned while I was still working at Dagenham. The second, the *Hudson Point* was not completed until after I had finished my history of the firm, but I received an invitation to a cocktail party on board her as she lay in Dagenham Dock prior to setting out on her maiden voyage to the West Indies. While the rest of the company present seemed intent on serious drinking, the Managing Director, John Carmichael, and I set out on a tour of exploration. The *Hudson Point* had the usual layout of a bulk carrier with engine-room, crew's quarters and dining saloon right aft and bridge-house for'ard, a series of enormous cargo hatches occupying the space between. We were investigating the bridge-house where I found that directly below the Captain's cabin there was a second cabin, as large as a bedroom in a house, having twin sleeping berths and its own bathroom, shower and loo. Over the doorway to this palatial apartment were carved the words: OWNER'S CABIN. 'Does the Owner ever travel?' I asked Carmichael, half enviously and half in jest. 'No', he replied, 'I shouldn't think so', and then he added as an after-thought, 'Why, would you like to?' So it came about that January 1958 saw Sonia and myself embarking on the *Hudson Point* for a voyage to the West Indies.

Having left our two sons, Richard and Timothy, at Stanley Pontlarge in charge of a nanny, we joined our ship at Readhead's yard on the Tyne whither she had gone for her first re-fit. This was the first time I had seen a shipyard at close quarters and I was astounded by the primitive and dangerous working conditions, the dirt and the apparent disorder and muddle that appeared to prevail. Most of the dock was unprotected from the weather and the ground was covered by a slippery mixture of thin mud and suspended oil. On this surface electric arc welding cables snaked about everywhere for the unwary to trip over, perhaps to fall into the unprotected depths of a large dry dock. We went aboard the *Hudson Point* to find that the ship's fitters had finished their work but had left an indescribable mess everywhere. New paintwork was covered with oily fingermarks, the decks were strewn with balls of filthy cotton waste and there were heaps of metal and wood shavings in corners. The crew appeared to take this state of affairs quite philosophically. Apparently it was usual because the shipyard worker argues that once the ship puts to sea her crew will have all the time in the world to clean up after him.

We met the Master, Captain Platt, a genial Tynesider who had graduated from the coastal coal trade, and the young Shetland Islander who was Chief Engineer. It was explained to us that as the ship did not officially carry passengers we would have to sign on as steward and stewardess. In the afternoon, the *Hudson Point* moved to the bunkering berth and then, at 11 p.m., finally cast off, moving slowly towards the mouth of the river where she was swung to adjust compasses. This done we set course down the east coast but caught no glimpse of land the following day owing to bad visibility.

When, at 11.30 p.m. that night, we rounded the North Foreland and entered the English Channel, I was up on the bridge gazing in absolute fascination at the radar screen. It was my first acquaintance with radar in action and I could not have chosen a better moment. There, outlined in white on the sides of the screen were the familiar outlines of the channel coasts, while over the black void between there moved like so many luminous water-boatmen, numerous points of light from each of which small arrowheads of wake fanned out. I had no idea that these narrow seas carried so much traffic and to my inexperienced eye it all looked very fraught, imminent collisions appearing inevitable. But the radar screen, like a map, is on a small scale and in this respect conveys an alarmist impression to those unfamiliar with it. In fact, we scarcely glimpsed the lights of another ship in our passage down channel.

When the reluctant January daylight came there was a thick mist over the land and distant foghorns were groaning and grunting. Once a corridor opened in the mist to starboard to reveal some vicious fangs of rock which we were told were the Casquets. Distantly, we could hear the melancholy clangour of a bell buoy. This was the last sight and sound we had of Europe.

As soon as we got out into the open Atlantic we ran into heavy weather which lasted for four days and nights and was made worse by the fact that we were travelling light ship with only water ballast to steady her. It seemed to me extremely rough, though the crew assured me that it was nothing unusual for the North Atlantic in January. The weather proved too much for Sonia who had to retire to her berth. So long as she remained in a horizontal position she felt alright, but as soon as she got up she began to feel sea-sick. Fortunately I am a good sailor and was quite unaffected. At first I thought it was all rather exciting, but after four days of it I had grown heartily sick of rough weather. I found the sheer physical strain of keeping my balance extraordinarily tiring and by the end of the day felt as stiff as after a twenty mile walk. Again, sleep, for me at any rate, became almost impossible. Because the ship was both rolling and pitching it made little difference whether one lay fore and aft or transversely. The berths in our cabin (they were virtually twin beds) were disposed fore and aft which meant that every time the ship rose to a wave I found myself sliding down in the bed, while as she descended into a trough I found my head pressed firmly against the bedhead.

I spent quite a lot of this stormy time up on the bridge. The outlook forward through the whirling spinners was hypnotic as a succession of great waves attacked the port bow of the *Hudson Point*, causing the whole ship to tremble under their impact and sending a pother of white water creaming over the bows only to pour from the scuppers as she recovered from the blow. We were travelling on a set course by automatic pilot and although I have an ineradicable mistrust of such gadgetry, particularly on ships, I could not help admiring the way this device held the ship to her proper course under such conditions. The effect of the wind and the battering seas was that the ship kept on tending to veer away to starboard. Each time this happened there was a rapid whirring, clicking sound as of the striking train of a large clock starting up as the pilot, or 'Iron Man' as the crew nicknamed it, took instant corrective action and the wheel spun as though turned by a phantom helmsman. Yet no human hand upon the wheel could have reacted so accurately or with such unfailing promptitude.

It was at this time I discovered that life in the exclusive bridge-house was not without certain disadvantages. The prostrate Sonia's needs were supplied by a devoted steward, but Captain Platt and I must needs battle our way aft to the dining saloon along the length of the open deck, clinging to the lee rail and trying to dodge the clouds of flying spray. In the dining saloon, which was right aft, a new phenomenon was manifest as the ship pitched which I found very alarming the first time I experienced it. The whole saloon would suddenly seem to fall by several feet, not all at once but in a series of shuddering jolts, a foot at a time. At this the crew would remark jocularly that 'the old girl's falling down stairs' which, in fact, was exactly what it felt like. It was due, they explained, to the whip in the empty steel hull.

My only regret, as an enthusiast, was that the *Hudson Point* was not a steamer. She was propelled by an eight-cylinder Doxford opposed piston diesel engine which was coupled to an exhaust heat boiler to provide deck steam for winches etc. I grudgingly had to give this engine full marks for its relative silence and lack of vibration as it kept slogging away through fair weather and foul. One of my vintage car friends owned an Edwardian Gobron-Brillié car with an opposed piston engine, and, except for the difference in scale, it was interesting to see how closely the layout of the modern Doxford followed this pioneer design.* Only one feature of this Doxford alarmed me at first sight. The upper pistons were water-cooled. As the stroke of these pistons was quite considerable this water was supplied to them through rubber pipes, each between two and three feet long. On entering the engine room at deck level, standing on the iron staircase and looking down upon the main engine, the first thing to catch the eye were these eight rubber pipes, snaking away like so many captive writhing serpents at each stroke of the engine. I felt they could not possibly withstand such an ordeal for very long, but I evidently underestimated the properties of modern synthetic rubbers for, in reply to my question, the Chief said he had never known one fail although they were changed as a precautionary measure after each round voyage.

At length we left the winter storms behind, emerging into calm and sunlit blue waters. Soon we were able to sit out in the

---

*   In an engine of this type the explosion takes place in the middle of the cylinder between two pistons which are thus driven apart. The upper pistons drive a common crankshaft by means of piston rods, crossheads and connecting rods. In a large marine diesel, one of the great advantages of this layout is that the explosion forces are equalized by the two pistons. There is thus no tendency, as there is on an orthodox engine, for the explosion to lift the cylinder head and block off the crankcase. Hence the latter can be made much lighter.

sun in deck chairs in the lee of the bridgehouse watching the
flying fishes flutter from wave-crest to wave-crest. It was at
this time that we sighted our first ship since leaving the
English Channel. This was another surprise, for the phrase
'the North Atlantic shipping lanes' had given me the naïve
impression that we should be encountering a constant stream
of fellow-voyagers. Now I was learning the truth that, despite
all man's trafficking, an ocean remains a very wide and lonely
place.

When the *Hudson Point* was passing down channel she had
still to receive her loading orders and the crew had speculated
whether their destination might be Cuba, a prospect which,
from previous experience, they regarded with disfavour as that
country was still under the Batista regime. So it was a relief
when orders came through that we were to make for the port
of Barahona in San Domingo not far from the border of Haiti.
Eventually and almost miraculously it seemed to me – the
little town and port, crouched beneath high and densely
wooded hills loomed up dead ahead. Captain Platt moved the
telegraph from full to slow ahead and, for the first time for
many days, the familiar rhythm of the Doxford slowed and the
ship's wake died. We continued to drift ahead while the
Captain and I studied the harbour through binoculars – for
this was the ship's first visit. We watched two dark figures,
who had been reclining at their ease on the sun-drenched
quay, suddenly awakened to frantic activity as the bray of our
siren echoed among the surrounding hills. They ran down
some steps and piled into a small white launch, one madly
cranking the engine while the other frantically fumbled with
mooring lines. The Barahona harbour pilot had been alerted
and was on his way.

Although the *Hudson Point* was a very small ship as modern
bulk carriers go, being a mere 10,000 tons burden, her arrival
caused something of a sensation in Barahona as she was said to
be the largest ship ever to enter the port. We discovered that
the principle of bulk carriage had not yet been accepted by the
West Indians. Not only did it spell formidable labour

problems but the installation of new and costly mechanical handling equipment. So every day an elderly Baldwin metre gauge wood-burning steam locomotive, with a tall balloon stack, shuttled to and fro between the quay and Barahona's one sugar mill freighted with stacks of bagged sugar. These sugar sacks were swung aboard four at a time by the ship's derricks. On board, the enormous hatch covers were only opened to the extent of about eighteen inches, just sufficient to allow a grating to be inserted in the gap. Two native loaders received the sacks from the derrick and, while one withdrew the draw-string from the neck of each sack, the other up-ended it over the grating so that its contents fell into the cavernous hold beneath. The whole operation looked as tedious as trying to fill a large bath with a teaspoon, but it suited us for, as was proved on our return to Dagenham, had the right equipment been available we should scarcely have had time to put a foot ashore.

When we realized how long the loading was going to take, we had the optimistic notion that we might visit the ruined palace of the black emperor Christophe in the interior of Haiti, but when we learned that we should have to hire mules and that the journey would take at least two days, we reluctantly abandoned the idea and confined ourselves to things nearer to hand. With Captain Platt we were the guests of the local Rotarians who held a dinner for us in a Barahona restaurant. It was here that we tasted the local coffee for the first time and fully endorsed our hosts' claim that it was the finest in the world. So enamoured were we of this discovery that Sonia determined to take a bag of the green beans back with us so that they could be freshly roasted at home. We combed the open market and every provision shop in the town in vain. The fact that we could not speak Spanish did not make this quest any easier, but finally we were directed towards an ironmonger's shop. Here, surprisingly, we found our quarry, for in these unlikely surroundings there reposed a great sack full of green coffee beans. At dusk we liked to sit in the small town square under the palm trees, watching with amusement the nightly parade of the youth of Barahona, the boys circulating in one direction and the girls, graceful and beautifully dressed, in the other. Apart from an occasional shy interchange of glances, there appeared to be no communication whatever between the two sexes.

We were befriended by the Spanish manager of the sugar mill who showed us over his mill and also arranged a footplate trip for us on a Baldwin diesel locomotive up into the sugar plantations. I was surprised both by the extent of the plantations and by the size and complexity of the railway system which served them. Our friend also introduced us to Mrs Grant, the only English resident of Barahona. This very remarkable old lady lived alone in a bungalow overlooking the harbour. The widow of a former sugar plantation owner, she was a survivor of the days when the greater part of the sugar industry of the West Indies was owned either by the English or by the Americans. She received us most graciously but with a surprising degree of detachment considering we were probably the first people of her own blood she had seen for months. We sat chatting and sipping cups of china tea for all the world as though we were near neighbours making a polite call. Her bungalow translated us into Edwardian England, or rather the Ewardian Empire's version of England. It was obvious that she stood very high in the estimation of our Spanish friend and that she was still a force to be reckoned with in Barahona. But we speculated long on the considerations that had induced her, after her husband's death, to go on living entirely alone in this alien community.

Just before our ship sailed for home we had an opportunity to see the capital of San Domingo, then known as Cuidad Trujillo after the reigning dictator. We visited the city's two historic buildings to survive the hurricanes, the cathedral and the palace of Diego Columbus, both built in coral limestone of a most ravishing colour. That evening, after darkness fell, we also visited the new city which dictator Trujillo had caused to be built on the outskirts of the old. This was a weird experience. It consisted of a grid pattern of almost absurdly

wide avenues with groups of modern statuary on islands at
each intersection. These avenues were flanked by modern
high-rise buildings. Not only were the roads brilliantly lit, but
every window of the buildings which flanked them blazed with
light. The air was filled with the sound of sickly canned music
issuing from invisible loudspeakers. What made this modern
city so very odd was that there was not a single solitary soul to
be seen in it; no cars on the avenues, no people on the
pavements or framed in those blazing windows. It might have
been a city of the dead. We agreed that it was more than odd,
it was decidedly sinister and we could not get away from the
place quickly enough.

The voyage home was uneventful and, where Sonia was
concerned, much more comfortable as the *Hudson Point*, now
that she was fully freighted with sugar, behaved in a much
more decorous manner. It was now March so we hoped that
we had avoided the worst of the winter, but our hopes were
dashed when we passed up channel through a raging blizzard.
We docked at Dagenham at about 10.30 p.m. and by 11.30
a.m. next morning, when we bade farewell to Captain Platt
and left the ship, her cargo had been three-parts discharged by
the dock's 12-ton grabbing cranes loading into an endless
string of lighters. The whole voyage had been a most interesting and worthwhile experience but one which I have no desire
to repeat. For it taught me something of the deadly monotony
of life in the merchant navy, a monotony that is made worse by
the characteristics of modern shipping, by all those technical
aids to navigation and by that ever increasing speed of
turn-round upon which modern economics insists.

As I had previously had nothing whatever to do with the
shipping industry, it was something of a coincidence that the
very next commission I obtained was to write a centenary
history for a well-known firm of ship store dealers named
Burnyeat Ltd. The Burnyeats are a very old Cumberland
family whose name can be traced back to the sixteenth century
and the founder of the firm was William Burnyeat who opened
his ship store business in the then flourishing Cumbrian port

of Whitehaven. This William served his time at sea until he was twenty-one when he took over a butchery business in the vanished Georges Market at Whitehaven from his widowed mother in 1840. Precisely when he started in the ship store trade was uncertain at the time I undertook the assignment. The firm's letter heading and its considerable fleet of vans proudly announced 'Established 1861' yet I could find no shred of evidence to support such a claim in the firm's archives, a circumstance I found somewhat embarrassing as I had been commissioned on the assumption that 1961 would be their centenary year. I have never undertaken such a history where there was less documentary evidence to work upon. All that was known about William Burnyeat was that at the time he started his ship store business he was already a man of considerable substance. He owned land on which he reared his own stock for the butchery; he had a considerable investment in local mining companies and, above all, in shipping. At that time, when a new ship was laid down, it was customary to divide her estimated capital cost into sixty-four shares and William Burnyeat eventually became known in shipping circles as 'the greatest sixty-fourther of them all'. In addition to these considerable shareholdings, William Burnyeat was known to have owned and worked at least two ships, the barque *Sarah Burnyeat*, and the brigantine *Emily Burnyeat*, named after his wife and daughter respectively.

There was so much hearsay and so little hard evidence about William Burnyeat's career in Whitehaven that there seemed to be nothing for it but an investigation on the spot so, having bespoken a room in Whitehaven's only listed hotel, one day in the early autumn of 1957 I headed the Alvis north for Cumberland. I was able to kill three birds with one stone on this one northern trip for, when my work at Whitehaven was done, I went on to stay with the Nobles at Walwick Hall where I was able, not only to do some research for my Stephenson biography as I have already mentioned, but also some work on the history of Burnyeat Ltd's branch depot and offices on the Newcastle quays.

One amusing little incident occurred as I was driving into Cumberland. I had unwisely allowed the level of petrol in the scuttle tank of the Alvis to fall extremely low with the inevitable result that, half way up a long hill on the approach to Millom, petrol failed to reach the carburettor and the car came to an ignominious halt. As there was no sign of a petrol pump, in these circumstances there was nothing to be done but to free-wheel back to the foot of the hill, turn the car round, and then ascend backwards. I was making a rapid ascent in reverse gear (for the Alvis has a high ratio reverse) when I was overhauled, but not passed, by a baker's delivery van. The baker and I found ourselves regarding each other, eye-ball to eye-ball over our respective steering wheels, he with an expression of mingled fear and bewilderment that was comical to behold. He was obviously not accustomed to the spectacle of men in strange looking motor cars going up hills backwards and when I smiled and waved to reassure him that everything was under control it appeared to have the opposite effect from that intended. The hill ended in an abrupt summit where there was a view of a long descent with, in the distance, an undoubted filling station on the outskirts of Millom. There was also a convenient side turning at the top for me to reverse into, waving the van past. When I passed the baker at a rate of knots on the long, straight descent he must have been more than ever convinced that I was a lunatic. He probably had drinks on the story for weeks afterwards.

I had never been to Whitehaven before and found it precisely the sort of place to appeal to me. I have always been strangely fascinated and moved by places of bygone industrial activity. It is as though they remain forever haunted by that tide of fierce and often terrifying energy which had created them and then passed on. It was this quality which had first attracted me to Ironbridge during the war and which now attracted me to Whitehaven. The port had begun to grow in the latter part of the eighteenth century until it became one of the first six in the kingdom, flourishing exceedingly as a consequence of the exploitation of neighbouring resources of coal and haematite ore. Whitehaven coal mines, extending under the sea, were one of the wonders of the early industrial revolution period. At the time of which I write, one of these pits was still working, its gaunt stack and winding gear dramatically crowning a headland jutting out into the sea on the south side of the harbour. Wagons of coal were lowered from it down to harbour level by a perilous-looking, sharply curved and graded cable-operated incline. On the opposite side of the harbour was a second colliery which had been closed and its workings sealed following a terrible disaster.

Such was the prosperity of Whitehaven that eventually no less than seven massive stone piers were built – one of them by Sir John Rennie – to contain and shelter its growing volume of shipping. On these piers there stand charming little stone lighthouses. It was the rapid rise to wealth and fame of the port of Liverpool that sealed the fate of Whitehaven. The writing was on the wall when the two uncrowned kings of the port, the brothers Thomas and Jonathan Brocklebank, ship-owners and shipbuilders, removed their business to Liverpool. The astute William Burnyeat was not long in following them and Liverpool has remained to this day the headquarters of the company he founded.

My hotel was close to the waterfront and after I had dined I set out on foot in the deep dusk of an autumn evening to explore the harbour. The walls of the row of eighteenth- and early nineteenth-century houses that overlooked the basin of the inner harbour supported gas lanterns whose mantles flared and flickered in the breeze blowing off the sea. Except that the capacious basins contained only two small steam cargo ships, it was a scene that can have changed very little since the heyday of Whitehaven. I determined to walk out to the distant extremity of the southern piers and from that vantage look back at the town. It was quite a way, and as I walked on I soon passed out of range of the last gaslamp and it became quite dark although I could just see the colliery and its headgear looming against the night sky on the headland to my left. I stopped to look up at the colliery and as I did so I heard, for a moment only, the sound of footsteps behind me. It was as though I had caught an echo of my own footfalls except that this sound was the unmistakable dot-and-carry-one of a man with a wooden leg. When I moved forward, the sound began again, yet whenever I stopped it stopped. It was a strange experience to be followed in this way on a walk which I knew, and as my pursuer must have known, would end at the pier head. At such a time of night the piers were completely deserted and I confess that I experienced a slight *frisson* of fear.

About a hundred yards from the pierhead I found some stone steps on my left which led to a narrow walkway at a higher level on the pier wall leading to a lookout over the open sea beyond. I swiftly turned aside up these steps and ran on tip-toe to the lookout. Short of jumping into the sea I could go no further. I listened and for a moment there was nothing but the sound of the sea breeze in my ears, but then I heard the clear sound of the one-legged man laboriously ascending those stone stairs. As is usual in the case of true stories of this kind, the ending was anticlimactic in the extreme. My pursuer turned out to be no sinister character out of *Treasure Island* but an old Whitehaven salt in a heavy blue seaman's jersey whose wits were fuddled either by age or alcohol so that he had seen fit to follow me thus far, like the ancient mariner, until I became literally a captive audience for his yarns. I was so relieved that I have not remembered one word of what he said.

Next morning my insatiable urge to explore the port of Whitehaven led me to make an extraordinarily lucky chance discovery. I was peering through the cobweb-blurred panes of a window of an old and ramshackle wooden hut on the quay. To my amazement I saw, standing out from the rusting and mouldering junk within like a rose among nettles, the beautiful, freshly painted figure-head of a woman. Three old men were seated on a bench nearby gazing ruminatively out over the empty harbour, so I asked them who owned the hut. Mr Keenagh, an old ships' rigger, I was told. He had retired from business now, but if I cared to wait around he would most likely be down before long. Sure enough, an ancient bent figure presently appeared and proceeded to unlock the door of his hut.

Asking him to forgive my curiosity, I explained how the figure-head had attracted my attention and asked him if he could tell me anything of its history. The old man chuckled, 'Ain't she lovely?' he asked rhetorically, 'you don't know who she is so I'll tell you – that's Emily Burnyeat that is.' I could hardly believe my ears, but old Mr Keenagh went on to assure me that this was indeed the figure-head of William Burnyeat's brigantine. For years it had lain gathering dust in the sail loft of the Keenagh family business, but when the loft was either sold up or pulled down, he had rescued it, removing it to his hut where, with loving care, he had restored the figure to its former glory. It became clear that the old man had fallen in love with the effigy and was terrified lest someone should take her away from him and 'put her in some museum' I had to assure him that I had no such intention and he finally allowed his darling to be taken out of his hut, perched on the edge of the quay wall and photographed in colour for the cover of *Mariners' Market*, as my Burnyeat history was called.

I still had to find out where and when William Burnyeat had started his ship store business. In an investigation of this kind the public librarian is usually helpful and Mr Hay of the Whitehaven Library was no exception. At his suggestion I was soon looking through piles of dusty bound volumes of the local newspaper, *The Cumberland Pacquet and Ware's Whitehaven Advertiser*, searching the announcements on the front pages. I do not know what made me go back earlier than 1861, but it was fortunate that I did so, for before very long – eureka! – there was the vital clue, an advertisement inserted by William Burnyeat announcing the opening of new and commodious premises at 23 King Street, Whitehaven. This was dated December 1851, so the firm was just ten years older than had been assumed.

It remained to find the whereabouts of 23 King Street and then see whether any traces of William Burnyeat's occupancy were still to be found. King Street was, and still is, the main shopping street of the town and Mr Hay, who was by now as hot and keen upon the scent as I was, explained that, although the street had long ago been re-numbered, we had only to go along to the Lowther Estate Office and ask to see an estate map of the right date in order to pinpoint No. 23. The Lowthers own the whole of Whitehaven and, sure enough, their Estate Office produced a superb map of the town, *c.* 1860, on which every property was identified. By cross referencing to a modern street map it was easy to establish the whereabouts of No. 23.

When we walked down King Street to discover that the premises were now occupied by a cheap multiple clothier, all plywood panelling and plate glass, our spirits sank. Had this ever been a butcher's shop? We asked the startled youth in the winkle-picker shoes behind the counter. Not that he knew of; the business had not been there very long and had succeeded a tobacconist and confectioner. But, he added, we could take a look round the back if we liked. As he spoke he opened a door behind the counter to reveal an enormous whitewashed slaughter house, its ceiling supported by cast-iron columns, still carrying the large hooks from which William Burnyeat had suspended his carcasses. It became clear to us now that the modern clothier's shop only occupied a fraction of the original premises and that there were buildings at the back, most of them now falling derelict, sufficient to house not only the butchery business from Georges Market but that stock of provisions and chandlery which an expanding ship store business would require. I was particularly intrigued by a curious building in the yard outside the slaughter house. This consisted of a row of what appeared to be single, self-contained rooms, three in number, each with a front door opening onto a balcony equipped with a cast-iron balustrade and approached by a short flight of steps. The youth followed my gaze 'The older folk what comes in here', he volunteered, 'call them "the Captain's Flats".' So, this had all been a part of the service. For a consideration William Burnyeat would provide his captain, cronies and customers with a room ashore while their ships were in port without attracting unwelcome attention. Such a man deserved his success. Unfortunately 'the Captains' Flats' were derelict when I saw them so they have doubtless been demolished long since.

Although I was trained as a mechanical engineer, the commissions I found most enjoyable and interesting were those concerned with some big new civil engineering project. These usually consisted of writing the text of an illustrated booklet, published to coincide with the official opening by HM The Queen or some other grandee and commissioned either by the main contractors, by the consulting engineers or, in some cases, by the committee responsible to local government for the project. I preferred such assignments because any work of civil engineering is necessarily unique; it is a one-off job whether it be a great bridge, a towering masonry dam or a tunnel beneath a river. Although the modern civil engineer can call to his aid equipment and plant such as his nineteenth-century predecessor never dreamed of, because he is dealing with natural things, earth, rock, air and water, his work remains subject to imponderable hazards which often cannot be foreseen and which, when they arise, he must wrestle with as best he may. For this reason, although great civil engineering works seldom excite the admiration and public acclaim that they did in the nineteenth century, there is usually an element of the heroic in the story of their successful completion.

My first commission of this kind was to write the story of the building of Britain's first motorway, the M1, for the main contractors, John Laing & Sons. When this new road was put out to tender in 1957 it was divided into four contracts of approximately equal length because it was felt that a single contract for the whole $52\frac{1}{2}$ miles of road would be beyond competitive reach. However, Laings tendered for the four contracts and, greatly to their surprise, won all of them. It was one of the biggest civil engineering jobs ever to be awarded to a single British contractor. Laings established site offices at Chalton, Newport Pagnell, Collingtree and Walton on each of the four contracts, that at Newport Pagnell also serving as the headquarters and nerve centre for the whole gigantic operation. It was to be a fight against time for, England being a late starter where motorways were concerned, it had evidently been decided to make up for lost time and completion date was only nineteen months from 24 March 1958 when the Minister of Transport inaugurated the work.

So far as I was concerned the job could not have started at a more apposite time, for I had then just completed my researches into the construction of Robert Stephenson's London & Birmingham Railway and the opportunity to study a very similar example of modern construction being carried out on a closely parallel route would be most instructive. The two ceremonies inaugurating construction symbolized the difference between the two undertakings. Whereas the customary ceremonial barrow and spade was used on Stephenson's railway in 1834, work on the M1 began when the Minister of Transport pressed a button, sounding a horn which summoned the bulldozers into action. Although the new motorway was only half the length of the railway, the formation width was more than double so that the two are strictly comparable. A total of 25,000 men, the equivalent of 225 per route mile, toiled for four years on the 112 miles of railway. By contrast, the maximum number engaged on the $52\frac{1}{2}$ miles of motorway never exceeded 4,700 and the work was completed on time. The explanation, of course, is the use of mechanical power. Plant totalling 80,000 hp was used on the M1 which meant that each man employed wielded approximately 20 hp.

Laings broke down their four contract lengths of road into 'sub-projects' of four miles each as they considered this the maximum which could be effectively supervised by one man. The four main contract site offices and the small sub-project offices were, of course, linked by telephone, while a helicopter, on charter from BEA, was used to provide rapid physical communication between these offices. Robert Stephenson had likewise divided the London & Birmingham into four divisions, each in charge of an engineer. Each of these divisions was in turn divided into two districts over which there presided an assistant engineer with a staff of three sub-assistants under him. The administration of both these great works of civil engineering, separated though they were by nearly 125 years, was thus strikingly similar. But what amazed me, having seen the M1 under construction, was how such a system could possibly have functioned at a time when there was no method of communication faster than a man on horseback. It is this fact that makes the achievement of the railway builders seem almost miraculous.

I flew over the line of the road twice by helicopter which was a novel experience for me as I had never travelled in this type of vehicle before. On the first occasion it was in a small machine with only three passenger seats powered by an Alvis Leonides engine. I thoroughly enjoyed this flight, the only drawback being the fearful mechanical commotion. So high was the noise level that conversation was only made possible by headphones and throat microphones. My second flight was far less pleasurable. On a very hot June day and after a heavy lunch, we took off from Laings' sportsfield at Elstree in a very much larger helicopter bearing a dozen or so VIPs. The passenger cabin, like a fat seed-pod hanging below the rotor, swung continuously to and fro like a pendulum and its interior was almost unbearably stuffy. I found the motion so uncongenial that I came nearer to being sick than I have ever been at sea.

The consulting engineer for the M1 was Sir Owen Williams, one of the very few living men (if any) who, like Telford and other pioneers, combined the roles of civil engineer and architect. He was also a great character with an impish sense of humour. I had several long conversations with him including a luncheon at the house he had rented for the duration of the contract in the Northamptonshire village of Milton Melzor

which I had known very well as a boy.* He claimed to have
been responsible for the design and construction of more new
bridges in Scotland than any engineer since Telford and he
delighted to tell the story of the occasion when, accompanied
by his faithful dog, he had gone to examine a suspension
bridge over the river Garry at the western end of the Great
Glen. As he walked onto the bridge, his dog positively refused
to accompany him but lay on its belly in the approach roadway
whining piteously. 'And when I examined the bridge', said Sir
Owen, 'By God the dog was right!' This story must have got
around locally, for when Sir Owen's new replacement bridge
was formally opened by Cameron of Lochiel escorted by a
detachment of pipers, in his formal speech Lochiel said how
delighted he was that Sir Owen had been able to be present
and then added drily that he noticed the engineer had wisely
left his dog at home.

I like to think that my old duck's-back Alvis was the first car
to travel the length of the M1 from Slip End, near Luton, to
the junction between the so-called 'Birmingham Spur' and the
existing A45 trunk road at Dunchurch. There was certainly
plenty of contractor's traffic in Land Rovers to be seen on the
road by this time, but for obvious reasons this was mostly
short distance. I wanted to see the progress of the work at
close quarters, also to visit the four site offices, and it struck
me that an open vintage car with good ground clearance would
be an ideal vehicle for such a tour of inspection. By keeping a
good look out for distant obstructions and switching from one
carriage way to another as occasion demanded, I got along
famously, sometimes travelling on the levelled earth formation, sometimes on the sub-base of lean concrete and
sometimes rolling smoothly along on a short stretch of completed road. It was when I neared the village of Milton that I
thought I had met my Waterloo. For the plate girder bridge
carrying the Roade–Northampton railway line over the motorway had only been rolled into position the previous week-end

* See *Landscape with Machines*, p. 63.

and the 'dumpling' of old embankment beneath it had still to
be removed. I had drawn to a disconsolate standstill when a
bronzed and muscled giant in a singlet, the modern successor
of Stephenson's railway navvies, gave me a reassuring wave
and clambered up into an enormous bulldozer. With a cloud of
black smoke and a thunderous roar he started this machine
whereupon, signalling me to follow him, he headed full-tilt at
the bank ahead. Feeling like a small launch in the wake of an
Atlantic liner, I did as I was bidden. The seemingly so solid
earth parted as miraculously as the waters of the Red Sea and
in a few moments we were through. With a creak and screech
of tracks my friend in need swung his great machine abruptly
to one side and waved me enthusiastically forward. The road
was clear ahead and I was on my way.

When I stopped at Walton, the most northerly of the four
site offices, situated near the Watford Gap where the Birmingham Spur and the M1 proper divide, I was particularly
curious to know how work had progressed in an area notorious
in civil engineering history. Here the contractors for Crick
Tunnel on the old Grand Union Canal had been compelled to
adopt a different line when one of their preliminary shafts had
struck a water-bearing quicksand. Robert Stephenson knew of
this and, hoping to avoid such a hazard, selected a line for his
railway tunnel at Kilsby, further to the south. As is well
known, this tactic proved vain and Stephenson's great battle
against the Kilsby quicksand has become one of the epics of
railway history.

Almost covering one wall of the Welton site office was a
large scale map of the division. While I was chatting to the
engineer in charge, I noticed that the line of the Birmingham
Spur passed over the top of Kilsby Tunnel* and this
prompted me to ask whether he had experienced any particular trouble on that stretch of road. He looked at me sharply.
'What makes you ask that?' he asked, and then went on, 'I'll

---

* One of the great brick ventilation shafts of the railway tunnel may be
seen close beside the road at this point.

say we have, in fact we call that "tiger country" up there.' The
road is in shallow cutting thereabouts and he went on to
explain to me how, when they had excavated this almost down
to formation level, they had suddenly struck a totally unexpected
quicksand. This had involved pumping, drainage, further
excavation and finally the importation of hundreds of tons of
fill to restore the correct level. This is an illustration of the
strange fact that civil engineers are so often taken unawares
through their failure to benefit from the experience of their
forerunners. This engineer had never heard the story of
Kilsby Tunnel until I told him. In just the same way,
although he knew about Crick Tunnel, even the great Robert
Stephenson had evidently never heard of William Jessop's
long battle against rotten, water-bearing oolite when he was
driving the Grand Junction Canal Tunnel under Blisworth
Hill. Otherwise Stephenson would not have been taken by
surprise when he encountered the same difficult conditions in
driving the Blisworth railway cutting nearby. Apart from
Kilsby, this cutting was the biggest trouble spot on the
London & Birmingham. Bourne's engraving of the cutting
shows rocks supported by timber props, and eventually most
of the cutting sides had to be held back by massive retaining
walls.

I had passed through 'tiger country' and was almost within
sight of my goal at Dunchurch when I had to stop because
both carriageways ahead appeared to be completely blocked
either with heaps of road surfacing material or machinery of
one kind or another, rollers, pavers and graders. I was sitting
on the back of the Alvis with my feet on the seat, peering
ahead over the top of the screen and pondering what I should
do, when I observed an individual who looked like the district
engineer advancing purposefully in my direction. I was quite
prepared for him to ask me brusquely what the hell I thought I
was doing there; instead he remarked, in a delightful Irish
brogue, 'I'm afraid we're not open yet', for all the world as
though he were a polite landlord and I a member of the public
who had strayed into his bar during closing hours. Having

delivered himself of this blinding glimpse of the obvious, and when I had explained the purpose of my journey, this charming Irishman proceeded, with miraculous efficiency, to clear a path for the Alvis through the chaos of machines ahead, shooing them aside like so many cumbersome elephants. In a very few minutes I was on the A45, had turned to the left and was heading home to Gloucestershire down the lonely miles of the Roman Fosse Way.

After the M1 was finished, I subsequently wrote the text of booklets to celebrate the completion of the new Severn Bridge, the Tyne Tunnel and, much more recently, the first of the new twin road tunnels under the Mersey between Wallasey and Liverpool. Following so soon after my work on those pioneers of the suspension bridge Thomas Telford and I.K. Brunel, I naturally found the Severn Bridge assignment particularly interesting.

In the second half of the nineteenth century, the initiative in the design of long span suspension bridges passed from England to the United States thanks to the American A.W. Roebling, inventor of the modern system of cable suspension and builder of the Brooklyn Bridge. Hence when the first modern suspension bridge in Britain was built across the Forth, British engineers played safe by adopting American methods using a deep lattice girder deck which had to be laboriously assembled piecemeal across the Forth. But for an accident, the new Severn Bridge would have been similar to the Forth. A model of that design had been sent down to the National Physical Laboratory for wind tunnel tests but, when Sir Gilbert Roberts of Freeman, Fox & Partners inquired as to the results of these tests he was dismayed to learn that due to an insecure anchorage the model had been blown out of the wind tunnel and completely destroyed. This was a major set-back, for to make another model would take time whereas the wind tunnel had been 'booked' only for a brief period. It was at this juncture that Sir Gilbert conceived the idea of substituting, for the conventional lattice girder construction, a deck made up of a series of prefabricated steel box sections which could be welded together *in situ* and which in cross section would resemble an aerofoil and so offer minimal resistance to cross winds. To make a series of simple wooden models of such box sections for testing in the wind tunnel in order to arrive at the best form was very quickly done. So the design of the Severn Bridge, which won back for Britain the decisive leadership in this field, was determined.

The actual deck sections were fabricated in Fairfield's yard at Cheptstow, where, long ago, the ironwork for Brunel's Chepstow Bridge had been wrought, and these were then launched into the Wye and towed by tugs to the bridge site. There, each in turn was hoisted aloft, attached to the suspension cables, and then welded to its neighbour. To ascend to the very summit of the tall steel suspension towers as I did and watch this operation going on far below was an ever-memorable experience.

The Severn Bridge is a great, original feat of engineering. It is most unfortunate that it was so soon followed by other bridges of prefabricated and box-girder structure but of most unsatisfactory design. This was shown by two cases of failure, in this country and Australia, where the use of calculators and computers alone in their design led to disaster. Had they been subjected to practical tests such as those applied by Stephenson, Hodgkinson and Fairbairn to a model of the Menai Bridge box girder in 1846, so disastrous and ignominious a series of failures might never have occurred.

Sonia and I were invited to attend the ceremonial opening of the Severn Bridge by the Queen at Aust, following which she drove over the bridge to perform an exactly similar ceremony on the other side and so propitiate the Welsh. When she had returned to the English side, loudspeakers announced that we were free to walk onto the bridge if we wished. From each bank a dense crowd surged onto the bridge to meet and mingle in the centre. The effect of this unusual load upon the bridge was most remarkable. One could feel the movement of the deck which was set up and both feel and see the fact that every suspension cable was quivering like harp string with a curious high frequency vibration. Such an experience made it easy to understand why an early, and admittedly defective, chain suspension bridge had collapsed beneath the measured tread of an army platoon, thus leading to the 'break step' rule. What would have been the effect, I wondered, if this huge crowd had all been walking in step?

It was not very long after this that I was in Newcastle having a brief introductory talk to the secretary of the joint committee, consisting of representatives of the counties of Northumberland and Durham, which was responsible for the administration of the new Tyne Tunnel works. He was telling me of the arrangements that were being made for the opening by the Queen, whereupon, remembering the Severn Bridge affair, I remarked that at least on this occasion she would not have to perform twice over. 'Don't you believe it!', he retorted, and in the event she had to do just that in order to satisfy both Durham and Northumberland. I had not reckoned upon the strength of county loyalties, particularly in the north of England.

Of these three great civil engineering projects, the latest was the driving of the first of two new twin tunnels under the Mersey. In the novel methods used and in the unexpected and daunting difficulties encountered and triumphantly overcome, it was this work which, in my opinion, could most worthily be compared with those of the heroic age of engineering when any major project was a venture into the unknown.

A pilot tunnel, which was first driven by conventional means beneath the Mersey, revealed the fact that, apart from a short section of boulder clay at the Liverpool end, the entire tunnel would be cut through soft red Bunter sandstone. Bearing this in mind, when the contract was put out to tender, the consulting engineers, Messrs Mott, Hay & Anderson, specified that the tunnel should be driven by mechanical means. No subaqueous tunnel on such a scale (7,000 ft long, 33 ft 2 in unlined diameter) had ever been driven by mechanical means before. The contract was won by a British firm of contractors who specialized in tunnel work and who, in order to carry out this job, had formed a partnership with an American firm who owned the world's largest tunnel boring machine. This had previously successfully driven five tunnels, each 1,500 ft long, in connection with the huge Mangla Dam project in Pakistan, and for this reason it became known as the Mangla Mole. It weighed 350 tons, was 45 foot long and, under favourable conditions, it was capable of cutting at the rate of four feet per hour. It presented to the rock face a cutting head resembling a giant lathe face plate on which were mounted radially a series of conical steel cutters. This face plate was originally solid, but one of the modifications carried out after it had been shipped to England was the insertion of a central hole through which it was possible to crawl into the pilot tunnel ahead. By this means the machine could be kept on its true course by directing a laser beam from the pilot tunnel through this central hole. In the case of the Mangla tunnels there had been no pilot bore so there was no necessity for such a provision. Hydraulic rams were capable of exerting a thrust of 500 tons on the cutting head which was rotated by ten electric motors of 100 horsepower each. Besides the propelling rams, the rear part of the machine included hydraulic arms for placing the tunnel lining segments in position and the endless bucket conveyor used to remove spoil from the working face directly to waiting trucks behind the machine.

From this brief description it may be judged how exciting it was when, clad in unfamiliar protective clothing and feeling rather like Charlie Chaplin trapped amid the cog wheels in *Modern Times*, I threaded my way through the intricacies of this huge machine and finally crawled through the hole in the cutting head to find myself in the dripping cavern of the pilot tunnel beneath the Mersey. I have never encountered working conditions so unpleasant or so potentially dangerous; it was very wet, very muddy, claustrophobic and dark despite the bright electric lights, and one seemed to be menaced on every side by angular and potentially lethal pieces of machinery.

Whereas the Mangla tunnels had been dry, the Bunter sandstone under the Mersey was fissured and faulty, admitting water in considerable quantity and it was this fact which nearly spelled disaster. Despite all efforts to prevent it, so long as it was working the Mole was constantly drenched with an abrasive slurry of water and sand. This proved to be too much for the protective seals to exclude and the giant machine had reached the midpoint of its drive under the river when the bearing behind the cutting head failed. This was a massive roller thrust bearing, 15 ft in diameter and weighing six tons. The pessimists, who were in the majority, shook their heads sadly. The breakdown had occurred at the end of a 2,500 ft tunnel no larger than the machine itself. Of the two alternatives, to replace the bearing on the spot or to dismantle the machine completely and withdraw it piecemeal by the way it had come, both seemed at first thought Herculean and almost impossible. Nevertheless, the brave decision was made to attempt to replace the bearing despite the fact that it was a shrink fit on its shaft having a negative tolerance of five thousandths of an inch. Naturally this demanded fitting conditions of almost clinical cleanliness and accuracy.

A cavern was first excavated round the Mole and a protective roof of corrugated iron and polythene sheeting attached to a series of steel arch ribs to protect the machine from water and grit. When this roof was completed there was six feet clearance over the top of the Mole. It was vital to the success of the whole operation that the cutting head should be held in an absolutely vertical position before its support was retracted. To this end it was welded to two steel beams securely concreted into the rock. A spare bearing had accompanied the Mole from Pakistan, but when it was unwrapped it was found that a number of rollers were badly corroded due to the failure of the protective grease and no less than forty new rollers had to be made to replace them. The six-ton bearing was then manoeuvred horizontally over the top of the Mole and finally lowered to the necessary vertical position by means of chain hoists moving on steel runway beams welded to the centre of the arch ribs. In this fashion was the bearing successfully fitted and the Mole duly completed its drive beneath the Mersey. This breakdown occurred on 20 February 1970 and yet the Mole was able to complete its drive on the 4 March following. This was a feat worthy to be compared with Sir Marc Brunel's struggles against adversity in his Thames Tunnel and that old engineer would surely have admired the energy and resources with which the emergency was met.

As a result of my writing for industry I sometimes found myself in somewhat unusual situations. For instance, when I was writing a history for a well known London-based firm of civil engineering contractors, they were insistent that I should interview their erstwhile chief civil engineer who had recently retired and bought a farm near Perth. So I travelled by night sleeper from Euston, taking a taxi from Perth station to the farm which lay on the fertile levels of Strath Earne against a magnificent backdrop of mountains. It was a brilliantly sunny morning in the early autumn with an invigorating nip in the air and those outlying peaks of the Highlands, Ben Chonzia and Ben Vorlich showed up blue and majestic in the distance. I had never seen a 'strong' Scottish farm before and admired its great ranges of substantial stone-built covered yards and buildings, the latter including a circular one which had originally housed a horse-engine for driving the barn machinery.

Although I was hospitably received, the engineer was obviously too pre-occupied with farming matters to discuss his past career. When an agitated stockman arrived to inform him that one of his pedigree Aberdeen Angus cows was just about to calve, he hurried out of the house, saying to me over his shoulder 'Come on, you may be able to help.' Before I knew where I was I found myself hauling with all my might on a rope attached to the emergent legs of a half-born calf while the engineer and the stockman assisted the cow more directly. I had never taken part in such an exercise before and it all seemed so brutal that I felt certain the little creature would be born dead. Yet having eventually fallen onto the deep layer of straw in the byre, it was staggering onto its spindly legs in a surprisingly short space of time and the engineer, now in high good humour, was leading me back to the house where he soon became expansively reminiscent.

Among other things he described to me how he had dismantled the old Chelsea suspension bridge prior to erecting the present one which was completed in 1937. Having removed the deck of the bridge piecemeal, the problem was how to dismantle the massive suspension chains with the minimum disruption to river traffic. To do this he slung cables across the river beneath the chains and on these placed a timber staging. He then tautened these cables until the staging had taken the weight of the chains so that their link pins could readily be removed. He was obviously pleased with his ingenuity and was a little dashed when I told him that more than a century ago Thomas Telford had used precisely the same procedure, but in reverse, in order to assemble the chains of his Conway suspension bridge. This was yet another example of the failure of engineers to profit from their own history.

When I wrote at the beginning of this chapter that writing for industry had led me into some embarrassing situations, it was not of delivering calves that I was thinking. Such embarrassments were invariably caused by conflicts between the need to meet the wishes of my client and my own conscience as a writer and historian. It is significant that in the case of the smaller companies such a conflict never arose. They would be well satisfied by an honest history of their company, warts and all, whereas the executives of a large group of companies would commission me to write a history whereas what, in fact, they wanted was an unreal exercise in public relations in which nothing to the company's discredit had ever occurred. A commercial enterprise, like the individuals of which it is composed, has its ups and downs, its faults and its failures as well as its successes, and any history that pretends otherwise not only must ring false but also makes very dull reading. It is the equivalent of the worst kind of Victorian biography in which the subject is portrayed as an inhuman paragon of all the virtues. The directors of one large group even went to the length of asking me to suppress my account of a disastrous factory explosion even though it had occurred during the Great War, long before the company concerned had become a memeber of the group. In this particular case I had been commissioned to write a text of about 60,000 words which was none too long in view of the size of the company, controlling as it did many plants both in this country and overseas. Yet when presented with the result after a year's hard work, the Board could not agree to its publication and suggested it should be cut to 10,000 words. It was at this point that I withdrew, suggesting that such a short text would be better done by their own Public Relations Department. Exactly the same thing had happened earlier in the case of another large, nationally known company; the Board could not agree to publication so my typescript lies gathering dust on some forgotten shelf.

In both these cases my handsome fee was paid in full, yet an author naturally feels that he has wasted precious time if the result of his labours never sees the light. The root of the trouble with such large companies is that the unfortunate author they commission suffers acutely from too many cooks. Copies of his typescript are circulated, sometimes to every member of the Board and sometimes to every managing director of however many subsidiary companies there may be. Each of these individuals feels compelled to justify his existence by making some criticisms and, as these often contradict each other, the wretched author becomes distracted to the point of despair.

Nevertheless, I have found writing for industry an interesting and worthwhile exercise, and I do not mean this solely in the monetary sense. By providing me with valuable knowledge of what was going on in the engineering world of today, such experience has helped me to see the engineering past in more correct perspective than would be the case if I were to become wholly pre-occupied with that past. Moreover, like my wartime job with the Ministry of Supply, it gave me a first-hand knowledge of industrial conditions while remaining myself independent and detached. I became aware, for example, of the folly of the modern fallacy that the bigger the business the more efficient it becomes. This is the outcome of the 'economy of scale' argument advanced by economist and accountant. They may be able to prove that it is much cheaper to produce 5,000 tonkle valves a week than 500, but what their figures can never show is the catastrophic result in human terms, the wastage of creative talent either in repetitive or unproductive administrative tasks, the lack of a sense of responsibility due to the breakdown of communications between employer and employee. No 'Personnel Department' however efficient can ever compensate for the latter failure. Above all, comparing this experience with my earlier one, I was dismayed to find to what an extent the accountant had usurped the place of the engineer in the conduct of large industries. When interviewing such new men of power in the Boardroom, I must confess I found them uniformly cold, unsympathetic and often more than a little sinister.

7

The Fight for Stanley Pontlarge

When I lived afloat I was always fearful that my boat might suddenly spring a leak and sink under me. There was a terrible occasion one winter while we were moored at Banbury when I stepped out of bed on a dark morning into water. I thought the end had come but it turned out that I had neglected to shut the sea-cock and that frost had split the pipe connecting this cock to the circulating pump. Shivering in pyjamas and dressing gown, I manned the bilge pump and soon disposed of the water which fortunately had not risen high enough to cover the carpet in our sitting cabin.

Again, because *Cressy* was old I was kept constantly at work with paint and putty or tar to prevent rainwater invading our cabins from sides or roof. For these reasons I have to admit that there were times when I found myself secretly envying the householder, protected by more durable materials than wood and surely based on firm ground. When we moved into Stanley Pontlarge, however, I very soon learned that a house can be as big a source of anxiety as a boat, particularly if it is an ancient one in a state of disrepair.

The antique plumbing gave cause for anxiety. One Saturday morning the galvanized steel cold water storage tank in a cupboard in the bathroom began to drip ominously from the bottom, from which it was evident that it must be paper thin. The old builder who had worked for my parents had retired, so we had to telephone for a strange builder from

Winchcombe. He arrived, accompanied by his plumber and, on being shown the drip, before anyone could stop him he had pushed his first finger straight through the bottom of the tank. 'You shouldn't 'a done that' remarked his plumber reproachfully as torrents of water gushed everywhere. 'Well, what do we do now?' I asked, exasperated. The precious pair shook their heads sadly, saying in unison 'Sat'day arternoon; can't do nothin' till Monday mornin'.' I was left to make a temporary repair by sticking a large patch cut from an old inner tube on the inside of the tank bottom. This lasted until a more efficient plumber installed a new tank on the following Monday.

But our chief worry was whether we should continue to have a roof over our heads. I should not like to guess how long it had been since any substantial repair work had been carried out on the roof. Many of the old cleft laths had broken, the inside plastering had fallen away and, as I mentioned earlier, most of the oak pegs by which the stone tiles were hung upon the laths had fallen out. The roof over the later, eighteenth-century, wing of the house was of 45° pitch and not ceiled on the inside in any way with the result that snow blew under the slates in quantity every winter. Many years before, my parents had appealed to their old builder to do something about this, whereupon he had 'torched' the slates upon the outside, a cheap and simple, but unsightly and injudicious remedy. In any case, much of this torching had since cracked and fallen away with the result that the snow trouble was now almost as bad as before. The older, medieval wing had a much more steeply pitched roof and we would sometimes be alarmed to hear a sound like a miniature landslip as one, or sometimes a whole patch, of stone slates slipped off the roof to crash either onto the garden side of the house or, more seriously, into the lane which ran close beside the back of the house. If anyone happened to be passing at the time we should have been liable for a serious claim for damages, but most fortunately this never happened.

After a particularly bad fall on the older part of the roof I summoned a Winchcombe builder to repair it. Obviously there could be no way of making a sound and permanent repair. All he could do was to push the peg-less slates back as best he could and apply some mortar to hold them there. When he had done this he came down his ladders white and shaking saying he had never seen a roof in such bad condition and that it was only by the mercy of providence that he had not brought half the roof down with him. It was obvious that something would have to be done so I asked whether the slates could be re-hung. The builder shook his head and assured me that the existing slates were all too rotten to be re-used and that to remake the roof with new stone slates would be prohibitively expensive if not impossible. He strongly advised me to re-roof with concrete tiles. Poor though I was, I refused to contemplate such a course which seemed to me as serious a crime as to chromium plate the nickel radiator on a vintage car.

It was Sam Clutton who pointed the way out of this dilemma when he advised me to seek the aid of the Society for the Protection of Ancient Buildings whose response was to send down one of their consultant architects. The choice of architect could not have been more appropriate for he arrived in a modern 3-litre Alvis and was, it transpired, a lifelong Alvis enthusiast, so this common interest put us on the best of terms immediately. On seeing the timbering of the roof he expressed the greatest surprise and appreciation, attributing it to the fourteenth century if not earlier. When asked on what grounds he dated it so early, he pointed to the massive size of the ridge piece or 'roof tree', explaining that it was only the earlier medieval builders who had yet to learn the fact that such stout ridge pieces were not necessary as they carried no more load than the weight of the ridge tiles. He would, he said, make the strongest recommendation to the society that they should endorse an application from me for a grant from the Historic Buildings Council.

The next development was that I received a most un-bureaucratic letter from an inspector in what was then the Ancient Monuments Department of the Ministry of Works.

He proposed a visit, explained that it was his job to evaluate the historic and architectural merit of a building and that he proposed to bring with him a colleague who would estimate the amount of work involved and its cost. He finished his letter by saying he was a fellow member of the VSCC and that he had long hoped for an opportunity of meeting me. On the occasion of his visit we spent a great deal of time closeted in my study discussing the merits and demerits of different makes of steam car while his colleague stumped up and down impatiently in the corridor outside. In fairness I should add that he did look at our roof and was as impressed as the SPAB architect had been, with the result that we were duly awarded a grant. This was an immense stroke of good fortune, for although I was just able to afford my share of the cost, I certainly could not have afforded the whole sum but would have been forced to adopt some cheap and unsightly expedient if the house were not to become uninhabitable.

On the recommendation of the SPAB architect, two brothers from Tyrley, a small village near Haw Bridge on the Severn, were contracted to do the work. They had lately re-slated the roof of the Ashleworth Tithe Barn for the National Trust and ours was a small job by comparison. When I told them what the Winchcombe builder had said on the subject of the slates being rotten and unusable, they smiled and explained that had I accepted his offer to re-roof with concrete tiles he would undoubtedly have removed the originals 'to get them out of the way' and then sold them for a high price. By trimming some of them down to a smaller size if necessary, they estimated that they would be able to re-lay at least 90 per cent of the original slates, a forecast which proved suprisingly accurate. They were superlative craftsmen, so neat, precise and orderly that it was a delight to watch them at work. As most people are aware, in traditional Cotswold roofing the slate courses diminish in size from eaves to ridge, a fact which contributes greatly to the beauty of the finished roof. Our builders had a name for each size of slate and when, in 1957, they had reached the ridge on the second side and they had laid the last and smallest course (known as the 'Farewells' because they represented the end of the job) we broached a bottle of wine with them in celebration.

I had feared that when the roof was stripped it would be seen that some of the medieval timbering needed replacement, but in the event it was only necessary to renew one rafter. The builders did find, however, that the timber supporting the single dormer window in the roof, which was inserted in the seventeenth century, was rotten. But instead of pulling long faces as do most of their kind on making such an unexpected discovery, these craftsmen took it in their stride and in no time at all, it seemed, they had supported the weight of the dormer on jacks and packing and replaced the timber.

Over the next ten years the roof of the eighteenth-century wing deteriorated far faster than we had anticipated. Finally, it became the object of a second Historic Buildings Council grant and was reconstructed by the same builders. Because of that injudicious external torching, I had feared that a much higher porportion of slates would have to be replaced than had been the case on the older roof. However, in the event, the mortar flaked away from the slates very readily so that the proportion re-used was as high as before.

With a sound roof over our heads which will probably last for another two generations, we have been able to carry through, as our means have allowed, a long overdue programme of internal improvement, restoration and redecoration which the old house richly deserved. When I remember the words of H.J. Massingham's injunction to me on the subject so many years ago, at least I now feel I have honoured them to the full.

In return for the public money which had been expended on the house, we are under obligation to admit interested visitors by prior appointment during the summer months and are somewhat embarrassed when they naturally ask us what is the history of the medieval portion. The answer is that nobody knows for certain so that we can only conjecture. It is very unusual to find so early and so small a house built in what, in those days, must have been the grand manner. The interior is surprisingly spacious and the ceiling heights generous. Unlike the eighteenth-century wing which is built of rubble stone, the walls are of dressed stone laid in courses, albeit rather irregular ones. Sometimes a large squared block of stone may appear which extends over the height of two, or even three, courses. Again much of this stone is of a most attractive and unusual colour for this district, so that we speculate whether it may not have come from Caen in Normandy to be shipped up the Severn as was the stone of which Tewkesbury Abbey was built.

The manor belonged successively to the Abbeys of Winchcombe and Hayles, and my father always maintained that it had been built by one or other of these monasteries to house the priest who served the small Norman chapel of ease nearby. Built into the fabric of the free-standing chimney at the south end of the house is a small, carved niche, which obviously once contained an image, also a stone with a mass dial inscribed upon it. My father used to point to these as proof positive of his theory, whereas they are nothing of the kind. This area is littered with carved fragments dated from the time when Winchcombe Abbey was dissolved and its fabric became a convenient quarry.

We have come to the conclusion that a much more plausible theory is that it was originally a Court House where the manorial courts were held. The words 'Court House' certainly appear here on the earliest maps of the district, while one old document refers to 'that Stanley where the Court House is'. Since Sonia and I have lived here we have discovered traces of a blocked up arched entrance at first-floor level in the north gable end which had been rendered invisible externally by the building of the eighteenth-century cottage against it. The timberwork of the ceilings on the first floor are clearly of seventeenth-century date and the single west-facing dormer in the roof was added at the same time to afford extra light. Our theory is, therefore, that there was originally one large hall, open to the splendid roof, on the first floor reached by a tallet or outside stair, probably of stone, at the north end. Here, presumably, the manorial courts were held. On the ground floor there was originally one large room of the same floor area as the hall above and with a great open fireplace in the south gable. This is now divided into hall and drawing room by a partition wall of brick, presumably built at the time the building was converted into a cottage and an interior staircase put in, perhaps in the 1780s when we think the second cottage was built. Originally, however, we believe it was used as a single living room by whoever was responsible for looking after the Court House.

This manor was originally awarded by William the Conqueror to one of his henchmen Robert de Pont l'Arch, hence the curious name. Pont l'Arch is a town on the Seine near Rouen and boasts a railway station so called. Curiously enough, I was shown a photograh of a stone-built farmhouse in Normandy with a stone outside stairway which bears an almost uncanny resemblance to this house. The only major difference is that the roof is of thatch, but judging by the unusual height of the gable-end capstones above the line of the present stone slate roof, I speculate whether, when first built, our roof may not have also been thatched.

As a family we are devoted to this ancient house. But for its unique quality and its associations with my boyhood I would have found abandoning *Cressy* and going 'on the bank' very much harder than I did. But I confess that there have been many times when I have wished that, like *Cressy*, I could move it away to some more congenial surroundings. For the changes that have taken place in the surrounding countryside since the Rolt family moved into this house have been greater than any its windows have seen over the past five centuries with the possible sole exception of those brought about by the enclosure movement. And most of them have not been for the better where the vigour of English rural life and the beauty of the landscape is concerned. I do not pretend that they are unique, however. Unfortunately they are only a typical example of the revolution that has taken place in the English countryside as a whole, with the exception of a few of the more remote and favoured areas where the same process of change has not yet become noticeable.

In the first volume of this autobiography I gave some description of this part of Gloucestershire as it was when my parents first moved into this house and their friends and relatives thought them crazy to bury themselves in such remote country. No one could describe it as remote today, even though we do, at least, have the good fortune to live up a dead-end road and so are spared the ceaseless, distracting noise of passing motor traffic. But the road to Cheltenham with which our lane connects is no longer a narrow and dusty one but a widened tarmac highway carrying buses and an ever increasing volume of motor cars, most of them commuters.

It was during the last war that this drastic process of change really began. There were two principal factors involved. First, there was the growth of the aircraft industry in the vicinity of Gloucester, Cheltenham and Tewkesbury. The grid system made this possible and the fact that Gloucestershire was considered a safe area where bombing was concerned made it desirable. Secondly, the need to produce more food from our own land without increasing manpower began that process of mechanizing agriculture which has now effectually depopulated the fields.

There is in the Cheltenham Art Gallery a rare picture, said to have been painted in the early eighteenth century, which shows the villagers at work in their common fields lying between our Cotswold slopes and Bredon Hill. This shows that in those pre-enclosure days they were, as Langland would have said, 'fair fields full of folk'. There is even a company of morris dancers performing in the foreground. The fact that they are still known as Gretton Fields and Alderton Fields presumably commemorates the days when they were owned in common by these villages, but mechanization has completed the process which enclosure began and the fields are now emptied of life. They reflect this in their unkempt hedgerows and generally neglected appearance, such as the empty plastic fertilizer bags which litter the choked ditches. For unlike the equipment of the industrial machine shop, agricultural machines, although they may be faster and more economical, seldom do the job better than the older method they have superceded, in this case the man and the horse. For example, one man with a tractor equipped with an efficient modern hydraulically-controlled hedge-cutting machine can, in a few hours 'brush' a length of hedgerow that would take the same man as many days to trim by hand, but no machine has yet been devised which can lay a hedge and as this manual skill is rapidly dying out, hedges soon thin out and begin to look 'woody' and unsightly. Also, whereas the man could recognize and spare young saplings such as elm or holly, the machine cannot, so we can look forward to a day when there will be no more hedgerow timber and may realize when it is too late what a contribution this made to the beauty of the English landscape.

Despite the effects of enclosure, fifty years ago the population of the neighbouring villages was all directly employed in agriculture or else in some ancillary trade or craft which either served the local people, like the cobbler or the thatcher, or the local farming community, like the blacksmith, the wheelwright or the saddler. This common interest gave the village an organic link with the countryside around it besides welding it into a community. Now, in this area at least, this common interest has gone and our neighbouring villages, Bishops Cleeve, Gotherington, Gretton, Alderton, bloated with new building, have no links with the countryside and, because they have become mere dormitories for commuters, little communal life and only a nominal identity.

Because of mis-application of the well-intentioned Slum Clearance Act by a zealous Medical Officer of Health, most of the old village cottages I knew were condemned on grounds of their low ceilings, or lack of through ventilation. Even with the aid of the available local authority grants, their occupants could not afford alterations which would conform with local regulations. Consequently, such houses have been acquired by those who could afford reconstruction, executives or retired business men, with the result that they have been 'prettified' beyond recognition and embellished with such things as bogus wrought iron work of welded steel strip, carriage lanterns or wooden wheelbarrows filled with flowers. Meanwhile such old village families as have survived this upheaval live in council houses on the village outskirts from whence they are collected and delivered daily by special coaches which take them to work in the nearby factories.

By that process known as 'judicious infilling' whereby every available orchard or paddock in or around the village has been built upon, these raddled relics of the old villages I used to know are now surrounded upon every side by new houses. In the mistaken belief that they will thereby conform to the traiditonal style, most of these buildings are built in what I call pre-digested stone (blocks made from cement with an aggregate of pulverized Cotswold stone) or from sawn blocks of the genuine article. Apart from the fact that the former never appears to weather but retains indefinitely its raw yellow colour, the effect of both is equally unpleasing, especially when it is associated, as it usually is, with modern standard steel-framed windows and concrete roofing tiles. Although the blocks are produced in different lengths so that the coursing may be varied, a variation so produced naturally looks too regular and contrived while the surface texture is unpleasantly smooth. Presumably in an unsuccessful attempt to obviate this visual defect, some of these new houses are built from blocks whose external faces are rusticated so that their joints are slightly recessed. If anything the effect produced is even less pleasant than that of smooth blocks, especially as these roughened blocks are usually laid in cement mortar of a darker colour. The beautiful old Cotswold town of Winchcombe is now beset on three sides by a great area of new housing estates and, because site values and buildng costs have soared, in the more recently built houses all attempt at aping the regional vernacular has been abandoned. After so much ghastly good taste it is almost a relief to see such unashamed jerry building.

When a village has been 'infilled' in this way, it is the turn of the local council to step in by installing concrete lamp posts, side-walks with tarmac surfaces and high concrete kerbs, and conventional road name-boards for what were once quiet country lanes. Thus the whole village loses its rural identity to become a detached satellite suburb.

Except at weekends, these erstwhile villages and newly built suburbs are never fully populated. Weekends appear to be devoted to gardening, the ritual washing of cars or to watching the telly and the only vestige of communal life the customary foregathering in the village pub on Saturday nights or, more particularly, on Sunday noons.

I have described in *Landscape with Machines* how, as a boy, it was my delight in summer to ensconce myself in a seat I had made in one of the apple trees in our orchard and to watch the trains go by on the Cheltenham–Honeybourne line of the GWR which passes our house. The story of the decline and fall of this railway since nationalization reads like a tale told by an idiot although, I suppose, it could be paralleled in many parts of the country. In addition to expresses between Birmingham and the West Country or South Wales there was a regular local service of 'push-and-pull' trains which served all stations and halts between Cheltenham and Honeybourne. These trains were well patronized, particularly by housewives and school children, because they not only offered a quick service to Cheltenham but also to Gloucester by means of convenient connections at Cheltenham Malvern Road. To my certain knowledge many children used to travel daily to school in Gloucester from Gretton Halt and many adults from the village used to visit Gloucester market every week by this means. One could even travel to Paddington from Gretton Halt without too much inconvenience. I remember doing this on several occasions during our earliest years as a family at Stanley Pontlarge when, for one reason or another, it was inconvenient to take a car for the day, either to London or to be parked at a main line station. One left Gretton at 8 a.m., changing to a through train at Evesham and, in the reverse direction, off an evening express at Moreton-in-Marsh. But all this came to an abrupt end when in 1955 or '56, the Western Region decided to put in hand major civil engineering works.

When the line was built between 1900 and 1906 the contractors, Messrs Walter Scott & Middleton, made two fatal mistakes; they failed to ensure effective drainage of the cuttings and they did not remove from them at formation level the sticky clay which is found all along the base of the north Cotswold escarpment which the railway follows. Water-logged clay makes a chronically unstable base for permanent way and despite constant re-ballasting and tamping there had been endless trouble with sleepers 'pumping' or working, a slurry of clay and water spurting up as a train passed over them. It was also as a result of this treacherous clay that there had been much trouble with cutting slopes slipping. Now at last the Western Region decided to take the bull by the horns and put an end to these troubles by laying improved drains, by building retaining walls where necessary, and by the costly process known as 'track blanketing' which consists of removing the offending clay and replacing it by more suitable material. As a result of all this work, as Mark Smith, the then chief civil engineer, admitted to me, more money per mile was spent on the Cheltenham–Honeybourne line than on any other section of the Western Region over the period that had elapsed since the last war.

But – and it is a very large but   whereas if the GWR had tackled such an operation they would undoubtedly have planned it in such a way that single line working was maintained, the engineers of the Western Region had total occupation of the line for months. Meanwhile, through goods and passenger traffic was diverted over the old Midland route between Cheltenham and Birmingham, while our local train service was simply suspended until further notice. Now, if you suddenly decide to shut up your shop for six months or so, when you do decide to unlock the door again you cannot expect to see your faithful customers standing in a queue outside. Yet it was precisely this that the Western Region did appear to expect and were surprised to find that they had lost the local traffic to double-decker buses plying on an unclassified and totally inadequate road and taking nearly twice as long over the journey to Cheltenham.

While the civil engineering works were in progress, the 'push-and-pull' trains, which had worked the local service for years, were scrapped. They had been popular with the locals and, because of their ability to run in either direction at will, they were peculiarly suited to this particular service which entailed a reversal at Cheltenham Malvern Road so that trains could start and terminate at Cheltenham St James. When services were at last resumed, the unit used consisted of two standard GWR non-corridor thirds hauled by a 2-6-2 tank locomotive.

With this combination of a more expensive vehicle and fewer passengers the next move became inevitable – an application to withdraw local services and close all intermediate stations. This became the subject of a Transport Users Consultative Committee inquiry which I attended. From the outset it was clear that the result was a foregone conclusion. We were kept waiting in a cold and dreary room near Gloucester station until long after the inquiry was due before the members of the committee and the local officials of the Western Region came in together, laughing and joking among themselves. It struck me then that we were wasting our time; that while we had been sitting shivering, they had been settling the whole matter on an 'old boy' basis next door. To our questions they returned, with completely straight faces, replies so asinine in their illogicality that they insulted our intelligence. For instance, when asked why they did not replace the costly steam train with a small diesel rail-car such as they were running at that time on the Tetbury branch, we received the *Alice-in-Wonderland* reply that such a car would be insufficient to carry the traffic at present offering at peak periods. So we lost our local train service and all the stations and halts were demolished with almost indecent haste. Through passenger traffic lasted longer and my two sons were

born just soon enough to see and to appreciate as I had done
the sight of a steam-hauled Penzance express ('The Cornish-
man') thundering past our orchard. It was hauled by a *Castle*
class locomotive now instead of the four-coupled *County* class
engines of my own youth. But this proved to be only a brief
interregnum before all passenger trains were switched to the
Midland route and this late-built and most costly of railways
was relegated to 'freight only' status. At the time of writing the
big diesel locomotives still go grumbling by, though they have
become invisible such is the wilderness of bramble bushes and
sapling trees that has grown up on the railway banks which the
local gang once scythed and made into hay each year. These
diesels draw their trains of antique freight vehicles at far too
fast a rate, and as there is only one surviving signal box in the
twenty miles between Honeybourne and Cheltenham, there
are no eagle-eyed signalmen to give early warning of a hot box.
Consequently this malady is chronic and we recently had one
of such magnitude that not only did the axle box disintegrate
entirely, but the spring then cut through the axle causing
major derailment and much damage to the track. The damage
was eventually made good, but there are regular rumours of
closure.

Meanwhile, so many of the villagers, now even the council
house dwellers, have motor cars that our local bus service, like
the train service before it, is running at a loss. Many people
blame the private car for the decline in rural public services
whereas the boot is often on the other foot; certainly in this
area. I can think of many local people who would never have
invested in a car, which they could ill afford, had it not been
for the fact that a speedy and efficient train service was cut off
at a single stroke. An aggravating factor here was the closure of
Cheltenham's central railway station. What is now the only
station, Cheltenham Lansdown, is an impossible distance
away from the central local bus station, and as its rail services
to Gloucester are now infrequent, it is virtually useless to the
commuter. Dr Beeching and his ilk have a great deal to answer
for.

So far I have described some of the changes that have taken
place in the country round about. Where Stanley Pontlarge
itself is concerned, the threat so far has not been from new
housing development, but from the new mechanized agriculture and factory farming, the effects of which on the
landscape have been as dire as that of the new housing estates
in pre-digested stone. To some extent, of course, we sacrifice
the landscape to our own comfort and convenience. I am
reminded of this with an acute sense of guilt every time I look
from my windows at the cat's cradle of poles and wires with
which Stanley Pontlarge has been disfigured as the price of
mains electricity and the telephone. But the so-called agricultural disfigurement has been far worse. In the previous
volume of this autobiography, *Landscape with Canals*, I
described how our neighbour Mr Bowl of Manor Farm could
be seen leading his sheep down the lane wearing a smock and
carrying a crook. Alas, under modern conditions traditional
mixed farming, as he used to practice it, has become no longer
economic, particularly on this belt of heavy clay land at the
foot of the north Cotswold escarpment. It was to compensate
for this natural handicap that some of the local farmers,
including, unfortunately, at Stanley Pontlarge, took up
factory farming.

When we first came to this house fifty-two years ago, our
only neighbours, apart from the Bowl family at Manor Farm,
were a Mr and Mrs Johnson who owned a small farm then
known as the Close which was virtually no bigger than a
small-holding. Sadly, the Johnsons lost both their sons in the
Great War as a wall tablet in the little Norman church testifies.
Consequently, there being no one to succeed him, Mr Johnson
sold his farm to a man who, although of local extraction, had
previously run a greengrocer's business in the Birmingham
area and it was he who began factory farming. Our eastern
windows look directly over the lane onto a green meadow
where, in Mr Johnson's day, his Jersey cows had grazed. Now,
under the new regime, there grew up in this once attractive
meadow a hideous conurbation of Nissen huts and other

ex-army portable buildings while what was left of the field gradually became a wilderness of nettles and thistles. For many years these buildings were used as battery chicken houses. During this period Stanley Pontlarge after dark resembled some large factory on night shift, to be seen from afar across the vale, the buildings blazing with light so that the wretched birds, imprisoned in their wire cages, would be persuaded by the illusion of daylight to continue laying throughout the twenty-four hours. When eventually battery chickens ceased to pay, the buildings were converted into intensive pig fattening units. At least this put an end to the lights at night, but the smell and the swarms of flies which we had to suffer each summer were worse than before. Apart from the fact that their muck was periodically spread on the surrounding fields, (a highly malodorous proceeding) neither chickens nor pigs had any organic relationship with the surrounding countryside whatsoever so that their 'concentration camps' might equally well have been situated in a town except that no townsman would tolerate so great a nuisance. Neither were ever allowed to see the light of day and their feeding stuffs were imported in ever larger lorries which came grinding up the hill past our house. The pigs arriving for fattening and those departing for slaughter travelled by the same means in huge cattle transporters.

Most of our visitors would mistake this example of the new farming for a derelict army camp and sympathize with us accordingly. The County Planning Officer, when appealed to on the matter, viewed it from my windows and, having admitted that he had seen nothing worse in the entire county, shook his head quite sadly and said that as they were agricultural buildings he was quite unable to help us. But there was an ironical twist to this as he went on to explain. He did have a measure of control over agricultural buildings erected within a certain distance of a classified road. In other words, if the road past our house had been a major highway howling with traffic we might have been spared this eyesore, but because it was a quiet country lane leading nowhere we had to learn to live with our affliction.

At about the same time we had another example of the curious philosopy that this planning policy reveals. This was a dispute over the route of a new 'super grid' overhead line from Melksham to Hams Hall. The issue was whether, in descending from the Cotswold escarpment into the vale, the line should run on the east or the west side of Langley Hill. While the easterly route would pass near new housing estates on the outskirts of Winchcombe, the westerly course meant that the huge pylons would march through a wild and lovely valley known as Frogalls Bottom, then pass between us and Dixton Hill before striding off across the vale in the direction of Bredon. At the public inquiry at Winchcombe, those of us who opposed the westerly route argued that it was surely better to carry the line through country already encroached on by new housing development than to impose it on a virgin and beautiful countryside. But we lost the day, the argument being that if the pylons took the easterly route, far more people would see them from their windows.

If the planning philosophy exemplified by our 'concentration camp' and by the pylons was to be applied on a nationwide scale it would surely mean that, with the sole exception of our National Parks, the whole of our English landscape would eventually be defaced by a thin coating of undesirable 'things in fields' instead of confining such things, so far as possible, to areas of existing industrial and urban development. Apart from this general consideration, I have always felt strongly that the immediate surroundings of any historic building such as ours on which public money has been spent should be subject to special planning protection. This view, which I have constantly pressed on the SPAB, was not prompted in the first place by the selfish considerations of my own case, but by the sight, many years ago, of a large and unsightly caravan site established cheek by jowl with the ruins of Valle Crucis Abbey in North Wales which the then Ancient Monuments Department of the Ministry of Works had lately restored. This was a flagrant example, but many other ancient buildings still suffer in this way.

Our local factory farmer flourished as the green bay tree and eventually acquired part of the lands and all the farm buildings of the Manor Farm in addition. He then initiated a series of actions which I could not do other than oppose with the consequence that we soon found ourselves in the thick of that most unpleasant of all situations – a bitter feud between neighbours.

When my father had bought his Alvis in 1925, because there was no suitable land near the house,* he asked his neighbour, Farmer Bowl, whether he might put up a wooden garage on a small patch of waste land in front of the Manor Farm buildings. Permission was freely granted and the existence of our garage was accepted by successive tenants and owners until our factory farmer came upon the scene. Then, without a direct word spoken, I received a letter from his solicitor instructing me, either to remove the garage within seven days or pay his client an exorbitant rental. In such circumstances I could not do other than consult my London solicitor, an old friend of my IWA days. On being told how long the garage had stood there, he pointed out that I had established a squatter's right to the garage. In reply to increasingly lengthy and threatening letters from my opponent's solicitor, he would reply very briefly: 'I shall require evidence of title' or, 'I still await evidence of title' until the farmer finally gave up the struggle. Naturally this contest did nothing to improve the atmosphere at Stanley Pontlarge.

Things got to such a pitch that if Sonia and I went away for a holiday we used to dread what fresh horror we might find when we returned. On one such occasion we got back to find the farmer and his son digging a trench in the lane beside our little church so as to lay a high concrete kerb. He had obviously acquired a job lot of these kerbs somewhere. I was

---

* I have since been able to put up an inconspicuous two-car garage on a strip of additional land I have purchased and added to the property.

appalled. Apart from the fact that I loathed the prospect of our lane being given the semblance of a suburban street, I felt he had no right to tamper with a public highway. So I asked him to stop and, on being met with a refusal, rang up the local road surveyor who came over at once and ordered the work to stop. Finally, in consultation with the vicar and the local authority, a compromise was reached whereby a line of inclined and inconspicuous granite setts was laid by the local roadmen to form an edging to the strip of mown grass outside the church.

The effect of these two defeats on our opponent was that his bitterness towards us knew no bounds, so much so that, believe it or not, we thought our house might very probably burn down. Despite the warnings of the local fire prevention officer, on two successive Guy Fawkes' nights he built an enormous bonfire, as high as a two storey house, in his ruined field in a position only a dozen yards away from my house. On the first occasion we had arranged to be away and could only hope that the wind would be in our favour. In fact it was not and my mother was so terrified by the showers of sparks that flew over our roof-top that she sought the aid of our friendly neighbour from the Manor Farm house who very nobly patrolled my property until the fire died down. On the second occasion we were at home and again there was a strong east wind which blew sparks onto and over our roof in such a flowing river and with such violence that there was a very real risk that they would set fire to the roof timbers. In these circumstances I felt I had no option but to call the Winchcombe fire brigade. They arrived very promptly and, while some of the firemen went up into our roof, others quickly and calmly extinguished the bonfire with their hoses, ignoring the fire-crackers and the abuse hurled at them by the fire-raisers who seemed by this time to be almost demented. It was a most unpleasant situation.

One of our neighbour's least endearing characteristics from my point of view was his propensity for cutting down trees. He persuaded British Railways Estate Department to fell a fine row of trees that stood on railway property opposite our orchard on the pretext that they were shadowing his wheat-field. In this case I lost the day. I only knew of his intention when I heard the deadly sound of the chain saws buzzing, though I did my utmost to bring about an eleventh hour reprieve.

If there is anything calculated to raise my blood pressure it is the maiming or hacking down of trees, and here local philistines are not the only culprits. From my study window one day I noticed an officious-looking individual strolling about in the orchard belonging to my neighbour at the Manor Farmhouse. He was also peering in a suspicious manner over the drystone wall that divides the orchard from my garden. Always acutely mistrustful of such official snoopers, it was not many seconds before I was inquiring about his business. It appeared that he was an official of the Midlands Electricity Board and he calmly announced that he was proposing to fell – at the Board's expense, of course – three large old perry pear trees, two in my neighbour's orchard and a third, a particu-larly beautiful tree, that shades the lawn at the end of our garden. He explained that there had been so many cases of accidents caused to people gathering fruit for Showerings of Shepton Mallet through their aluminium ladders making contact with overhead power lines that his Board had ruled that all large fruit trees in the proximity of power lines should be felled. Now although the fruit of these trees is rarely used now, they are objects of delight at all seasons, while in spring, when they are covered with clots of white blossom, they take on a beauty that would have ravished Samuel Palmer. So I informed this official that, while I could not speak for my neighbour, he would cut down my tree only over my dead body, a reply whose vehemence evidently surprised him exceedingly. It was clear that he thought me eccentric to say the least. This particular story has a happy ending, for my neighbour supported me as I thought he would and, at the price of adding an extra pole to our wirescape, the cables in the vicinity were insulated and the trees spared.

I am aware that the foregoing account of what has befallen

this particular part of the Gloucestershire countryside makes sad reading. In this case time has not given but has taken away its rural character. Yet no one who has loved the landscape of England as I have could honestly fail to put on record the sweeping changes that have come about in the last thirty years, particularly as they are but a microcosm of what has occurred, or is in the process of occurring, in England as a whole. I console myself with the fact that I am old enough to remember the older, rural Gloucestershire that has been temporarily submerged. These memories, once given by time, time is powerless to erase. I write 'temporarily submerged' because, unlike the older Gloucestershire, the urban tide that has swept over it represents a society so unstable that it will ebb away as quickly as it came. I give it three generations at the most.

So far as Stanley Pontlarge itself is concerned, this chapter has a happier ending. Our local factory farmer has retired and his land and buildings have been acquired by a more amenable neighbour. Thanks to the munificence of the Landmark Trust*, it seems very likely at the time of writing that our view will soon be greatly improved, that the unsightly huddle of sheds in the fields opposite will disappear so that it will once again become a green pasture and that the present cat's cradle of poles and wires will be banished underground. Even if I should not live to see such a transformation completed, it is good to know that Stanley Pontlarge will once again look much as it did when first I saw it as a boy over fifty years ago.

---

*   See next chapter for a full account of this Trust's activities.

8
Reflections

From Marlborough's eyes the streams of dotage flow,
And Swift expires a driv'ller and a show
Samuel Johnson

If his subject expires at the height of his powers when life is still at full flood it is very much easier for a biographer or autobiographer to shape his book into a satisfactory artistic unity. Would our perennial interest in those romantic figures, Byron and Shelley, be so great had they not both died young and on a foreign shore at Missolonghi and at Spezzia? Despite the unquestionable brilliance of the Brontës, would we find that ill-fated family quite so fascinating had its early-flowering genius lived on into old age? To bring this question within the orbit of my own work, I do not think that my biography of Brunel would have been so successful a piece of literature had it not been rounded off by its subject's dramatic death while still at the height of his powers, coinciding as it did with the first sea trial of his most ambitious but ill-starred achievement, the *Great Eastern*. Conversely, I found my biography of Telford a far more difficult book to bring to a satisfactory conclusion simply because its subject continued to live and to practise into old age. His design for a Clifton suspension bridge, so correctly scorned by the young and up-and-coming Brunel, was surely the equivalent of the work of painter, poet or novelist whose talents fail with advancing years. Whether they are aware of such failure or not, the situation is equally tragic. But this is the common tragedy of the human condition and one that it is not easy for the biographer to turn to dramatic account. Men such as W.B. Yeats, whose poetry continued to change and develop into old age, are the exception rather than the rule.

It is in childhood and youth that an author's readers take delight, not second childhood. As we grow older we naturally tend to become more conservative and less venturesome when it comes to setting our hands to some new work. We tend to talk more and to do less and, for the readers of biography or autobiography, the doing is always more interesting than the talking. It would seem that the older people grow the more the committees they are invited to serve upon. This activity gives them the illusion of 'doing' without the physical effort. Such invitations assume that the recipient is a wise man, but unfortunately your habitual committee man all too often suffers from what I can only describe as a 'corridors of power' complex. He cherishes the belief, that when he comes to the committee room he is influencing the course of history by shaping events and the destinies of men. Yet the committee minutes seldom support such illusions of consequence but make dull reading.

Since 1956 or so I have been, as I still am, a member of many committees, mainly devoted to some aspect or other of what is generally called 'the amenity world', in other words that small minority concerned to fight against the philistines and the destroyers with the object of preserving what is left of the English landscape and those infinitely varied and meaningful man-made things associated with that landscape which represent the English tradition. To say that my part in these activities would make dull reading is not to imply that such bodies do not do a good job. They most certainly do.

Only three of these committees deserve mention here because they are, or were, connected with personal interests of long standing. These are The Inland Waterways Redevelopment Committee, The Council for British Archaeology's Industrial Archaeology Research Committee and, lastly, the Science Museum Advisory Council.

I served on the Inland Waterways Redevelopment Committee from 1959 until 1962. It was appointed by the then

Minister of Transport, Mr Ernest Marples, to advise him what was best to be done about certain derelict, or at least moribund, sections of the canal system. Our periodic tours of inspection, which took us all over the country from Kendal in Westmoreland to Taunton in Somerset, were most enjoyable and instructive. Enjoyable, because my colleagues were all such interesting, intelligent and likeable men, especially our chairman, Admiral Parham, who personified everything I expected a retired Admiral of the Royal Navy to be like. He used to come out with the most delightful nautical phrases. It was interesting because it made me intimately acquainted from the towpath with precisely those waterways which *Cressy* had been unable to visit, and so greatly increased my first-hand knowledge of England's canal system. The so-called redevelopment schemes were mostly concerned with eliminating canals by infilling and the majority were prepared by the Inland Waterways Executive, although two came from local authorities. Those put to us by the former included figures showing profit and loss, the latter always featuring an item headed 'Head Office Expenses, Proportion'. This increased steadily from year to year, indicating to me that, while the waterway system contracted, the administrative machinery responsible for it did not, and I speculated whether our shrunken railway system was burdened in the same way. If it was, then the process of creeping paralysis initiated by Dr Beeching becomes easier to understand.

A proposal to infill the Ashton Canal came from Manchester Corporation and a similar scheme for the Pocklington Canal from the city fathers of Sheffield. Both were remarkable for their ineptitude, a fact I found saddening because, in principle, I am all in favour of the decentralization of government. The city engineer of Manchester described his scheme for the Ashton Canal, which consisted of constructing a series of concrete basins, or 'lagoons' as he called them, to supply the various canal-side mills which depended on the canal for water. These were to be connected to each other by lengths of buried pipeline, but this was where he had failed to do his homework. The canal is (or it was at that date) in the vicinity of an active colliery and we had therefore ascertained beforehand from the NCB the subsidence anticipated in the area over the next twenty years and learned that it was considerable. I forget the actual figures now, but it was something of the order of six feet. When we asked the engineer whether his pipes could withstand that amount of settlement without fracture, the corporation's scheme collapsed like a house of cards.

Sheffield Corporation proposed to use the Pocklington Canal as a convenient dump for semi-liquid slurry from their nearby water-softening plant on the Derwent. The engineer responsible for this scheme explained how he proposed to lay a porous pipe in the bed of the canal before dumping began. This would allow the moisture in the slurry to drain away, leaving a solid residue to be covered with a layer of earth so that the site of the canal could gradually be restored to agriculture. At this point a representative of the local drainage board rose and asked the engineer if he was aware that a substantial portion of the canal was regularly flooded in winter. Once again the engineer was completely confounded and another 'redevelopment' scheme collapsed in ruins.

In these two cases, as in most of those for infilling advanced by the Inland Waterways Executive, we rejected the schemes as either impracticable or too costly, recommending restoration in whole or in part as a cheaper and more desirable alternative on the grounds of multiple use – land drainage, water supply and amenity. We also supported two out of three positive restoration proposals submitted to us by the Stratford Canal Society, the Kennet & Avon Canal Trust and the Derby Canal Society. The lower part of the Stratford Canal was subsequently restored and is now owned by the National Trust.* The Kennet & Avon is a much bigger and tougher proposition. We recommended that restoration work should begin at both ends with the idea that the canal could start earning revenue from pleasure traffic as soon as possible and although this has been adopted there are still some years to go before the two sundered

---

*   [Later returned to British Waterways.]

ends are joined.* Only in the case of the Derby Canal did we come to the regretful conclusion that the canal was too far gone to make restoration a practical proposition.

It was towards the end of this committee's life that a conservative government abolished the British Transport Commission as transport overlord and replaced the old executive by a newly appointed and autonomous British Waterways Board whose members, including as they did Admiral Parham and my old friend Charles Hadfield, pursued a far more positive policy than their predecessors. It was to this new Board that our committee's recommendations were passed and as many of them have since been acted upon, I feel that we really did achieve something worthwhile.

The Council for British Archaeology is a government-assisted body whose object it is to encourage, promote and co-ordinate research and field work into sites of every period from the remotely prehistoric onwards. It is also concerned with the recording of threatened sites and with their preservation where possible. To this end it works closely with government representatives of those departments concerned with the preservation of historic monuments. In December 1959 the CBA organized an Industrial Archaeology Conference at which it was decided to add to its various 'period' committees an Industrial Archaeology Research Committee. To this committee I naturally gravitated, for it was recruited on an *ad hoc* basis from anyone who seemed likely to make a useful contribution. I had been interested in this subject long before it acquired its present cumbersome but aposite title. For although my primary interests had been vintage cars, canals and railways, these had soon widened to include all the visual three-dimensional evidence of the industrial revolution in Britain. If I were asked what single event had been responsible for firing this wider enthusiasm, I think I would say that it was my first visit to the Ironbridge area during the last war.

The present and growing popularity of industrial

* [The canal was re-opened by the Queen in 1989.]

archaeology may be said to stem from the setting up of this committee. One of its first objectives was to persuade the government of the day to finance a national survey of industrial monuments. To this end I spoke about the significance of these monuments to the Conservative Arts & Amenities Committee at the House of Commons in March 1962. Exactly a year later, at the instigation of Pat Lucan, I addressed the Labour Party equivalent to the same tune. It was a consequence of such campaigning that the national survey was authorized with my friend Rex Wailes as survey officer. It was remarkable how, as he travelled the length and breadth of the country carrying out his survey, local societies seemed to spring up in his wake wherever he went so that what had been a minority interest, in the passage of very few years, became a popular nationwide pursuit engaging people from every walk of life. I had only one personal experience of the way in which this movement snowballed when I joined Rex Wailes in addressing a meeting at Stroud where a Gloucestershire Society for Industrial Archaeology was founded there and then.

How to account for this sudden popularity? Many reasons have been given: that because the industrial revolution – surely the most significant revolution in man's history – began in this country, we possess industrial monuments of unique significance. Also, that the process of change and the forces of destruction have gained such momentum that these monuments are very much at risk and that unless forces could be mobilized to defend them, all too frequently it was a case of here today but gone tomorrow. This is all true, but speaking for myself I would say that what has all along attracted me to industrial monuments, be they beam engines or buildings, is their quality. Their social consequences may have been disastrous; they may have been built by grossly underpaid labour, working overlong hours and living under appalling conditions, yet they reveal the most superb and painstaking craftsmanship. Work of such quality is almost poetic in its significance, especially bearing in mind the conditions under which it was done. Such workmanship surely reveals that even the humble artisan shared the conviction that he was helping to build a new and better world. It is bitterly ironical that, in fact, the world they helped to create would have no time for the craftsman and little appreciation for his handiwork. It is a world which, just at this time (1962) wantonly destroyed the Euston Arch. This great arch was the supreme industrial monument because it was a memorial to the craftsmanship and the aspirations of all those thousands who, captained by Robert Stephenson, had laboured to build Britain's first main line. On the part of the philistines who connived at its destruction it was a compulsive, ritual act of repudiation of all those values which the arch stood for. But their vandalism has recoiled on their own heads for, by revealing the magnitude of the threat, the destruction of the Euston Arch has mobilized the opposition forces with the effect that such a thing would not happen today.

Because the steam railway was the one form of transport that we indisputably pioneered in England, I have for a long while been convinced that Britain of all countries ought to possess a National Railway Museum that would worthily represent a national heritage that changed the world. The existing set-up whereby such a museum became the responsibility of our nationalized railway system was entirely due to Lord Hurcomb, the first Chairman of the Transport Commission, who displayed a great respect for the railway past, a quality in which his successors have shown themselves sadly lacking. Because they are so manifestly inferior to their great predecessors who created our railways, is, I believe, the psychological reason for their almost pathological concern to destroy all evidence of that past. In what other way is it possible to account for the needless destruction of the Euston Arch, that supreme symbol of past greatness, and of much else besides? They justify such acts with jargon about the need to create a new and progressive public image. Yet what image, one might ask, has their mean work succeeded in creating? It struck me as sheer folly to entrust to such men the great heritage of the railway past, especially when they declared quite openly that it was their job to run a railway and not to run a museum, a statement in which there is, at least, a certain logic.

After years of indecision and argument over a site for a new railway museum, the BTC finally offered its unfortunate Curator of Relics a disused bus garage at Clapham as a man flings a dog a bone. A less suitable place for a railway museum it would be difficult to conceive. Lacking any form of rail access, it was impossible to move any large object into or out of the museum except at vast expense, with the result that all the steam locomotives and rolling stock became frozen like so many ships in bottles. For the same reason it was impossible to make Clapham a live steam museum despite the fact that some of the locomotive exhibits there were in steamable condition. Nevertheless, the Clapham scheme went ahead but, even when it had been set out as well as it could be, it remained closed to the public for some months because the then chairman, Sir Brian Robertson, sensible of British Railways' heavy deficit, felt that the public might see the new museum as a piece of needless extravagance.

These briefly were the reasons why I decided to make the creation of a National Railway Museum the object of my latest, and probably my last, campaign. The opportunity to fire an opening shot occurred in 1960 when I read the Conservative government's Bill abolishing the British Transport Commission and setting up autonomous Boards in its place. Now the Relics and Records Departments had hitherto been administered directly by the BTC, as was only natural since they were originally intended to cover all forms of transport. Yet there was no mention of them in the new Bill, nor any clue as to who would be responsible for them in the future. It was obvious to me that the drafters had been unaware of their existence. On consulting an MP friend of mine as to what would be the best course to take, he explained that such questions, as to who should be responsible for what, were usually decided by the Prime Minister personally and he went on to suggest that if I would draft a suitable letter, he would send it over with his signature to Mr Harold Macmillan. This I duly did, pointing out the omission and suggesting that the opportunity should be taken to transfer the relics to the then Ministry of Education, now the Department of Education and Science (DES). It was evident from his reply that the PM did not accept this proposition though he promised action of some unspecified kind. In the event this took a most unsatisfactory form. He made the new Railways Board temporarily responsible for the relics and charged them to prepare a scheme for their long term future and submit it for approval to the Ministry of Transport by a specified date. Many people besides myself felt that this was a wrong decision and that such a scheme should have been directed to the Ministry of Education and not to the Transport Ministry which was not in the least interested in the future of museum collections.

This was the state of play when, by the greatest piece of good fortune, I was invited to join the Science Museum Advisory Council which gave me a unique opportunity to press my view of a National Railway Museum as an 'out station' of the Science Museum. At the same time I was able to lobby sympathetic MPs on the Conservative Arts and Amenities Committee whom I had met earlier in connection with the Industrial Monuments Survey. The latter effort culminated when a party of MPs were taken by bus from the House to Clapham to view the collection. As a result of this visit, they said they were prepared to back such a scheme provided it could be shown that it was workable. The then Director of the Science Museum, Sir David Follett, also favoured the scheme and was able to begin exploratory talks with Mr John Scholes who was responsible for the Clapham Museum. All this activity was just as well because the so-called 'scheme' submitted to the Ministry of Transport proved to be little more than an application for a mandate to disperse the Clapham Collection. Of the other two collections for which the Railways Board was temporarily responsible, the new Great Western Museum at Swindon and the original Railways Museum at York, responsibility for the former passed to Swindon Corporation, but the future of the latter remained doubtful.

Negotiations were still going on when a general election took place and a Labour Government took office. To my great satisfaction, however, the Transport Bill introduced by this new government contained clauses authorizing the transfer of the Clapham and York collections to the Science Museum and their removal to a new museum building sited in York. With the choice of York as a site for the new National Railway Museum I had nothing to do except to endorse it as a member of the Advisory council. It was a part of the bargain between the government and British Railways that, in return for being relieved of their responsibility for the collection, they should provide a new museum building on a suitable site, financing the operation by the sale of the Clapham property. A reconstruction of the existing steam motive power depot at York was proposed by British Railways and approved by the Science Museum. Personally I had no strong feelings as to where the new museum should be. A much more important thing to my mind was that the building should be suited to the display of large locomotives and that it should have good access to some railway that was most unlikely to be closed, thus enabling the exhibits to be moved around or got out of the museum and put into steam. None of the three existing museums possessed these essential attributes whereas the new museum building at York, with its two turntables and radiating tracks, certainly did. What was equally important was that it offered the possibility of future expansion which the old sites did not. Unless a museum has room to expand its collection, eventually it becomes fossilized and dead.

So far all appeared to be going well, but the powers that be were soon to learn what I had already learned by bitter experience – that whatever you may do you cannot please the railway enthusiasts. They contain more wrong-headed cranks per thousand than any other body of men I have ever encountered. As soon as the York proposal became known a babel of confused protest broke out from their ranks. Some, for reasons best known to themselves, began a 'save Clapham' campaign; others argued that the new museum should not be confined to railways but should represent all forms of transport. Apart from the fact that such a museum, if truly representative, would have to be of huge and bewildering size, it ignored the fact that other forms of transport were already adequately catered for by existing specialist museums at Stoke Bruerne (canals), Beaulieu (cars), Crich (trams) and Hendon (aircraft). Almost the only aspect not catered for was the theme of urban transport, but these protestors ignored the fact that the Science Museum Advisory Council had already agreed that the London Transport exhibits at Clapham should remain in store in London with a view to their eventual display in a museum of just this character sited in the London area. In fact, most of them are already on display at Osterley. Yet another body of enthusiasts maintained that the new museum must be in the London area and, despite the fact that it was up to British Railways to provide the site, gratuitously advocated alternatives.

Most unfortunately, when the Labour Government's Transport Bill was in debate, the guillotine put an end to it before the clauses concerned with the setting up of the York Museum had been considered. Yet another change of government gave the dissidents their opportunity and they appealed to the ombudsman on the ground that the issue had never been discussed. By this time work on the new museum building had already begun, but owing to this ill-judged intervention, it was now suspended while, so that justice should be seen to be done, Lord Eccles, the new minister responsible, weighed the York scheme against the rival proposals It was the York scheme which ultimately prevailed. When work was eventually resumed, the target date for completion was 1975, the 150th anniversary of the opening of the Stockton & Darlington Railway. Owing to the current recession, it now seems unlikely that this target will be achieved.*

One of the sad things about growing old is the loss of friends. In recent years I have suffered a number of such casualties. Two of them were Harry Rose and Mark Newth, the only surviving friends of my school-days, the others representative of my varied interests: Laurence Pomeroy of the VSCC, Pat Lucan, a friend from the early days of the IWA, and from the railway world that delightful character Tommy Salt, railway enthusiast, veteran car-owner and champion of the Welshpool

* [The York Railway Museum was opened by The Duke of Edinburgh in September 1975.]

& Llanfair Light Railway, David Northesk, Edward Thomas, that old and staunch ally, and George Tibbitts, the Warwick solicitor, a most endearing character who for many years acted as honorary solicitor to the Talyllyn Railway Company. Dear old George wrestled indefatigably on behalf of the company, most notably over the acquisition of land for the extension of the railway to Nant Gwernol and it is sad that he did not live to see his work completed and the extension actually under construction as it is now. The latest loss has been Sir Arthur Elton from the world of industrial archaeology. He was best known for his work in the film industry, but what I most valued in him was his rare appreciation for the art of the industrial revolution, an appreciation which I share but in which I have benefited immensely from his tremendous enthusiasm for, and knowledge of, this neglected but fascinating aspect of the subject.

Yet I count myself fortunate that in my case I have made new friends to redress such losses. I think of two particularly whose friendship has proved especially valuable and life-enhancing, Doctor Richard Harper of Barnstaple and J.L.E. Smith. To call them new friends is misleading, for on leafing through past diaries to discover when it was that I first met them, I find with a shock that it will soon be twenty years since they came into my life with such rewarding results.

I met Dick Harper at Llanthony Abbey in 1956. It was on the occasion when I first introduced Sonia to a place that had exercised so great an influence on me, both in my childhood and on my return thither which I have described earlier. Ten years had then elapsed since my last visit, and as we drove down in the Alvis on a perfect June day, I recall a growing feeling of trepidation as to what changes might have occurred since my last visit. I need not have worried. Nothing had changed. The old tranquillity and the old magic still invested the place.* I

---

*   Alas, this is not longer altogether true today. As a result of the making of a road over the Gospel Pass, where there was previously only a grassy track, the valley has been invaded by an increasing volume of people and motor cars at holiday times and summer weekends, a trend that has

usually looked forward to meeting congenial company there, but our meeting Dick Harper and his wife was an unexpected bonus and proved the beginning of a most valued and enduring friendship.

Dick Harper, it appeared, was a regular visitor although we had never coincided before. It became clear that he had been drawn to the place in the same fashion as I had been, and this common attachment was the starting point of our friendship. He had for years been a great student of evolutionary theory so that his heroes were Darwin and Mendel and, like a good evolutionist, he professed no religious belief. Although I have never subscribed to any particular religious creed, I consider my own philosophy to be fundamentally religious and anti-materialistic, and as that philosophy had largely grown out of my love for the Black Mountains and Llanthony, the fact that he and I should find so much common ground may seem unlikely. Yet it might surprise Dick to know that I consider him one of the wisest and most saintly men. I found in him a great reverence for life in all its forms and that basic humility that recognizes the limitations of man's knowledge and his power. While professing no religion, he has the keenest awareness of the mystery of life and it was here that we found common ground. He has a long-cherished theory, still not accepted by the medical world, of the influence of evolutionary vestiges upon illness. Many modern diseases including cancer are, he believes, due to ancient evolutionary mechanisms in the human body which, having long lost their original purpose, are triggered off under modern conditions of stress to operate in a harmful manner. Although I have little knowledge either of evolution or of medicine, we have had long discussions on this subject which I find utterly fascinating and convincing. I am quite certain that although Dick's theories may not win acceptance in his lifetime, they will eventually revolutionize our

---

become more marked since the Severn Bridge was opened. At such times the valley and the abbey have become a place to be avoided, although one can still easily find solitude on the mountains.

knowledge of the origins of many diseases and thus profoundly change methods of treatment.

The recollections of our discussions as we strolled together in the high-banked lanes around Llanthony after dinner, when the sun was setting behind the mountains and the summer dusk was falling, are now among my most cherished memories, for owing to advancing years and ill-health Dick Harper can no longer travel so far afield from his native Devon. Yet we still keep in touch both by telephone and letter. Although they are very different characters, this exchange of correspondence reminds me of that earlier exchange of letters with the late H.J. Massingham which I found so stimulating during the last war.

It must have been shortly after I first met Dick Harper that my old friend Sam Clutton expressed a wish to see Eddie Moore 'plating' scythe blades under his water-powered tilt hammer at Middle Mill, near Belbroughton. I had first met Eddie Moore of Middle Mill during the war and knew that he was about to retire and that with his retirement the mill would close, so it was a question of now or never for anyone who wished to see this ancient process in action. So it was arranged that Sam would drive up from London and meet us for lunch at the Bell Inn at Bell End, between Bromsgrove and Stourbridge. Later, he telephoned to ask if he might bring an interested friend with him. This friend turned out to be John Smith. We found we shared so many interests that it was a case of friendship at first sight. When I look back over the years that have since passed, no single individual has done more to enrich and enhance them. To say any more than this would be to embarrass him.

At the end of his entry in *Who's Who*, John names his favourite recreation as 'Improving the View' and this is not just a humorous quirk but is quite literally true. So far as my experience goes he has contributed more towards the preservation of the English landscape and its buildings, including its industrial monuments, than any man living, though so unobtrusively that few people are aware of the fact. If other rich men applied their wealth to such good purpose, England would be transformed. He is extremely perceptive, and possesses an insatiable appetite for the individualistic, the eccentric and the bizarre both in people and things, for all, in short, that adds a spice to life. For this reason he has given his support to a great variety of unusual enthusiasms and causes. At the time I first met him, John was playing an extremely active part in the National Trust and, as a member of the IWA, was also deeply interested in canals. He served with me on the Inland Waterways Redevelopment Committee, and it was he who was responsible for persuading the National Trust to become responsible for the Stratford Canal.

In 1963, John became disenchanted with the National Trust and though after a while he returned to this particular fold, there was an interim when his abundant energies lacked an outlet. He has often allowed me to stay at his London house in Smith Square when my business in town required me to stay overnight. It was sometime during this year that I arrived there to find him poring over the columns of *World's Fair* and, on inquiring the reason, he told me that he was planning to organize a Great Steam Fair in the grounds of his house, Shottesbrooke Park, at White Waltham, near Maidenhead. It was to be a once-only event the like of which had never before been seen, certainly not in the period following the last war. To this end he went to immense time and trouble to track down the best examples of such traditional fairground 'rides' as still survived, gallopers, a scenic railway, steam yachts, a helter-skelter, a big wheel and so forth. This painstaking quest also included appropriate side-shows and, in this department, he succeeded in discovering rarities such as a flea circus which few people would have believed still to exist. He even contrived a 'bioscope', the fairground parent of the cinema, actually showing short early films to the accompaniment of appropriate piano music provided by an elderly man who was one of the last survivors of the days of the small-town silent screen. To power this bioscope, which was complete with high-kicking dancing girls and a bowler-hatted barker with a big drum, an enthusiast lent and manned an authentic example of the type of steam generating set which was originally used for such shows.

For supplying power to the big rides, such as the gallopers, or the scenic railway, John had to rely upon the amateur owners of showman's engines as, although these rides were traditional, their professional owners had long ceased to rely on steam power to travel and to power them. The ubiquitous diesel had taken over. The amateurs responded magnificently to the idea, but the professionals, naturally, were much more cautious, especially as many of them had to make long journeys far from their accustomed circuit in order to appear at Shottesbrooke. They would not do so to satisfy what they regarded as a rich man's whim unless they were guaranteed against loss. This meant that if the Great Steam Fair proved a failure due to public apathy, bad weather or a combination of both, John stood to lose a very substantial sum of money.

The Great Steam Fair was finally scheduled to open on the last weekend in August 1964, opening on Friday 28 August and closing on the following Sunday evening. On the preceding Thursday afternoon, Sonia, myself and our two boys motored down to Shottesbrooke from Stanley Pontlarge to render such help as we could. It was an absolutely unforgettable occasion. The weather was perfect throughout, while it became evident from the moment of opening that the fair was going to prove overwhelmingly popular. So much so that at times the roads round about became blocked by traffic queues and it was just as well that there was almost unlimited car-parking space available in the park. The fair itself was laid out in the space immediately in front of the house and included attractions such as Harry Lee's Steam Yachts which a younger generation of southerners had never seen. For Harry Lee had hitherto confined himself to travelling in Yorkshire and had never come south before. Incidentally, his steam yachts really were what they claimed to be, being the only major ride to be steam-powered, The other rides drew their power from a ring main supplied by an impressive row of gleaming showman's engines, Fowlers and Burrells, drawn up in front of the stable block.

It was over this supply of power that the only real hitch occurred in the arrangements, although only a very few of the public realized the fact. As the enthusiastic owners of these engines very soon discovered, it was one thing to take their engines to a traction engine rally and display them quietly turning over or slowly perambulating a parade ground; to be asked to work them hard and continuously from noon until well after dark proved a very different proposition. With one significant exception, these amateur enginemen proved unequal to the task, and although they managed to keep their glittering monsters ticking over to the admiration of the crowds, the amount of current they were able to pump into the ring main was quite inadequate. Fortunately, one of the professional showmen, perhaps a pessimist, had brought along a powerful diesel generator and this, discreetly concealed from the public eye in a nearby shrubbery, made good the deficiency. Most owners of the showman's engines blamed the coal for their shortcomings. John had asked my advice on what coal to provide, and from my past steam experience I had recommended Welsh Steam which was supplied to all engines throughout the duration of the fair by a small Garrett steam tractor and trailer. It was soon apparent that most owners were unaccustomed to the use of such fuel and kept up too thick a fire with the effect that they complained bitterly of burnt firebars. Had they applied the rule of 'little and often' they would have had little trouble. If any of these owners should happen to read this and feel aggrieved by my remarks, I can only point to the exception, the engine belonging to my old friend, the late Tommy Hunt of the Griffin Foundry, Oldbury.

Tommy Hunt was a splendid Black Country character with whom I had first become acquainted through our mutual interest in the Talyllyn Railway. In that connection he had proved a tower of strength, promptly supplying anything the railway might need in the way of castings from his foundry at no cost. When John was planning his fair, I had told him that Tommy was a 'must' and the latter had responded by bringing down his magnificent Gavioli fairground organ with a small Burrell showman's engine to draw it and power it. In addition to this outfit, Tommy also brought down his Foster showman's engine. This stood apart from its fellows and, because it was less showily finished than they, it attracted less public attention. Only the knowledgeable could appreciate the fact that whereas the other engines was merely turning over most of the time, the Foster, as could be heard from its exhaust beats, was working hard, pumping its full quota of current into the main. As Tommy remarked to me in his broad Black Country accent, it was just a question of knowing how.

Both Sonia and I were kept busy, usually by relieving other volunteer helpers so that they could have a break. Sonia assisted with the ox roasting, while I found myself performing several unusual roles such as taking a turn in the paybox on the bioscope. Little did I think I should ever find myself working beside a vociferous barker and two high-kicking dancing girls. From my position beside the entrance I could hear the piano tinkling away inside so I was amazed when the old accompanist suddenly emerged and, with a broad wink at me, sloped off in the direction of the nearest beer tent. Suffering as he did from an unslakeable thirst, he had had the forethought to provide a tape recording of himself and the necessary reproduction equipment so that he could gratify his periodic craving without ostensibly interrupting his performance.

Our work for the fair was enough to give us the satisfaction of feeling we were active participants, but not so exacting that we could not enjoy the fair to the full. Walking around, it was astonishing how many friends and acquaintances I met. They were representatives of all my varied interests, vintage cars, railways, canals and even the world of publishing. It seemed that they all found common ground in the fascination of this fair. It was for them as for me a never to be forgotten occasion, a kind of feast of Crispian where those absentees, hearing accounts of it afterwards, would 'think themselves accurs'd they were not here'. For John had no intention of making it an annual event and most people realized they were experiencing an unrepeatable occasion. Nevertheless, its success had an important long term effect. With the sole exception of the Travelling Circus, which alone might have done better had the weather not been so perfect, John did not have to pay out any guarantee money to the professionals and the money they had earned over the three days made them realize the value of traditional 'rides' as nothing else could. Potential organizers and amateur owners of suitable fairground equipment were also suitably impressed, with the effect that 'Old Time Steam Fairs' have ever since been popular annual fixtures in many parts of the country and showmen like Harry Lee no long confine the appearance of their rides to a particular district. Yet, in the minds of participants and spectators alike, there will always be one one Great Steam Fair. One night, accompanied by the Smith family, we climbed up to the roof of the house after dusk had fallen to look down at the panoramic view of the fair spread out below, the rides and side-shows outlined with multi-coloured lights and the bright glare of arc lamps lighting up the shifting crowd and the smoke and steam of the engines that drifted overhead. It was this picture that I carried away.

It was in the year following this unique event that John and his wife Christian started the Landmark Trust 'for preserving small buildings, structures or sites of historic interest, architectural merit, or amenity value, and where possible finding new uses for them; and for protecting and promoting the enjoyment of places of historic interest or natural beauty'. This is financed by a more general charitable trust which they had founded a few years earlier. This Landmark Trust was not intended to compete with the National Trust in which John has again become active. On the contrary, the Landmark acts as a kind of safety net by saving those small properties which, for lack of any endowment or for some other reason, the National Trust is unable to assist. In this way the two Trusts frequently act in concert. In the case of most of the properties which the Landmark has acquired since 1965, they are funished either wholly or in part and so made available for short term letting. This gives practical expression to the word 'enjoyment' in the Trust's aims for, as John has so rightly written 'to appreciate a place properly it is not enough to see it briefly by day; it is essential to go to sleep there and wake up there and be there in all lights and weathers.' He adds that many of those who stay in a Landmark 'just for a holiday return with an interest in "conservation" which will last them all their lives and greatly benefit us all.'

I have mentioned the Landmark Trust in some detail because, since 1965, it has become very much a part of our lives. For soon after the Trust was founded Sonia was asked if she would be responsible for furnishing its properties and this proved a most fascinating and exacting job in which I have naturally taken a close and often active interest, just as she has done in my own activities. With the needs of different properties in mind, she buys furniture at local auctions, has it renovated where necessary, and arranges for its delivery to what was once the laundry of Sudeley Castle, near Winchcombe, which the Trust rents as a store. Here, when the collection of furniture for a particular property is complete, it is loaded for delivery to Cornwall, North Wales or East Anglia as the case may be. Where a large property is involved, the delivery is done by professional removers, but usually the amount of furniture needed is not too great and in such cases she has hired a self-drive van, and, having loaded up, we have set off together for our destination, sharing the driving between us.

I have said that this job is exacting and challenging because Landmark properties vary so widely in character and period. Also, because the bulk of the Trust's resources must necessarily be devoted to restoring its properties, coupled with the fact that they are destined to be occupied by a long succession of tenants, to furnish a place with pieces wholly 'in period' is out of the question, particularly at present day prices. Consequently, to furnish appropriately places so varied in character as a medieval tower on the walls of Caernarvon, a gothic temple at Stowe, the eighteenth-century Luttrell's folly tower on the shore of Southampton Water, the engine house of the old Danescombe Mine near Calstock, the Egyptian House at Penzance, an eighteenth-century cotton mill in Edale, or the stationmaster's house at Alton station requires considerable thought, ingenuity and discernment. It has frequently happened that, having set

out the furniture in such places, Sonia and I have camped for
the night in them before starting on the long journey home. In
this way we have become the first to occupy them and the first to
appreciate their unique quality. It has been for us both a most
rewarding exercise. It has been, as John puts it, equivalent 'to
making a new home half a dozen times a year'. This comment
stresses the laborious part of the job; its satisfaction comes in
seeing a bare room suddenly come to life and acquire a character
so right and so natural that it might have been there from the
beginning. I have said that John is unusually perceptive, but
why he chose Sonia for this particular job is a mystery because I
do not myself know from what source this talent springs and
neither does she. I have speculated that it may come from her
past theatrical experience, but she denies this. I have often
helped to load into a van what struck my untutored eye as a
depressing load of assorted junk, yet when furniture and
pictures are unloaded and put in their intended places, they are
mysteriously transformed.

The Landmark Trust also assists by donation other worthy
causes to an extent that is not widely realized. The extension to
our Narrow Gauge Railway Museum at Towyn; the restoration
and removal to Penrhyn Castle of an ancient locomotive *Fire
Queen* from Dinorwic; the rescue of the cruiser *Belfast* and her
removal to a permanent mooring on London River opposite the
Tower; the transfer of the two Beam Blowing engines from the
Lilleshall Ironworks to the Blists Hill site of the Ironbridge
Gorge Museum. But the most important donation of all, in my
opinion, was the very large contribution made by the Landmark towards the repair of Abraham Darby's famous iron
bridge, the first in the world, at Coalbrookdale.

The state of the iron bridge, the most important industrial
monument in Britain, had been the cause of great concern for
many years. The Ironbridge Gorge is geologically unstable
and, as a result, the massive stone abutment on the Ironbridge
side of the river was slowly but remorselessly moving inwards,
bringing increasing pressure to bear upon the bridge causing
some of the cast-iron arch ribs to crack. For years the bridge had

been scheduled as an ancient monument, but this failed to mend matters. Rescue was obviously going to be a very expensive operation and for years the Shropshire County Council and the Ancient Monuments Department were locked in fruitless argument as to which should bear the brunt of the cost. The department argued that as the responsible authority for highways and bridges in the area, the county council should assume prime responsibility. To this the county council replied that it was not prepared to spend a great deal of ratepayers' money on a bridge that had been closed to vehicular traffic for many years. On the contrary, as the bridge was scheduled as an ancient monument it was clearly up to the department to initiate repair work. This stalemate dragged on for so long that many of us feared that the bridge would lie in fragments at the bottom of the river by the time it was resolved. It was the Landmark Trust's donation which was really responsible for setting in motion the present costly rescue operation which includes the construction of an inverted reinforced concrete arch beneath the river to hold back the abutment.

Another recent event which has given me immense pleasure and satisfaction has been the dramatic salvage of Brunel's *Great Britain* from the Falkland Islands and her voyage home to her native Bristol where she now lies in the dock where she was built and where she is now being restored to the condition in which she was launched. I confess I was lukewarm about this project when it was first mooted, arguing that so much money was needed to save industrial monuments at home, most notably the iron bridge, that we could ill afford such an extremely costly salvage operation. However, when the munificent Jack Hayward came forward with his offer to meet the entire cost of bringing the ship home, the whole situation was completely transformed where I was concerned and the *Great Britain* Project now has no more loyal and enthusiastic supporter.

In my biography of Brunel I told how, after being damaged by a storm when rounding the Horn in 1886, the gallant old ship managed to limp back to the Falkland Islands where she was condemned and converted by the Falkland Islands Company into a hulk, a floating store for wool and coal. I also told how, following an unsuccessful attempt to raise funds on the part of the then governor of the islands, in 1937 she was towed away to nearby Sparrow Cove where she was holed, beached and left at the mercy of the sea. There, I wrote, 'the indestructible hull of Brunel's splendid ship may still be seen'. But what I did not realize when I wrote these words was just how indestructible she was and envisaged a rusting skeleton of bare ribs. It was not until 1964 that I realized just how complete her hull still was when I was sent a set of photographs of her taken recently by the Admiralty fishery protection vessel, HMS *Protector*. Yet it was apparent to me from these pictures that she could not last much longer. For a close examination of the photographs revealed that the hull had been seriously weakened when the ship had been converted into a storage hulk by the cutting of an access door in her starboard side amidships, and she was beginning to 'hog' and must eventually break her back. The reason for this became apparent when the hull was inspected on the spot by Dr Ewan Corlett, the naval architect, a man who has since become the technical brain behind the project and who knows more about the history of the *Great Britain* and her construction than any man now living. The ship had been run into the cove in such a way that her bow was hard aground. Meanwhile the action of the tides over a period of nearly thirty years had been to scour away the shingle aft with the effect that the ship's stern was hanging in deep water. By the time of his visit, the hogging had become much worse than it was in the 1964 photograhs and a large and sinister crack had appeared in the vicinity of the access door. So the rescue operation, like that of the iron bridge, came only just in time.

Although they had been unable to save the ship, the islanders were proud of her – she was the only object of historical interest they had to show visitors. Also, they were extremely sceptical of the outcome of the salvage operation and some were not a little chagrined to see their one show-piece disappearing. Yet any hard feelings of this kind were very soon dissipated for, on behalf of the islanders, the governor presented to the project the ship's bell which had been brought ashore for safekeeping. It is now exhibited in Bristol where it has since acquired a fitting companion.

Only a short while ago I received a letter from a correspondent informing me that the bell of Brunel's first ship, the *Great Western*, was hanging in the hall of a large country house which had become the headquarters of the South Eastern Gas Board. How on earth had it got there and why had its presence passed without remark for so long? The story sounded so improbable that, as my correspondent had not seen the bell himself, I wrote back asking whether he could confirm by the evidence of his own eyes. Having received such confirmation, I passed the news on to Ewan Corlett with the result that the bell will shortly hang beside that of the *Great Britain*. I understand that the project has since tracked down the whereabouts of, not one but two *Great Eastern* bells, so that tangible reminders of all three of Brunel's great ships may soon be hanging side by side at Bristol.

It was in connection with the *Great Britain* that, by a curious coincidence, I made a discovery which carried me back to pre-war days. I had been invited to join the *Great Britain* Restoration Committee and drove down to Bath to attend its first meeting at Lord Strathcona's house in Lansdowne Crescent. Lord Strathcona was a leading member of the project and one of the lucky few who had gone out to the Falkland Islands at the time of the salvage operation. When I walked into the room in which the meeting was to be held in the company of my host, my eyes were at once drawn to an oil painting on the wall. This depicted, in side view, a 1903 Humberette which looked remarkably like the car I used to own and which I drove regularly in the Brighton Run in the thirties.* It was even painted in the same shade of green which I have used for all my vintage and veteran cars from my first G.N. onwards. I remarked on this similarity to Lord Strathcona whereupon he asked me if I could remember what the registration number

---

* See *Landscape with Machines*, plate 21.

was. 'FH 12', I replied promptly. 'Then that's the very same
car', he assured me, nodding in the direction of the picture, and
adding 'I'm the owner now.' Unfortunately, I could not see the
car itself because it was at that time garaged in Birmingham and
although I was promised a run in it for old times' sake, for one
reason or another this has never been achieved. I had lost track
of the old car completely and, although I have not seen it in the
flesh, it was nice to know that it was still in running order and in
good hands.

> Of dying man
> His living mind
> By writing deeds
> His children find.

I noticed, and noted down, this inscription over a cottage
doorway at Welcombe during the brief period that Sonia and I
spent at Aller Park in the spring of 1953. The lines now seem
prophetic although, not having the gift of prophecy, I cannot
think what made me use them to preface the first volume of this
autobigraphy. Any writer likes to console himself with the
reflection that his written words will long outlive him, that 'he
being dead yet speaketh'. But at the time I wrote that book I had
been lucky enough to pass the age of sixty without ever having
had any serious illness or seen the inside of a hospital. Some
racing driver has written, I think it may have been Charles
Jarrott in his classic book *Ten Years of Motor Racing*, that the
longer his car went on running perfectly the more convinced he
became that some dire mechanical disintegration was due, the
more disastrous for being so long postponed. Perhaps subcon-
sciously I harboured some such pessimistic notion about my
own health. If so it certainly proved to be correct. For nine
months after *Landscape with Machines* was published in the
summer of 1971 I had to go into hospital for what proved to be
only the first of a series of five major operations which,
separated by brief intervals when a return to normal health
seemed likely and I was able to lead a normal life, have been

spread over the past two years. During my second and third operations, which followed closely upon one another in the early autumn of 1972 I literally 'diced with death', to use a motor racing cliché. Now, in February 1974, sixteen months and two operations later, it has become clear that, although I won that particularly hard-fought game, I have not won the match and that my expectation of life may be measured in months rather than years. It is, after all, a match that we must all lose eventually, some to be hurried out of life suddenly and unexpectedly and others to await their end as philosophically as may be. As Dr Johnson said, the latter situation certainly 'concentrates the mind wonderfully'.

To undergo such an experience naturally raises the question whether the pain and discomfort suffered by the patient on the one hand, and on the other the skill of his surgeon aided by all the costly equipment and know-how of a modern hospital, are really worthwhile. To this my own answer is an unhesitating 'yes'. For one thing, but for this reprieve I could not have produced this book, much of which was written in hospital and all of it since my health broke down. More important than this, however, has been my intense enjoyment of life during the all too brief periods of reprieve. The reason for this is difficult to explain. Although I may have believed at such times that I was on the road to full recovery, I yet felt in some strange way like a *revenant*. It was as though the bonds attaching me to this world had already been loosed so that I possessed no longer any natural right to be alive. I found that I had lost my fear of death, and this I suppose is natural because it is not 'easeful death' itself which we fear but the pain and suffering associated with it and I have had my fill of that already. But because I no longer fear death does not mean that I have grown tired of life – far from it. Each day and its events, some of them quite trivial, has become infinitely precious to me. I have maintained all my varied interests, so far as this has been possible, with even greater enthusiasm. Above all, I have learned to value and appreciate my friends more than ever before. I must admit that I have always been more interested in things than in people and

the fact that I now feel quite otherwise is by no means wholly
due to the way they have rallied round Sonia and myself during
this time of adversity. Of this I will quote but one example.
Following my major operations in 1972, I reached the stage of
convalescence just as we were entering the dead of winter.
Quite unknown to us, a number of old friends in the VSCC had
clubbed together and offered us a three-week holiday in the
Algarve in southern Portugal, with a house and a car at our
disposal, something which we could not possibly have afforded.
As a consequence, we flew out of a grey England flecked with
patches of snow into a June climate where the sun shone from
cloudless skies. Not only did I return feeling twice the man I
was when I left England, but it was a shared experience of rare
pleasure which made all the darkness that had preceded it seem
worthwhile.

But the most important result of this shared adversity has
been its effect on the relationship between Sonia and myself. It
is impossible to describe this, for to say adversity has brought us
closer together, or that our relationship has been deepened and
mysteriously enriched, implies that it was in some way lacking
in depth before, which would be wholly untrue. On the
contrary, when I look back over the past twenty-three years I
realize the full extent of my good fortune in having such a
partner. They could never have been so happy and so fruitful
had they not been shared with her. So much so that I marvel
now that at the outset I could ever have harboured doubts as to
the strength and lasting quality of our relationship. Our only
regret now is that we did not meet sooner so that we could have
shared a greater part of our lives together. Looking back on our
lives before we met, I can see how we both made the same
mistake of consciously willing our former marriages. In a sense,
we both married the canals. Although it is true that I was deeply
attracted to Angela, the decisive factor was *Cressy* and the fact
that Angela took to a life afloat as a duck takes to water really
determined the outcome. Ironically, however, that she took to
the life as readily as she did, was a symptom of her incurable
wanderlust which was one of the many reasons why our

marriage finally broke down. As for Sonia, she married the canals in an even more literal sense by marrying a man who, as a canal boater himself, personified that way of life. This, for reasons even more obvious, was a marriage doomed to failure. The lesson we have learned from the past twenty-three years is that the strength and durability of a relationship between two people rests on the depth of that relationship and not on any preconceived notions, however romantic, as to how life should be lived. I know that for my part I became so obsessed with my 'design for living' on *Cressy* that I could not see beyond it, with the result that it ultimately ended in unhappiness. On the other hand, I began my life with Sonia under most inauspicious circumstances when we had no idea how the future would work out. That it has worked out so well, so fruitfully and so completely happily has been entirely due to the strength of our relationship.

If there is any truth in Dr Johnson's dictum which I quoted earlier, then this book is perhaps the better for having been written under such adverse circumstances. For it is natural at such a time to look back dispassionately over one's past life, to assess the gains and the losses and to ask oneself whether at any stage one should have acted otherwise. Reviewing my varied interests and the activities associated with them which I have pursued, although these have sometimes developed in ways that I could not possibly have foreseen and which, in some cases I do not now think wholly desirable, nevertheless I do not regret my part in them because I consider the gains to be much greater than the losses.

To take such causes in chronological order, they begin with the founding of the VSCC and the inauguration of Prescott. Where the VSCC is concerned it is somewhat ironical that it began as a very small club for poor men and is now a very large club for very rich men, at least so far as its most active members are concerned. This is no fault of the club but is simply due to changes in the society in which we live. In a world of mass production in which money steadily diminishes in value, a vintage car like any other surviving example of craftsmanship and quality, has come to be regarded as a gold-chip investment commanding a phenomenal price. Hence, such cars are frequently bought by investors who are not enthusiasts and who store the car where it can never be seen by the public and would not dream of driving it in anger. But, apart from this sad fact, the mere knowledge that their cars carry such an extravagant price tag must necessarily affect the thinking of even the most enthusiastic club members and unless they are very well-heeled it makes them hesitate to hazard their expensive properties by competing regularly in club events. It was quite otherwise in days when one could buy a good 30/98 Vauxhall for £50 or less.

As for Prescott Hill Climb,* it continues to give pleasure to thousands of motor racing enthusiasts each season. In the 1950s the course was extended by the construction of a new loop in the belief that it would make the hill more attractive for spectators. Personally, I doubt whether it has achieved this objective and I secretly regret it because the sense of continuity has been lost, records made today being no longer comparable with those set up earlier over the old course. By virtue of the gentleman's agreement made before the war, the VSCC still has the use of the hill for one meeting a year and it is significant that the club prefers to use the older and shorter course. In 1973, a special meeting was organized by the Bugatti Owners' Club over this short course to celebrate the 35th anniversary of the opening meeting. I was very glad that ill health did not prevent me from competing in this event by driving my faithful Alvis up the hill, just as I had done at that opening of the hill thirty-five years earlier. This car will be fifty years old this year (1974), and since the passing of *Cressy* it has become my oldest and best-loved material possession. Except during the war years, it has never been off the road except for periodic overhauls and, as the preceding chapters reveal, in all my activities it has been my faithful companion. To those who argue today that in order to conserve precious resources we should build our cars to last longer it has surely become an object lesson.

* See *Landscape with Machines*, p. 194.

Turning now to the canals, who could have envisaged the tremendous enthusiasm the IWA has now generated and the influence it now wields? Such activity is no longer confined to boating but to navvying; gangs of volunteers, often knee deep in mud, are to be found hard at work restoring derelict canals. What would have surprised us even more in 1947, such works now enjoys the blessing, and often the active cooperation of, British Waterways and local government. Nevertheless, one of the things I most regret when I recall the canals as I knew them is the passing of the working narrow boat. I realize now that even if our early effort to improve conditions for the boaters had been more successful, given the present economic climate, they could only have postponed by a few years the inevitable end of the narrow canals as a way of life. It was the fact that these canals were the territory of a colourful and unique community that made my years aboard *Cressy* so memorable. That is why the present 'cruiseway' system with its ever growing population of pleasure boats seems a poor thing compared with the canals I was fortunate to know. The moral is that you can preserve material objects, but you cannot preserve a way of life. Yet I console myself with the thought that, but for our effort, much of our canal system would either have been filled in or become neglected ditches choked with weeks and rubbish. Instead, they have been given a new lease of life, albeit a different one, and give to thousands a pleasure which has brought to their lives a fresh dimension. In particular, the Welsh Canal, where *Cressy* was the first boat to venture soon after the war, has now become the most popular of cruising waterways. So, despite its unhappy ending, on balance I do not regret my years of canal crusading. Such an ending cannot, after all, take away the value and satisfaction of the achievement.

After the working narrow boat, the thing I most regret is the passing of the steam locomotive. In retrospect, it seems to have happened so swiftly. When we founded the TRPS in 1950, the passing of a machine which had been an object of awe, wonderment and delight to me since earliest childhood seemed inconceivable and did not enter into my calculations at all. Yet the disappearance of steam from British Railways has attracted to the steam-hauled Talyllyn Railway an ever increasing flow of passengers. The success of the Talyllyn has also sparked off a great railway preservation movement, not only in this country but world-wide. I remember that when a scheme to re-open the Festiniog Railway came to successful fruition a few years after we had taken over the Talyllyn, I entertained misgivings as to whether there was a sufficient reservoir of enthusiasm and money to support two railways. Surveying the railway scene today this now seems a comical misjudgement. And yet I cannot help wondering, with the passage of time, whether it may be shown that the results would have been better if efforts had been more concentrated and less diffused. But railway enthusiasts are a peculiar breed. Each has his or her own particular pet railway and the mere fact that so many railways appear to have been successfully preserved becomes sufficient reason for starting yet another preservation society.

A big question mark that hangs over the long term future of preserved railways, particularly those of standard gauge, concerns their steam motive power. Who will cope with the locomotives when they need a major overhaul and, in parti cular, a new boiler? The number of steam locomotives, in this country alone, which enthusiasts have preserved is truly remarkable, yet I cannot help feeling that the future of many of them is by no means certain. Some quite short preserved lines seem to have collected locomotives far in excess of their real needs and I speculate whether this may not solely be due to too much zeal but to ensure the long term working future of the railway by building up a reserve of motive power so that when one locomotive has been run into the ground it will be possible to replace it by another. If this is the case then it is the negation of preservation.

My experience on the Talyllyn Railway has convinced me that it is impossible to preserve the life of a steam railway just as it has proved impossible to preserve the life of the narrow canal system. Both were fated either to die or to change. Like the canals, the preserved railways now handle a prodigious volume of pleasure traffic which has necessitated physical changes in the railway itself to enable it to cope and so subtly transformed its character. I am aware that when we took over the Talyllyn it already relied primarily on holiday-makers, but it performed a small local function. In 1951/52, when I was running the railway, we still carried local passengers down to Towyn on market days, while local Towyn tradesmen still brought parcels and sacks of meal to the Wharf station for delivery to farms up the line. Although such traffic made an infinitesimal contribution to our revenue, I valued it greatly and enjoyed entering particulars in the weighty leather bound parcels book which Edward Thomas had so scrupulously kept.

I mourn the disappearance of the rural branch line just as I do that of the working narrow boat. As is evident from the first part of this book, we and our friends made great use of branch lines when *Cressy* was moored in deep country. I remember with particular affection the Midland & South Western Junction Railway which we used in the early years of the war for journeys between Hungerford and Cheltenham, or the old Cambrian line from Whitchurch through Ellesmere to Oswestry over which we made many journeys during our pioneering voyages up the Welsh Canal. For me no preserved line can ever make up for the loss of such railways as these any more than a 'cruiseway' can be an effective substitute for a working narrow canal. Yet, here again, half a loaf is better than no bread and I do not regret the part I have played in the railway preservation movement. As in the case of the canals, such railways have given, and will continue to give, pleasure to many thousands of people and there is great satisfaction in that knowledge.

In reviewing *Landscape with Machines* in a provincial daily, a very dear and loyal friend of mine called me the 'Patron Saint of leisure hobbies' and the words were used as a headline for the review. That such a form of beatitude surprised me does not imply false modesty or that I do not appreciate the intended compliment. 'Hobbies' is a word that has never occurred to me in describing my varied activities, and in order to explain why this is so brings me to the influence of my ideas upon my actions. Although ideas are the mainspring of action, the space I have devoted to them in this book stands in about the same proportion as do *High Horse Riderless*, *The Clouded Mirror* and *Winterstoke* to my total literary output. I believe with Eric Gill that the artist is not a special kind of person but that every man is a special kind of artist given, I would add, the opportunity. It has been my aim in life to create such opportunities in a civilization which denies them. There is much talk nowadays about the wastage of precious natural resources brought about by the economic concept of unlimited growth* in a finite world. Yet nothing at all is said about the equally disastrous wastage of man's creative potential to which the same concept has led. It has been my aim from first to last to find outlets for that potential and not merely to find new ways of occupying leisure time.

In 1965 we celebrated the centenary of the Talyllyn Railway, and of the many events which were held at Towyn in that year it was the service of thanksgiving in Towyn parish church that remains most clearly in my mind. Plate-layers' tools and a wagon were arranged in the crossing of the church and, most appropriately, the service was conducted by the Revd W. Awdry, celebrated as the author of the 'little engine' books for children. He asked me to read the lesson for which he had so aptly chosen the famous passage in praise of craftsmen from Ecclesiasticus, Chapter 38. After describing the work of different craftsmen, the ploughman, the smith and the potter, it concludes as follows:

> All these put their trust in their hands; and each becometh wise in his own work. Without these shall not a city be inhabited, and men shall not sojourn nor walk up and down therein. They shall not be sought for in the council of the people, and in the assembly they shall not mount on high . . .

---

* This concept of unlimited growth is really another name for that assumption of automatic material progress which H.J. Massingham, myself and a few others denounced thirty years ago.

But they will maintain the fabric of the world; and in the handywork of their craft is their prayer.

So eloquently and in such magnificent language do these words express my own belief that I found myself profoundly moved; so much so that I could scarcely get the words out and nearly made a fool of myself in consequence.

It has been vastly encouraging to see such a multitude of volunteers from all walks of life happily engaged on so many different manual tasks. But projects of such magnitude cannot depend on the work of spare-time volunteers alone. More encouraging and significant to me have been the number of people who have given up well paid and promising careers in industry and come to work for one of these projects full-time, accepting a much lower salary and insecurity for the sake of the creative satisfaction that such work brings.

In *High Horse Riderless* I emphasized the importance of education in bringing about the changes I advocated and among the conclusions in which I summarized the book's argument was this one:

That the conflict developing between a generation so educated and conditions of life and work becoming increasingly stultifying may lie the foundation of a renaissance.

The outcome of my own activities is not the only sign that this is happening. An increasing number of the younger generation seem determined 'to do their own thing' despite the carrots dangled enticingly before them by the world of commerce and industrialism. At the moment, many of them fail to find their bearing and become mere aimless drifters, despised by the majority. Yet I cannot help feeling that these signs of revolt may prove in the long term to be a good thing. For, again, as I wrote in *High Horse Riderless*, 'we are witnessing, not the laborious construction of a new world, but the ruin of a civilization which, like a tower built upon a quicksand, sinks faster than we can add brick to brick.' This ruin appears to be coming about far more quickly than I could ever have believed. When it comes it can only be succeeded by some more self-sufficient form of society designed to make the fullest and best use of natural resources and human ability. It is in such a society that I believe those who have opted out will find their niches. It is certain to be a slow and painful process of transition, but less painful for those who have already contracted out than for those who still cling to the tenets of our consumer society where, in the words of Wordsworth, 'Getting and spending we lay waste our powers'. In order to produce more we must consume more and we are all urged along this fatal course by a vast advertising machine designed to make today's luxuries become tomorrow's necessities. Nor can we look to either of the main political parties to break this vicious circle because both are chiefly concerned in trying to win a bigger slice of a diminishing cake for their respective supporters. And yet an awareness of the necessity for fundamental change has become more speedily apparent than I had dreamed possible. For example, the word 'ecology', from being virtually meaningless to the majority thirty years ago, has now become almost an over-used cliché. But it is an easy matter to pay lip-service to inexorable ecological rules; to practise them, as we must, is a far harder and more difficult matter.

There was a time when I used to wonder what attracted me so powerfully about such old and traditional features of the English landscape as men and horses at plough, or innumerable watermills and windmills. Was it merely nostalgia, a yearning for the 'good old times' which never existed in fact? I now know that it was much more than this; that what attracted me about such things was their eternal quality. They did not depend, as our civilization depends, on the depletion of the world's limited resources of capital. If we are to survive as a species, it is to this simpler, harder and more realistic world that we must ultimately return.

To sum up, looking back over my life, I consider I have been singularly blessed. I have known the true meaning of love and I have been able to live a varied life of intense creativity. The thought that such creativity has brought pleasure to so many people is a great source of satisfaction and consolation to me at this moment. But this, so to say, has been a spin-off, for the source of my greatest satisfaction has been the creative work itself, quite apart from its results or rewards or such little celebrity as it may have won for me. I have had many good friends and made, to the best of my knowledge, very few enemies. I have not consciously wronged anyone and I have no regrets for opportunities lost or for what might have been. Hence when the end comes I think I shall experience a sense of sorrow such as one feels when a long and supremely happy holiday draws to a close, but certainly there can be no sense of bitterness, no remorse or regret. Certainly I have never succeeded in making much money, but money and true happiness seldom go together. Though it may be thought presumptuous of me to do so, I shall end this book by echoing the words of that great engineer, Richard Trevithick, as he lay dying at Dartford: 'However much I may be straitened in pecuniary circumstances, the great honour of being a useful subject can never be taken from me, which to me far exceeds riches.'